GENERATE
THOUSANDS
IN CASH ON YOUR STOCKS
BEFORE BUYING OR SELLING THEM

GENERATE
THOUSANDS
IN CASH ON YOUR STOCKS
BEFORE BUYING OR SELLING THEM

3rd revised edition

BY

DR. SAMIR ELIAS

First published 2001
Second revised edition, September 2003
Third revised edition, March 2007
Third revised edition, Updated August 2009

Printed in the United States

ISBN: 978-1-58597-424-5

Library of Congress Control Number: 2001097490

A division of Squire Publishers, Inc.
4500 College Blvd.
Leawood, KS 66211
1/888/888-7696
www.leatherspublishing.com

TABLE OF CONTENTS

Chapter 6

Chapter 7

Chapter 8

Chapter 9

Chapter 10

Chapter 11

Chapter 12

Chapter 13

Chapter 16

Chapter 16 *(Continued)*

Chapter 17

Chapter 19 *(Continued)*

Chapter 20

Epilogue 381

Index 384

INTRODUCTION

The past few years have certainly been very difficult for the average investor. Many have purchased stocks at much higher prices and are still facing losses. The question facing them is: " Should I sell or hold on and wait for losing stocks to come back?"

The answer to this question is not easy since no one wants to sell their stocks at a loss just to see them return to new highs. On the other hand, if a person does not sell now, they may have to wait many years to recover their losses and break even.

This book addresses several aspects of investing that are critical to success including:

(1) What you must do once you have purchased a stock to insure a profitable outcome.
(2) How to continuously reduce your cost basis while raising cash on stocks you are in the process of buying.
(3) How to capitalize on sentiment and price action to generate explosive profits.
(4) How to easily decide when to buy or sell a long term investment by doing a simple calculation each week.

Once you have decided to act and buy a stock, do you have a strategy on how to effectively manage your position? Or do you place your stock in a "lock box" to be opened only when you decide to sell?

It amazes me that when people place money in a bank or fixed investment their primary concern is what the return on their money is, but for some reason this does not apply when they invest in stocks. They would rather sit and wait, hoping the stock goes up so they can sell and cash in.

Whenever you buy a stock, it is critical that you continuously generate cash by renting out your stock using what we call in market language "covered call writing." This is a safe strategy that allows you to achieve annual returns of 20% or more on your stocks in addition to any capital gains you may realize.

In effect, next to the timing of your purchase, this is the most important action you need to take to achieve superior returns. In this book I dedicate several sections to explain this strategy and offer timing tools to maximize the premiums or "rents" you charge. Each technique is supported by actual examples from my personal trades.

Another important strategy to enhance your profits is to get paid in cash for a promise to buy a stock at a certain price before actually buying it. This is what is dubbed in stock market language as "selling put options." By learning how to effectively use this approach, you will be able to profit in several ways:

(1) Recover substantial stock losses without using any of your own cash.

(2) Use other people's money to average down on stocks you own.

(3) Buy stocks below market price.

This book introduces you to several ways, including half-half put selling, boxing, fading momentum and other strategies to maximize profits while limiting risk.

In addition, I will use several examples to illustrate how you can generate thousands of dollars every month by combining both covered call writing and put selling.

If you are a short term trader, you can also learn how to use tailor-made combination strategies such as inverted collars and bull put spreads to control the downside on your position.

Although the techniques described above will enhance your profits, nothing can replace the thrill of buying a stock that is about to explode to the upside, giving you 100% or more profit in a short time. I have dedicated two chapters in this book on how to quantify sentiment and then use it in combination with price action to find such stocks. In addition, you will learn how to leverage your profit by using effective option strategies. You will also be able to further supercharge your profits by recognizing stocks that are undergoing a short squeeze and an earnings squeeze.

In Chapter 13, I will introduce you to time-tested strategies designed to maximize your profits while cutting your losses. These are concepts I have personally used successfully to achieve average monthly returns of 12% over the past five years. These include: price congestion and trend indicator to signal breakouts, divergent signals to predict shakeouts and upward reversals, multiple time frame analysis to avoid selling too soon and missing the lion's share of the profits, continuation volume spikes to signal multiple entry points into a stock, and several other approaches to profit.

These strategies are easy to use and are supported by real life examples to show you how they can effectively work in the real market.

If you have been a long term investor during the past few years, I do not have to convince you of the importance of knowing when to sell. Whether you are a self-directed individual investor with limited time to manage your stocks or you employ a full-time broker to do that, I have written Chapter 14 especially for you. This chapter will show you how by performing a simple calculation every week on each of your stocks you can easily tell whether it is time to buy or sell for the long term.

If your broker ever tells you to hold onto a losing stock because he thinks it is a long term winner, check the CD charts explained in Chapter 14 and you will be able to make the right decision.

For those who are interested in short to intermediate term trading, I have introduced several concepts and ideas to help you trade profitably. A chapter on the most profitable chart patterns with real life example has been included. Another chapter discusses practical applications of candlestick charts in combination with selected technical indicators to spot sudden trend reversals. I have also added a chapter entitled "Tricks of the Trade" where I discuss practical tricks I have learned through my trading experience. These simple techniques allow you to determine the short term direction of a stock, as well as estimate entry and exit prices.

In a new chapter on risk and money management, specific methods on setting stops outside the usual congestion areas to avoid them being run by savvy market professionals are introduced. Option strategies most effectively used for short term trading are also discussed with practical applications.

In this book I also share with you my own stock scanning criteria that filters thousands of available stocks into a limited number of trading candidates. I then demonstrate how to look at the resulting charts to determine the top candidates for trading using the technical indicators in this book.

With practice and a little imagination, you will be able to adapt these tools to your own specific case. To facilitate this, I have included Chapter 15 to show you by example how you can use the simple option strategies in this book to cash in on some common real life situations.

To maximize your benefit from this book, you will need to learn how to apply the appropriate strategies for your type of trading.

If you are a long term investor, you need to familiarize yourself with option strategies to reduce cost basis and continuously raise cash on your holdings. You also must be diligent about constructing CD charts every week for each long term stock you are holding and learn how to determine your exit points using these charts as explained in Chapter 14.

If you are a short term or intermediate term trader, you should familiarize yourself with the technical indicators discussed and their use. You also need to learn to use oscillators, time and price strategies and buy and sell envelopes to determine the short term direction of a stock as well as entry and exit prices.

Do not forget the chapter on limiting your risk using strategically placed stops and combination option strategies.

If you are interested in boosting your ability in picking trading candidates, you can review the stock scanning system I discussed and incorporate any parameters you find useful into your own stock filtering system.

Keep in mind that the objective of this book is combining

options with stock trading to enhance profits and limit risk. As such, the option strategies discussed here have been selected based on simplicity as well as effectiveness. If your interest lies in exclusively trading options, then you will need to use a more comprehensive option trading book that discusses in detail the 60 or more available option strategies.

In this book my aim is to give you innovative ideas and tools that have worked for me in real life rather than a rehash of what you can find in many other books.

It is my goal that after reading this book and implementing the investment, cash generation and trading concepts discussed, you will gain enough confidence to be able to make a sizable income in the market. I hope that your success will be a testimony that this goal has been met.

CHAPTER 1

Learn from the Past

BEFORE GOING INTO DETAILS on how to achieve the goals mentioned in the beginning of this book, it is critical to spend some time analyzing the experiences of recent years to learn from them so the same mistakes will not be repeated in the future.

In this section, I will give a review of the important criteria for buying or selling stocks so as to avoid being in this situation ever again. These principles are simple to apply, but surprisingly most individual investors choose to ignore them.

(1) **Fear and Greed**: Remember this: The time to *buy* stocks is when everyone else, including you, are the most scared, and the time to *sell* is when everyone else, including you, thinks that the sky is the limit for profits. Recent history in fact supports this theory. The best times to buy were the recession and Gulf war of 1991-1992, the Asian crisis of October 1998 and the Y2K scare of 1999. The best time to sell was in March 2000 when everyone thought the good times will never end and that high tech companies are immune to economic slowdown and interest rate increases.

(2) **The trend is your friend:** Two out of three stocks follow the market. So do not try to be a hero by going against the general trend of the market. If you are deciding to buy a stock, first look

1

at the direction of the index it trades in and only buy in an uptrend and sell short in a downtrend. It is amazing how many investors try to buck the trend and fail.

(3) **Don't catch a falling knife:** Buy stocks on their way up after forming a base and avoid buying stocks in a downward trend. Look for a successful re-test of the established low and subsequent reversal before buying, and do not buy if the stock makes a new low. This can be easily demonstrated using a simple example. Remember CSCO (Cisco Systems) went from $80 to $70 to $50 and eventually to $15. Many investors thought that $50, $40 and $30 were good prices just to see the stock down to $15. Each time on its way down the stock made a new low until it hit $15, went back up to $20 and re-tested the low around $15 again. The time to buy would be an upward reversal from $15 after the re-test. In a word, "Do not try to catch the bottom" and "Do not ever average down on your losers" until the conditions described above are met.

(4) **Thumbs up thumbs down:** Use analysts as contrarian indicators. Remember that analysts work for the firms that hire them and not for individual investors. In addition, they usually need to buy or sell large volumes of the stock they upgrade or downgrade, and guess who they want to buy it from or sell it to? Individual investors and fund managers. Stock upgrades near a high are a sign to sell while downgrades near a low are a sign to buy. In cases of upgrades near the low or downgrades near the high, wait a couple of days until a trend is apparent and the knee jerk reaction is over and decide accordingly.

(5) **The long-term trap:** I am sure you heard this many times from your expert broker: "Don't worry about short-term fluctuations in the market, you are investing for the long term." Did you know that if you bought CSCO (CISCO) at $80, now below

2

$30, you may need 10 years to recover your loss. If you bought INKT (INKTOMI) at its high of $240, eventually acquired by Yahoo for less than $3, you will never be able to break even. I don't know about you but I am not going to live forever. The fact is that your expert broker does not like to admit he is wrong any more than you do. Remember that he is playing with *your* money, not his, and he may be willing to let you lose it all to find out if he is right. Be sure to place loss limits of no more than 15%. That is, if a stock closes at 15% below your purchase price, sell it and replace it with a better choice.

(6) **Trading or investing:** Most brokers will tell you that you should not trade, but invest for the long haul. This is true in meaning that you should be in the market for the long-term but should not mean that you should fall in love with any stock, ignore taking profits, cutting losses and rotating into better sectors of the market. The fact that is being ignored by most experts is that since the proliferation of the Internet news travels quickly, and reactions by investors are instantaneous. In addition is the popularity of day trading which accounts for more than 25 percent of the total NASDAQ volume. It is thus normal to see a stock gain or lose 50 percent or more in few days or weeks. The days when you could buy Microsoft or Intel and hold for years and count on 10-20 percent return every year are gone with the emergence of the Internet. To be able to see the analogy more clearly, imagine yourself in a Formula One race driving a 1930 model car; would you be able to compete? Think about large institutions as Formula One car drivers; if they sell millions of shares of a stock, no matter how fundamentally sound it is, it will drop and you will have to act quickly to take profits or cut losses.

The lesson here is to hold onto a stock as long as it is in an upward trend; when you see it selling off on large volume or breaking below the previous low, you should get out and take your profit or loss. Do not try to justify holding onto the stock just because you think the fundamentals are good.

(7) **The present or the future:** An investor usually buys a stock based on the expectations that it will go higher in the future rather than what it is doing at the present. Unfortunately, most investors do this based on fundamental analysis of the stock and ignore technical analysis. Fundamental analysis gives you information on how the stock is doing at the present time but not what it will do in the future. When you decide to purchase a stock based on fundamentals only, you may be rationalizing in this manner "This company has a low price to earning ratio, it is growing revenue and earnings fast, so it is my expectations that things will continue in a similar manner into the future." The question is, will any one ring a bell when earnings slow down and the business atmosphere changes? Of course not. This is where technical analysis is useful by telling you how the price of the stock will move in the near future. *Fundamental analysis* tells you which stocks to buy, while *technical analysis* tells you when to buy them.

In fact, recent history proves this. In March of 2000 technology stocks were showing excellent growth and accelerating earnings with no end in sight. Many experts were saying that the prices were not too high because they are immune to any economic slow down and growth is worth paying a premium for. On the other hand, insiders and smart investors who were paying attention to the technicals were noticing that the NASDAQ was forming a double top between March and April of 2000 with decreasing volume on up days and increasing volume on down days. This was a clear indication that the technology stocks were about to reverse direction. In this case the technical behavior of the market predicted more than six months in advance the deterioration in the fundamentals of the stocks. It is thus critical to pay attention to the technical indicators before buying.

Detailed technical analysis will be addressed in later chapters of this book; however, you should keep an eye on two important indicators: Volume and Price.

Remember this: Price and volume should move together; anything to the contrary spells trouble. Follow these simple rules:

(1) In an uptrend, a reduction in volume as the price is rising indicates a pending reversal.

(2) In a downtrend, an increase in volume indicates a pending sell-off.

(3) A substantial reduction in volume after a steep sell-off indicates a pending upward reversal.

(8) **Smart money or stupid money**: Experts label individual investors as stupid money, while institutions and fund managers are seen as the smart money. In fact, the exact opposite is the truth and recent facts prove this. Remember Qualcomm (QCOM) the best performing stock in the S&P 500 in 1999. In October of 1998 It was trading at $20 with an average daily volume of 600,000 shares. Around April 1999, the stock was trading at $150 with over 8 million shares average daily volume. Now let me ask you this: how many individual investors can buy 10,000 or more blocks of shares of a $150 stock? Institutions continued the frenzy buying until the stock was driven to $800 and split 4 for 1. The stock was already overinflated at $150, and the "stupid money" mutual funds and Institutions were buying all the way up to $800. Smart individual investors who bought during 1998-1999 were selling their shares to the fund managers and making a killing. The lesson here is that if you are lucky enough to own a stock that eventually gets noticed and experiences heavy fund buying resulting in massive average daily volume increases over extended periods of time, take your profits and run.

(9) Your broker can make you broker: Let me make a suggestion to you. Set up an appointment with your financial advisor and ask him the following question: "I would like to have a consistent annual return of 20% and would like you to set up a plan for me to achieve that." Many brokers are likely to give you responses like, "This is not reasonable since the market has returned an average of 8-10% over the long term," or "To do this you will have to take a lot of risk, which I am sure you would not want to do." The answer you want to hear and should hear if your financial advisor has your best interest at heart is something like this: "I will be happy to do that and will have a plan set up and will discuss it with you as soon as I have it completed." The fact is that there are low-risk strategies to make 20% or more cash income from your winning or losing stocks each year without having to sell them. If this is true, why then wouldn't your broker tell you? There are two possible reasons: (1) He is unfamiliar with the strategies to be used; (2) He is aware of these strategies but they do not create lucrative enough commissions to make it worth his time. What I am saying here is use your broker for ideas and suggestions, but take control of your own financial future yourself. In addition, be sure to insist that he implements any new strategies that you are aware of that can increase your return.

(10) Do not average down to zero: How many times have you heard this from your financial advisor: "This stock is selling at a good price; it is down from $80 to $40 and I recommend you average down." I know many people who listened to this and averaged down to pennies and single digits. The only time you should average down is when the following conditions are in place:

(1) The stock has stopped dropping to new lows and has established a base.

(2) The stock is emerging from a base with a new uptrend.

In this book I will show you a simple technique that will signal the right time to average down and how to accomplish that without using your own cash.

(11) The diversification trap: Many experts including your financial advisor are likely to recommend diversification by buying mutual funds, especially if you do not have a large amount to invest. The fact is that picking a mutual fund is more difficult than picking an individual stock. Right now there are more than 8000 mutual funds available and each mutual fund has up to few hundred stocks in it. Faced with these choices you can see that it is easier to pick an individual stock than a fund. This fact has proof in recent history. For the past 10 years, the average annual returns for actively managed funds were 13%, for indexed funds it was 14.5% and for the S&P 500 they were 15.25%. In fact, 95% of the actively managed mutual funds could not beat buying the S&P 500 index (SPDR). What I am getting at here is that if you and your financial advisor can pick funds that can beat the index, then you should be able to pick winning stocks that will multiply your returns many times over. Most importantly, however, is that the techniques described in this book apply only to stocks and do not apply to mutual funds. Remember that the cash income you will make using strategies described here will give you 20% return and beat most funds without having to sell.

(12) The "Are You Close To Retirement Trap": As most individual investors know, it is almost standard recommendation by their financial advisor that they move money from growth into income as they get closer to retiring. They usually suggest that investors sell some of their stocks and move into bonds and CDs and be satisfied with 5-8% returns. This advice is the worst wealth destroyer that anyone can think of. With companies handing early retirement and people retiring earlier and living longer, these years should be the time to maximize your income rather than cut it down.

Let me ask you this: "Why would you want to sell stocks that served you well for years to replace them with a 5% return per year when you can keep them and safely earn 20% or more?"

In fact, stocks held by retirees and investors close to retirement are usually ideal for using the concepts in this book. The reason is that such stocks are usually blue chip stocks that produce higher premiums.

I am not suggesting that you never sell, but rather that you keep stocks that have been performing well. Once the long-term indicators discussed in Chapter 14 turn negative on a stock, you should sell it and replace it with a better candidate. Be sure, however, that you continuously generate cash using the concepts in this book on any stock you are holding.

This book will show you how you can generate 20% or more spendable cash on almost any stock.

Imagine that if you had a retirement portfolio of $500,000 in stocks and only applied the concepts described here to half of the portfolio ($250,000) that will give you an income of over $50,000 in cash.

CHAPTER 2

Generate 20% + Cash Return
Each Year Without Selling Your Stocks

Time is money: Most people are aware that there is time value to money. When you invest money in a bank, you earn interest on your investment. The same applies when you place money in a certificate of deposit (CD) or a money market fund. Bank interests usually range from 1-3% while CD and money market rates range from 4-6%.

In the case of owning stocks, most investors believe that unless a stock pays a dividend the only way to make a return on the money tied up in it is by selling and cashing out. This could not be further from reality. In fact, there is time value to money tied up in most stocks, and this money is available to an investor to cash out with the right strategies.

To illustrate this, let me use an everyday example.

Imagine that a person is about to move to a new city due to a job transfer. He is looking to rent a home to get familiar with the area before buying. A property manager shows him a home that he likes and decides to rent it immediately. The manager tells him that the rent is $1000/month and that there is a $500 deposit. Since the tenant cannot move right away, he suggests to the manager that he give him the $500 deposit to hold the house for a couple of months. The manager indicates to the tenant that he cannot do that since there is a new factory moving into town and rents are going up rapidly. In fact, The manager says he is sure he can get a minimum of $1300 in two months.

To get around this, the tenant makes the following proposal: He offers the manager 10% of the yearly rent or $1200 to give him the option to rent the house for a period of two months. If the two months expire and he does not rent the property, the manager keeps the $1200. If he rents the property within that time frame, the manager gets to keep the $1200 but will have to rent the tenant the house for $1000 instead of the market price of $1300.

The manager is selling the tenant an option to rent the home at a price of $1000/month with an expiration date of two months from the start of the agreement. His compensation is a $1200 premium that he gets to keep whether or not the tenant rents the home.

A similar analogy applies in the case of stocks. Say you own 1000 shares of Microsoft with present value of $70,000. You can sell the right to someone to buy your shares at a specified price in a limited time period for a premium. In stock market language, this is known as selling covered call options. In this case you are in the manager's role.

In summary, a covered call option gives the owner (buyer) the right to buy units of 100 shares of stock (contract) at a certain price (strike price) by a certain date (expiration date). You as the seller of the option get a cash premium for the sale.

Low Risk Cash: Selling covered call options is one of the lowest risk and safest ways to generate cash while holding stocks, in fact, it is almost a no-lose situation. Options have the reputation of being high risk investments; however, this is only true if you do not own the underlying stock. Anyone who tells you this is a high risk approach lacks the understanding of how this really works. The low risk character of these techniques will be more apparent in the case histories discussed in this book.

Cash to Keep: Let us go back to the example of selling call options on 1000 shares of Microsoft. If you look at June 2001 option quotes, you will find that on May 7, 2001, the price of the June calls on Microsoft at a $75 strike price were $2.00 a share. This means that if you sell a call on 1000 shares of Microsoft June $75 strike you get $2000 premium.

By the date of the option expiration (the third Friday of June) one of the following possibilities can occur:

(1) Microsoft never reaches the strike price of $75 and the option expires and you get to keep the $2000 and the stock.

(2) Microsoft drops in price to $65 or less, in which case you can buy the option back at a much lower price (around $0.30) for a total cost of $300 and pocket the $1700 difference. Please remember that small price increases or decreases in a stock result in much faster movement on the option.

(3) Microsoft goes over $75, in which case you will have two choices:

(a) If you want to sell the stock, you can let it be called and get to keep the $2000 from the premium plus the $75000 from selling the stock at $75.

(b) If you do not want to sell the stock, you buy the option back at a slightly higher price and you then sell a new call option at a higher strike say $80. This will allow you to pay for buying back the option and leave you with a premium for selling the new option. Remember that the price of the $80 strike is higher since the stock has moved from $70 to $75+.

Deciding which action to take to give you the best results depends on whether you have a profit you are willing to take on the stock or you have a loss and you are trying to generate cash while waiting for the stock to come back.

This Is Real Cash:

To illustrate how to apply the principles discussed effectively, I will show you how to generate cash on winning or losing stocks using actual past and present case histories. After studying these examples carefully, try to start by implementing these concepts on one of the stocks you own.

Please note that due to large variations in commissions charged by different brokers, they were left out of the calculations. I do recommend, however, that you use a discount broker if at all possible to maximize your returns.

Case History: Juniper Networks (JNPR)

An investor purchased 200 shares of Juniper Networks (JNPR) on 10/16/2000 at $243 a share for a total cost of $48600. He was looking to sell at a 50% profit, which means that the sell price target is around $360/share. What this person did not know is that the market was about to fall significantly.

While waiting for the target price to hopefully be reached, rather than keeping the $48,600 as dead money we will use covered call options to generate cash on this stock during the holding period. To start, the investor sells a January 2001 $260 strike price call for $29.75 a share, giving him proceeds of $29.75 x 200 = $5950.

ALERT: Why did we pick a strike price of $260 rather than $250 or $255 even though we could have gotten a higher premium by picking a lower strike? Remember that our objective is to have the option expire before the stock reaches the strike since we do not want to sell for less than 50% profit. The price we picked is close to a level representing the next resistance of the stock. As a rule of thumb, place a target price 10%-20% higher than the present market price. Locate the price resistance closest to that and pick the strike price one level above that resistance.

Going back to our case with Juniper. By selling the covered call we achieved two goals: (1) We received a $5950 cash premium to keep if the option expires. (2) We reduced our cost basis on the stock from $48600 to $48600-$5950 = $42650 and our per share price is now at $42650/200 = $213.25 a share. To get our 50% profit target we need to sell at $320 rather than $360.

Our game plan is now as follows:

(1) If Juniper rose to $260 a share, we will buy back the call using the proceeds from selling another call at $320 strike. This accomplishes three goals:

   (a) We prevent the stock from getting called and we get to keep it.

   (b) Picking the $320 strike allows us to achieve a 50% profit if the stock gets called next time.

   (c) We use no out-of-pocket cash to buy back our $260 call.

(2) If Juniper's price did not rise to $260 a share, we will buy back the call when it is worth 25% of the premium we received. This allows us to achieve two goals:

   (a) Immediately pocket a profit equivalent to the difference between the selling price of the call and the price we bought it back at.

   (b) Immediately sell another call with the same strike price and /or expiration date, allowing us to almost double up on profits during that time period.

As it turns out Juniper's price closed at $185 a share two weeks after we sold the $260 call. The price of the $260 call at this time was $6/share, which is less than 25% of the original price of $29.75. Thus we executed part 2 of the plan and purchased the call back at $6/share at a total cost of $1200.

Our cost now is at $213.25+$6.00 = $219.25 a share, and the cash premium we received to date is $5950-$1200 = $4750.

ALERT: Do not sell covered calls right after a steep fall in the stock price. Wait until it reaches 20% above its 20-day closing low to do that.

We waited until the stock rose from $165 to $216 where it closed on 11/3/2000, which was 31% above the $166 price of 10/30/2000. We then sold the February 2001 $260 call at $29.50 a share for a premium of $29.50 x 200 = $5900.

Now our total proceeds from selling covered calls are $4750 + $5900 = $10650, and our cost per share is reduced to $219.25-$29.50 = $189.75. Our target for 50% profit has now been reduced to $189.75 x 1.5 = $284.63 from $360.

What have we accomplished: We produced a cash income of $10,650 on an initial investment of $48,600 in four months. This is a return of 21% over four months or 63% per year, and we kept the stock to sell when the market recovers. Remember that we did this by selling only two calls; just imagine where our average price would be if we repeated this process.

Case History: LSI Logic (LSI)
This case is so current that the execution of this plan is in progress. I felt, however, that it will be beneficial to include it here to demonstrate that this approach works in difficult market conditions where most stocks are down by large percentages.

An investor purchased 5400 shares of LSI Logic (LSI) In July – October 1998 at an average price of $10/share for a total cost of $54000. The stock reached $90 a share in March of 2000; unfortunately, this investor decided not to sell to avoid paying capital gains taxes. The stock subsequently dropped to $16 a share and traded between $15 and $25 between November 2000 and August 2001.

ALERT: This investor could have avoided this situation if he applied the principles described in the beginning of this book. In March 2000 when LSI was at $90, analysts were placing a target of $115, the earnings and fundamentals looked good with great growth prospects. In addition, if you read LSI message boards on the Internet, you would have thought it will go up forever.

Remember what I mentioned in the introduction: analysts are a contrarian indicator, sell when greed is rampant, and fundamentals tell you the present situation but cannot predict the future. Technical indicators were showing signs of trouble. After the stock hit $90, it dropped back to $70 and went back up to $90 but could not break through. It subsequently went down and broke below $70 forming a new low. This was a clear sign to get out. Be sure you do not fall into a similar trap with your holdings.

Going back to the situation at hand with LSI, this investor felt bad that he did not sell and missed a big profit and did not want to sell at $25 or so. He decided that he is willing to accept selling at $50 for a five-fold profit on the stock in less than three years.

The plan is to sell covered calls to generate cash and reduce the basis for the cost of the stock so he can achieve his target profit at a lower target sell price.

Studying the charts showed a strong resistance at $22.5 and that price was picked as the strike price. However, with the stock at $16 we could not get much for the call, so we waited until the price was above $19. On April 18 we sold May 2001 calls at $22.5 strike for $1/share for a total premium of $5400. Please note that you are dealing here with a $20 stock and not $240 as the case with Juniper, which explains the much lower call price.

On April 20th 2001 right after the Federal reserve decreased interest rate by 1/2 point, the stock hit $22.40 (10 cents below the strike); however, it never hit the $22.50 strike. If that happened, we would have had to buy the call back and sell another call with a strike at $25.

ALERT: It is important to pick strike prices carefully. As you can see, we were able to avoid having the stock called or having to buy back the call by picking a strike price close to strong resistance at $22.5.

After receiving the premium upon option expiration, our total cost will be $54000-$5400 = $48600, which gives us a price of $9/share. To achieve a five-fold profit, our target sell price is down from $50 to $45. Now we wait to see what happens by May 18,2001, the expiration date of the option.

Finally, May 18th is here and LSI does not hit the strike price, so we get to keep the $5400 premium.

We will look for an opportunity to make more cash by selling covered calls for June or July. After some research on the stock, we decide that since July is earnings month we would want to protect ourselves in case of an unexpected run-up before earnings. We decide to set a minimum strike price of $25 for July. On the other hand, we set a minimum strike price of $22.5 for June since we do not expect any catalyst that will move the stock much higher than the strong resistance at $22.5.

Now we wait for a temporary bounce in the stock to execute this plan.

On May 21, 2001 the Nasdaq was up 105 points and LSI was up to $21.50. We decided to take advantage of the move in the stock and sell additional covered calls. We researched the option premiums and found that June $25 was at $0.30, June $22.5 at $0.95, and July $25 at $1.00. We do not want to risk the stock being called or having to buy the option back, so we eliminated the June $22.5 since it is too close to the current price. The July $25 call was worth more than three times the June $25 call with twice the time left, so we sold 54 contracts (5400 shares) July $25 call for $5400.

On May 29 and 30th the Nasdaq was down a total of 150 points and LSI was below $18. The July $25 call we sold at $1/share was now at $0.25/share, so we bought it back and locked in a profit of ($1-$0.25) x 5400 = $4500. Our total profit is now $9450 or 17.5% in five weeks (180%/year). In addition, our target selling price to achieve five-fold profit is down from $45 to $41.25.

ALERT: When selling calls during an earnings month, be conservative in picking strikes, especially if you feel there could be a catalyst that will move the stock against your position and risk the stock being called.

We will look now for another opportunity to repeat the process.

On June 8, 2001, Solomon Smith Barney raised their rating on the semiconductor sector. As a result, LSI moved to $22.5 which is a resistance level. Since the analyst upgrade occurred near resistance, we will view it as a contrarian indicator. We thus sold 54 contracts (5400 shares) July covered calls $25 strike at $1.05/share for a total premium of $5670.

ALERT: Using analysts as contrarian indicators is a highly effective technique. If you had access to Nasdaq level 2, you would have noticed that Solomon Smith Barney was a big seller on the day of the upgrade. Remember that analysts work for their firms and not you or me. They probably upgraded the stock since they have a large number of shares to sell.

Since July is an earnings month, we expect that any earnings warnings will come the last two weeks of June. With the Technology sector weak, we anticipate that any warnings from other technology companies will result in a drop in LSI share price. This will allow us to buy the calls back for a profit.

The Federal Reserve meeting and a decision on interest rates is scheduled for June 27,2001. We prefer to close our position before then to avoid any possible run-up in the stock and hence an increase in the option price in case of a higher-than-expected rate cut.

ALERT: Always keep an eye on the big picture and use general market trends and upcoming news to your advantage. Notice how we sold the calls on a bounce anticipating a drop will occur during earnings warning season. We also planned to close the position before the Federal Reserve meeting in case a surprise 1/2 point cut occurs.

As expected, several high technology companies issued earnings warnings (JDSU TLAB TMTA to mention a few) between June 14 and June 20,2001.

On 6/20/2001 LSI dropped below $18, and the call we sold at $1.05 on June 8th was now at $0.15. We thus bought the call back for a profit of ($1.05-0.15) x 5400 = $4860. Our cost basis is now at $8.25- $0.90 = $7.35/share.

What have we accomplished:

Our target selling price to achieve 500% profit has now been reduced from $50 to 5 x $7.35 = $36.75. We have raised a total of $5400 + $4050 + $4860 = $14310 since April 18, 2001. This is a return of 26% in two months or 160%/year.

We will now look for another chance to repeat the process to further reduce our cost basis on the stock.

The Federal Reserve decision on June 27 was for a 1/4 point cut which was in line with expectations, so no quick run-up in the market occurred. However, we will watch LSI carefully on June 28th and 29th for any possible move due to end of quarter re-balancing by mutual funds.

On Friday, June 29th, 2001, LSI moved up over $20. There were no specific news to justify the move, so we decided to wait until the close to gauge the strength of the stock. LSI pulled back to $18.80 at the close indicating selling pressure above $20.

On Monday, July 2nd, 2001, LSI moved above $20 again, so we decided to take advantage of the move and raise cash by selling covered calls at a strike corresponding to $22.5 resistance. July $22.5 had a premium of $0.30/share while August had a premium of $0.95/share, so we sold 54 contracts (5400 shares) August $22.5 strike calls at a premium of $0.95/share for a total of $5130. If this option expires our total cash is at $14310 + $5130 = $19,440. This is a return of 36% in 75 days or 173%/year.

On Thursday, July 5, Advanced Micro Devices and EMC issued earnings warnings after the market close. The Nasdaq dropped by 75 points on Friday. LSI was at $18.20 and the calls we sold on Monday were at $0.40/share. We now have a profit of ($0.95-$0.40) x 5400 = $2700 in four days. Since the market looks weak and we expect LSI will drop further on Monday, we will keep our position open. We will plan to lock our profit before the start of the semicon-ductor earnings season or when we have a 75% profit, whichever comes first.

ALERT: Always be on the lookout for news on stocks in a similar industry to the one you are selling calls on. To raise maximum cash on your stocks, you need to use news whether it is related to the stock, industry or the general market to lock your profit. The idea here is to repeat this process several times and not have to wait for the option to expire.

On July 9, 2001, Corning (GLW) issued an earnings warning, followed by another from Compaq on July 10. On July 11th the Nasdaq dropped to 1950, and the call we sold at $0.95 is now at $0.20 (less than our 25% target), so we locked in a profit of ($0.95 - $0.20) x 5400 = $4050. Remember that this call will expire on August 17, and it is much more profitable to lock our profit now and have a chance of repeating the process rather than wait another 45 days to make an additional $0.10/share.

ALERT: I cannot stress this enough. Do not get greedy and always buy back any call you already sold when it is at 25% of the premium you obtained.

Our total actual cash is now at $14310 + $4050 = $18360. A return of 34% in 75 days or 165 %/year. Our cost basis for the stock is now down to $7.35-$0.75 = $6.60. We are well on our way to zero cost basis.

On July 26, 2001, LSI came out with earnings that met expectations and announced that revenue growth will pick up in the fourth quarter. The next day the stock was up $1.70 and traded over 7 million shares (three times average volume), indicating strong upward momentum. We will be on the lookout to sell additional calls when we see signs of fading momentum while the stock is going higher.

On Wednesday, August 2nd, 2001, LSI traded over 7 million shares and the price moved up to $24. The premium for the September $25 strike calls moved to $1.50. We realized that getting this premium will reduce our cost basis to $6.60-$1.50 = $5.10 which will allow us to achieve our 500% target by selling at $25.

We therefore decided to sell 54 contracts (5400 shares) of $25 strike LSI September calls at $1.50 for a total premium of $8100.

UNBELIEVABLE! In less than 4 months we were able to reduce our cost basis from $10 to $5.10. If we keep the premium from the last calls we sold, our total cash generated is $18,360 + $8100 = $26,460 for a return of over 150%/year. In addition, by selling at $25 we will achieve our stated target of 500% profit on the stock.

CHAPTER 3

Increase Your Profits on Winning Stocks By Getting a Premium to Market Price

YOU CAN EFFECTIVELY USE selling covered call options to increase your profits on a winning stock by getting a premium to the market when taking profits. This is best illustrated by an actual case history.

Case History: Scientific Atlanta (SFA)

An investor purchased 2000 shares of Scientific Atlanta (SFA) on April 4, 2001, for $37/share at a cost of $74000. The price of $37 was picked since it represented an uptrend bounce from the $35 support. Previous history of the stock showed strong resistance at $60. In addition, review of the stock charts showed a $60 price was reached in January 2001 right after earnings.

First quarter earnings were scheduled on 4/19/2001 one day before option expiration. The investor thus plans to sell the shares right after earnings at $60 or higher for a total profit of ($60-$37) x 2000 = $46,000.

Our plan is to enhance the profit on the stock by selling covered calls as the stock approaches $60. Our target is to sell April SFA $60 calls as soon as the market price of the stock reaches $59-1/2.

April was a lucky charm for this investor, right before earnings, on April 17, 2001, the federal reserve had a surprise 1/2 point interest rate cut. The stock reached $59-1/2 a day after, and we sold the covered calls at $7/share for a premium of $14000. SFA came out with strong earnings as expected, the stock broke through $60 and was called. We got to keep the $14000 premium in addition to the $120,000 from the proceeds of the sale. By doing this, our original target profit of $46,000 is now $14000 + $46,000 = $60,000, which is equivalent to selling the stock at $67/share.

As it happens, the stock reached $62/share, but a few days later pulled back to $54/share. By using this strategy we were able to get a $10,000 premium above the highest price the stock reached during that time frame. Using this approach, we achieved a profit of $60,000 in 19 days in a choppy market.

Now I will use another case history to illustrate how using a combination of buying calls and selling covered calls can multiply your profits many times over on winning stocks with little or no additional cash investment beyond the original purchase price of the stock.

Case History: Chesapeake Energy (CHK)

In this case I will use a stock that I recommended to investors that follow my system on the Internet. I will show the reasoning behind picking the stock followed by the strategy I recommended to maximize profits.

In a difficult and mostly down market it is much harder to pick winning stocks. My first step was to identify the sectors that are moving up in this market. After reviewing many sectors, the energy sector stood out as a winner. I researched that sector to identify stocks with good fundamentals to evaluate. After screening several candidates I decided that Chesapeake Energy (CHK) looked the best. The company had a low price to earning ratio of 5.6, excellent earnings growth of 40% and have reported record earnings for the last quarter. They were in the "hot" natural gas sector which has been performing well, and this stock looks like it has been overlooked.

With the fundamentals looking strong, it was time to check whether it was the right time to buy. To do that we needed to look at technical indicators. The stock had strong support at $7.50 with a double bottom. It was also emerging from a base into an uptrend. The logarithmic relative performance line was showing strong positive slope. The price was at $8 which is not much higher than the $7.50 support limiting our downside. The stock was breaking out of an ascending triangle formation. Based on this, I issued a recommendation to buy this stock at $8 or lower.

ALERT: As discussed in the introduction of this book, use fundamental analysis to decide *what* to buy and technical analysis to decide *when* to buy. I may have used technical indicators you are not familiar with; however, my point here is that you should use some kind of technical indicator before timing any purchase.

At this point I wanted to boost potential profits for investors with little cash, so I recommended that they buy July $12.5 calls selling at $0.15/share.

ALERT: In cases where you feel confident about the direction of the stock but have limited cash, it is effective to supplement your stock purchase by buying calls. This will allow you to boost your profit significantly if the stock moves in your favor. It is critical, however, to limit your risk by paying attention to the following:

If the stock has not reached the strike price and the option is close to expiration, you can expect to get $0.05/share when you sell.

Use selling covered calls when the stock is moving higher at a later date to pay part of the cost (at least half if possible) of buying the calls. This will be clearer as you read through this example.

Our objective is to limit our loss on calls we buy to $0.05/share. If we assume that we will be able to pay one-half the cost of buying the calls by selling covered calls at a later date, the maximum price we would want to pay for buying calls on any stock is $0.20/share.

$0.20 (actual cost) − $0.10(Premium from covered call)

−$0.05 (selling price) = $0.05 (loss/share).

REVIEW: Remember that buying calls is an offensive strategy where time works against you, so it is critical that you control risk. Do not supplement your stock position with buying calls unless you can do that at $0.20/share or less. A prudent strategy is to pick the strike price corresponding to $0.20/share and then decide whether to buy the call.

ALERT 1: I picked July option rather than June for the following reasons (1) Earnings are coming out in mid-July and based on expectations from previous earnings the stock may run up beforehand. (2) July had much larger option open interest which will give added liquidity in case we need to sell.

ALERT 2: The main reason I picked the $12.5 and not $10 strike is that it was selling at $0.15 compared to $0.60 for the $10 strike. In case we are wrong our loss will be minimal; however, our gain could be 500-1000%.

Let us assume that an investor took my advice and purchased 2500 shares of CHK at $8 for a total cost of $20,000 on May 3, 2001. Three days later he supplemented the position with buying July $12.5 calls on 20,000 shares of CHK at $0.15 for a cost of $3000. The total cost is $23000.

ALERT: Buy a call option a few days after you buy the stock to be sure that the stock is moving in the right direction. This is a prudent strategy to minimize losses.

On May 14, CHK was trading at $9.15 and the call option was at $0.25. Our profit to this point was $2000 + $2875 = $4875 for a 21% gain in two weeks. The stock showed above average volume with a close near its high which indicates good strength.

To maximize profits our strategy will be as follows:
(1) As soon as the price breaks through $10, we will sell July $12.5 covered calls on the 2500 shares we own for an expected premium of $0.60/share or a total of $1500.

(2) If the stock reaches $10 but cannot decisively break through, we will sell the calls on 20,000 shares at an estimated $0.60/share for an approximate profit of $9000. Our total profit in this case will be $5000 (stock profit) + $9000 (call option profit) + $1500 (covered call premium) for a total of $15,500. A return of 67% in two months.

(3) If we are wrong and the stock makes a double top at $10 and slides to $8, we will buy back the covered call at $0.15 for a profit of $0.45/share or a total of $1125. Remember that we sold the 20,000 share call at a profit of $9000. However, at this point we do not have a profit on the stock. Our total profit thus is $10,125. We will sell the stock if the price breaks below the support of $7.50. So a worst case scenario will give us a profit of $10,125-$1250 = $8875.

ALERT: How did we come up with $0.60/share? The call option value for CHK at a strike of $10 was at $0.60 when the stock was at $7.80. We are approximating that the option will be worth about $0.60 when we are $2 below the strike and with at least one month left to expiration. Thus we are using $0.60 for a strike of $12.5 and an approximate price of $10 to $10.5. Be aware that this is just a ball park figure and the number could be anywhere between $0.50-$0.70.

(4) If the stock decisively breaks through 10 and moves higher, we will hold all our positions and implement the following strategy:

(a) We will sell the calls on the 20,000 shares at approximately $1.00/share or two weeks before expiration whichever comes first.

(b) We will hold the covered calls until expiration hoping that the stock will get called and we can keep the $1500 premium in addition to a profit of $11,250 on the stock if we sell at $12.50.

What will we achieve: By selling covered calls we were able to reduce our cost for the 20,000 share call buy to a total of $1500 which is $.075/share. Furthermore we will be able to achieve a profit of $8875 in the worst case or more than 38% in two months (220%/year).

If the best case scenario plays out, our profits will be $11,250 from selling the stock at $12.50, $1500 from the covered call premium that we get to keep and the profits from selling the 20,000 share calls at $1.00 a share or $17,000. Our total in this case is $29,750 for a profit of 170% in two months or over 750% in one year. That is how people become rich!

You guessed right, we left one possibility out. What if CHK never reaches $10 and stalls around $9 to $9.5. We will address this on page **45,** since we will need to use techniques that have not yet been discussed.

CHAPTER 4

Average Down Without Using
Out-of-Pocket Cash

BEFORE GOING INTO DETAILS on how this is done, it is important to know when to average down. Before you throw good money after bad, you want to be sure that the stock has bottomed out.

The 1030 Test: In fact, there is a simple test which I call the 1030 test. Remember Lucent down from $82 in early 2000 to $14 in late 2000. At that price most expert brokers were telling their clients to average down. If you look at the graph of Lucent, you can see that the 10-week moving average crossed below the 30-week moving average on 2/4/2000 and remained that way until Lucent reached $7 a share and then reversed. The 10-week moving average crossed above the 30-week moving average when the stock was about $8 in April 2001. Depending on whether you are a long or short term holder, the time to average down is when the 10-week, or day, moving average crosses above the 30-week, or day, moving average. You may not catch the exact bottom, but you will be within 10% and will limit your down risk. So before averaging down give it the 1030 test.

The 102030 Test: This is slightly more sophisticated than the 1030 test, but is a useful and more accurate indicator on when to sell or average down.

When a stock is in an uptrend, the moving averages are lined as follows: 10 period simple moving average MA(10) >20 period exponential moving average EMA (20) > 30 period exponential moving average EMA (30). When a downward reversal is about to occur, the MA(10) starts trending down and crossing the EMA (20) and EMA (30). Hence, if a stock is in an uptrend, this will be a signal to sell if you are a trader or to start selling covered calls if you do not want to sell your stock. This is an indication that the upward momentum is fading. The period used could be hours, days or weeks depending on whether you are a short term trader or longer term investor.

In a down trend the moving averages are lined up as follows: EMA (30)>EMA (20)>MA(10). When an upward reversal is about to occur, the MA(10) will start curving to the upside and crossing the EMA (20) and EMA(30). This is a signal to average down or start selling puts on the stock.

To further your understanding, below is a brief explanation of the concept of moving averages.

A Simple Moving Average (MA) is calculated by adding the different prices and dividing by the total period. As an example, a 10-day moving average is calculated by adding prices for 10 days and dividing by 10. In this case, each data point is assigned equal weighting on the average.

The equation for an **Exponential Moving Average (EMA)** may look complex, but it is actually easier to calculate than the simple moving average.

EMA = (EMA*(1-K)) + (Price *K), where K = 2/(1+N), N = number of days in average.

The way this works is as follows:

(1) Multiply yesterday's EMA by 1-K
(2) Multiply today's price by K
(3) Add the two results to get today's EMA

Note that each new price has more of an impact on the EMA than the MA.

You will not need to do any of the above calculations, since they are available on numerous internet sites as well as charting services provided by online brokers.

You will be able to see the chart of the three moving averages overlaid on the price chart. You can clearly verify how the averages line up based on the stock trend. Be sure that you clearly understand this concept since we will be using it to maximize our cash generation.

Dollar cost averaging may be a feasible way to turn a loser into a winner, but what if someone does not have the cash or the patience? In fact, there is a better way.

Let us go back to the manager tenant example given previously. This time the manager accepts the $500 deposit but says he is worried that if the tenant does not rent the house, prices may drop since there are rumors that a factory in town is closing. The manager proposes that if the tenant does not rent the house and he cannot get a tenant for at least the agreed to price of $1000 the tenant will have to pay him the $1000 rent for a full year whether he occupies the house or not. This seems stiff, but the tenant reluctantly agrees since he lives out of town and feels the house is in a good area.

In this case the tenant has purchased the option to rent this house at a price that may be above market in case he decides to exercise the option. The manager gets to keep the premium whether the tenant rents the house or not. In addition, if the tenant refuses to rent the house and another tenant cannot be located to rent it for at least $1000, he will have to pay the manager a year's rent.

A similar analogy applies to stocks. Let us say you own 1000 shares of Lucent at $50 for a $50,000 cost. Lucent has now dropped to $11. You decide that it is time to average down, so you sell someone the option to sell you Lucent at a price of $10 for a limited period of time in exchange for a premium. In stock market language this is known as selling put options. In this case you are in the tenant's role.

In summary, selling a put option gives the holder (buyer) the right to sell 100 Shares of stock (contract) at a specified price (strike price) by a certain date (expiration date). You as the seller of the option will get a premium for the sale. In return for that premium you agree to buy the shares if the market price drops below the strike price and they are assigned to you.

Cash to Keep While Averaging Down: Let us assume you own 1000 shares of Microsoft that you purchased at $100 a share. The stock drops to $45 and after applying the 1030 test you decide to average down if you can buy the stock at $40. You decide to sell a January $40 put option on Microsoft for $2/share for a premium of $2000. The following possibilities can occur before the expiration of the option:

    (1) Microsoft never drops below $40 and you keep the premium.
    (2) If Microsoft reaches $40 you will have two choices:
        (a) If you are willing to buy the stock, you can keep the premium and buy the stock at $40 if it gets assigned to you.
        (b) If you feel that Microsoft can drop much below $40 and you do not want to buy the stock at that price, you can buy the put back and sell another put at a lower strike.

ALERT: Sell put options only if you are willing to average down on the stock and be sure to give the stock the 1030 test before doing so. Always try to use a combination of selling puts and calls on stocks that have significantly gone down in price and you are willing to average down on. If you change your mind and do not want to average down after selling the put, be sure to buy it back and sell a new put at a lower strike.

The case history below shows that using a strategy including a combination of selling puts and calls can turn a disastrous loser into a possible winner over a relatively short time period. Please try to read this case history carefully more than once if need be to understand the reasoning and logic behind each decision. Doing this will help you implement this strategy much more easily on your holdings.

Case History: Mckesson (MCK)

An unlucky investor bought 500 shares of Mckesson (MCK) at its all-time high on 9/25/98 for $93 a share at a total cost of $46,500. A month later the stock fell to $70.56. Applying the 1030 test indicated that the stock had further to fall, so he decided to raise some cash by selling covered calls to help regain some of the paper loss.

The investor sold five contracts (500 shares) January 1999 $85 strike call for $2.82 a share for total proceeds of $1410. His cost per share now is at $93 − $2.82 = $90.18 and his total cost is $45,090.

ALERT: The $85 price was picked since it is almost 20% above the present market price of $70 and defines a strong resistance for the stock.

MCK closed at $85 in January but the stock was not called, so we kept the $1410 and sold April $90 call for $8.31/share for total proceeds of $4155. Now the price per share was at $90.18 − $8.31 = $81.87 and the total cost was $45,090 − $4155 = $40,935. If the stock got called, we would have let it go with a nice $8/share profit since the cost is down to $81.87.

Unfortunately, the stock dropped to $62.31 a share so we kept the $4155 and sold a July 1999 $75 call for $3.87 a share for total proceeds of $1935. Our share cost now is $81.87 − $3.87 = $78 and our total cost is $40935 − $1935 = $39,000.

REVIEW: Our total proceeds from selling calls now are $1410 + $4145 + $1935 = $7490 on an investment of $46,500 for a return of 16%. But we are not done yet.

Two weeks later disaster strikes and the stock drops to $35 a share and the call we sold at $3.87 is now worth only $0.40, so we buy it back at a cost of $0.40 x 500 = $200. Now our basis is $78.40 a share and total cost is $39,200.

We then sold the July 1999 $50 call for $3.41 a share for a total of $1705. The stock never got close to $50 and, in fact, fell to $30

31

by August 20,1999. Now our cost per share is $78.40 − $3.41 = $74.99 and our total cost is $39,200 − $1705 = $37,495.

We sold the February 2000 $45 call for $4.03 a share for a total of $2015. The stock fell to $19.94, so we kept the premium from the call. Our per share cost is now down to $74.99 − $4.03 = $70.96, and our total cost is $37,495-$2015 = $35,480.

REVIEW: Our total proceeds from selling covered calls is now $7490 − $200 + $1705 + $2015 = $11,010. This is a return of 24% on our original investment. Remember that this was achieved even though the stock kept falling.

We applied the 1030 test to the stock at $19.94, and we concluded that it was getting close to bottom. In fact, the bottom was reached on May 26 at $16.06. At this point with our cost basis still at $70.96, it was so much higher than the stock price that selling covered calls is no longer useful.

Instead of waiting for the stock to move up, we realized that we had over $11,000 in cash which is more than enough to buy 500 shares of stock. But there is a better way to handle this by selling puts.

We sold May 2000 $17.5 put at $1.07 for a total of $535. If the stock went below $17.50, it would be assigned to us. On 5/17/2000 the stock closed at $16.50, so we ended up buying 500 shares at $17.50 for a cost of $8750. Now we own 1000 shares at an average price of ($17.5 + $70.96)/2 -$1.07 = $43.16

REVIEW: We now have used $8750 from our cash proceeds to buy additional 500 shares and reduce our cost basis to $43.16 a share. To do this we used no out-of-pocket money and still have over $2000 in cash.

Since our average cost was still above the current price, we sold an October 2000 $15 put for $1.18, giving us proceeds of $1118 (remember we now own 1000 shares). The stock hit $25.50 by July 21, and our put was only worth $0.16 so we bought it back for $160.

Our per share cost is now at $43.16 − $1.18 + $0.16 = $42.14. Our cost for the total 1000 shares is at $42,140.

We decided we needed to speed up our cash generation, so we sold an October 2000 $22.5 put for $1.5 per share or a total of $1500 and two October $35 calls for $1.52 each or a total of $3040. The stock closed at $30 on expiration of the option. Since this is below $35 and above $22.5, we got to keep all premiums from both calls and puts.

Clarification: Selling one put option implies that you are selling put options on the amount of shares of stock you are holding. Selling two put options implies that you are doing that on twice the shares you hold. In the above example one put implies an option on 1000 shares and two calls imply options on 2000 shares.

ALERT 1: When selling puts and calls within the same expiration month, pick the strike price near resistance levels for the call and near support level for the put. The idea here is that we want the options to expire to minimize our chances of having to buy the option back.

ALERT 2: Using a combination put/call selling strategy is highly effective in cases where the stock you own has gone down significantly in price. Our objective is to generate maximum cash as quickly as possible to achieve break-even by lowering the cost basis of the stock. To do this, sell call options as the stock is moving higher and put options as it is moving lower.

ALERT 3: We have sold two times as many calls as puts in the above example for the following reasons. We anticipate that since the stock is trending down the call option will be the most likely to expire worthless or be bought back at a much lower price. Since it is our objective to raise maximum cash, we will want to sell more of the option that is likely to generate maximum profit based on our anticipated movement in the stock.

Remember that a put option will move lower as the stock rises in price, and that allows us to buy it back at a cheaper price and pocket the difference. On the other hand, a call option loses value with a drop in the stock price. It is thus our objective to sell more call options if we think the stock will go lower and put options if we expect a higher stock price.

Clarification: The last statement may seem contradictory to what we said before, relating to the timing of selling calls and puts. You need to sell calls as the stock is moving higher toward resistance and puts as it is moving lower toward support. The relative number of calls to puts you sell depends on what the longer term anticipated direction of the stock is by option expiration date.

Our cost per share now is $42.14 − $1.52 x 2 − $1.5 = $37.60 or a total cost of $37,600 for our 1000 shares.

We then repeated the process by selling two January 2001 $40 calls for $1.24 each and a January 2001 $20 put for $0.84. Our per share price is now down to $37.60 − $0.84 − $2.48 = $34.28.

REVIEW: We now have generated cash of $11010 + $535 + $1118 − $160 + $1500 + $3040 + $2480 + $840 = $20363 since we purchased the stock. We used $8750 to double up on the shares and still have over $11,000 to use to buy more shares or invest in a better stock.

ALERT: When using a combination of selling covered calls and puts, be sure that you sell the puts when the stock is going down and the calls when it is going up. You do not have to sell the puts and calls the same day as long as you use the same expiration month for the option. In addition, be sure that you sell the put at a strike price representing solid support for the stock.

What have we accomplished:

As you recall, we purchased 500 shares of MCK at $93, and even though the stock dropped to $16, we were able to generate a cash amount close to $ 20,000 on a stock that was a huge disaster. We used $8750 of the cash to buy 500 more shares, eventually reducing our cost basis to $34.28 a share. We also still have $11,790 in cash from the proceeds of selling calls and puts.

If you held onto the stock, assuming a 15% yearly appreciation it would have taken over 12 years to get back to $93 and break even.

I am sure you are curious how this ended. MCK moved from $27 on 1/19/01 to $34.5 on 2/8/01. We studied the technical signals on the stock and the whole market, and we decided to sell on 2/8/01 at $34.5 for a small profit of $220. We used the cash from selling MCK to buy 1000 shares of CIENA (CIEN) near its support at $35 on April 5 and sold on April 20 for $65 for a profit of $30,000.

As for MCK, it eventually dropped into the low 20's, and as of May 8, 2001 it was still around $32.

CHAPTER 5

An Extra Peek

I AM ADDING this section here to give you a peek into the thought process that goes into selling covered calls and puts to raise cash on stocks.

Case History: Qualcomm (QCOM)

I will use one stock as an example. Say I own 1000 shares of Qualcomm(QCOM) purchased at $45 a share. I feel strongly that the stock has potential to appreciate significantly by next year due to the coming spin-off later this year. Subsequently, I am not interested in selling at this point even at a profit. On April 27,2001, I watched the stock go up to $62.50, and since I do not want to sell the stock, I sold a $70 May 2001 covered call for $1.5/share or $1500 premium.

On Friday May 11,2001, the stock dropped to $57 and the call was worth only $0.10/share, but I decided not to buy back the call since there was only five days left to expiration. With the stock trending down, it is very unlikely that the $70 strike will be hit so I will get to keep the premium. In addition, I will save commissions just by letting the option expire.

I studied the charts on QCOM and determined that a strong support exists at $40. Short term charts indicated that the stock is more likely to drop further on Monday, May 14. So I devised the following plan of action:

(1) If what I expect happens, and the stock drops further Monday, I will sell two July puts (20 contracts) or 2000 shares at a premium of no less than $3000 based on Friday's close.

(2) On Tuesday, May 15,2001, the Federal reserve is meeting to decide on interest rate. The market is factoring in a 1/4 point cut. If there were to be a 1/2 point cut, the market is expected to temporarily go up. If that happens, I will sell a July $70 Call.

(3) The expiration date for the call I purchased on April 27 is getting very close. I will buy the call back if the stock hits $70 by Friday, May 18, 2001, the option expiration date. Even if that happens, I will make a good profit because of the short amount of time left on the option.

ALERT 1: Notice that I am selling puts when the stock is moving lower and calls when the stock is moving higher to maximize my cash premiums. I am also picking support as the strike for the put and resistance as the strike for the call.

ALERT 2: Do not buy calls back if the option is close to expiring unless you have to do that to avoid the stock being called if you do not want to sell. You will save commissions and make a higher profit if the option expires.

(4) Based on the charts and technical analysis, I am expecting that the stock will trade above $40 and below $70 by option expiration on July 21,2001, and I will get to keep both premiums.

(5) In the unlikely event that the stock hits $40 by July, I will buy back one of the puts and limit my purchase to an additional 1000 QCOM shares. In this case I will keep the premium from the call.

(6) If QCOM hits $70 by July expiration, I will buy the call back and sell another call at a higher strike. I will still be ahead since I will keep the premium from the two puts, and I will

pay for buying the call back with the proceeds of selling a new call.

Now I will wait until May 14,2001, to decide the plan to execute.

Fast forward and today is May 14,2001. As the charts predicted, QCOM dropped further to the intermediate support of $56. I sold two July $40 puts (20 Contracts or 2000 shares) for $1.75/share or $3500 premium.

ALERT 1: Why did I sell puts on twice the shares I have? The reason is that I am intending to buy 1000 shares more if the stock drops below $40. If that is not the case, I will have only sold one put or planned to purchase both back if the stock hits $40.

ALERT 2: Why did I pick July puts rather than June? The reason in this case is that June puts were worth $0.60 while July were worth $1.75. I am getting three times the premium by waiting twice the time. As a rule of thumb, if your premium is more than twice by waiting an additional month, go with the later date. This will allow you a higher premium in addition to commission savings.

I will now wait until Tuesday and the Federal reserve decision. If QCOM moves to $60 or higher, I will sell June or July $70 Call.

As they say, never say never. On Tuesday, May 15,2001, before the federal reserve decision, good news came out on QCOM. The stock was up 4 points and the May call that expires on Friday, May 18,2001, was worth $0.15. To avoid any chance that the stock will be called, I bought back the call for $150. So my premium is down from $1500 to $1350 which I get to keep. On the positive side, the puts I sold yesterday are worth $1.20, so I have a profit of $0.55 x 2000 = $1050 on the puts. Since the stock is moving higher, I will not buy these back yet.

I also checked the July $75 calls and they have moved to $2.85 due to the jump in the stock price. I will wait for the Federal Reserve decision and then sell the July $75 call for a $2800+ premium. Right after the federal reserve decision the July $75 call was at $3.00, so I sold 10 contracts (1000 shares) for a premium of $3000. I picked the $75 July calls rather that the $70 calls since they were selling at a good premium and that gave me an additional $5 before the stock can be called.

ALERT: If you have sold a covered call on **all** the shares of the stock you hold, do not sell another unless you are willing to buy both back if the strike price is hit. You must first close the original position or you are exposing yourself to a possible call for twice the amount of shares you have. This is what I have done here since with the good news coming out, if I sold another call I would risk having twice the shares I own called and will have to buy the stock at the market to produce additional shares.

What have we accomplished to this point: We have a total premium of $1350 (April 27 call) + $1050 (profit on 2 puts) + $3000 (premium on July $75 calls) for a total profit of $5400 in 18 days. Remember that we have only 1000 shares to work with.

On Friday, May 18, the option expiration day for the month of May, QCOM was at $65.50 which is between the price of $40 and $75. The puts were worth $0.70, so we have a profit of ($1.75 − $0.70) x 2000 = $2100 on our puts. We will leave the position open since the stock is moving higher.

We have devised the following plan of action to insure a profitable outcome no matter what the stock does:
(1) If the stock continues to go higher, we will buy back the $40 puts on the 2000 shares when they are worth 25% of the original premium and we will keep 75% of that amount as profit. We expect this to happen if the stock moves to $70.
(2) If the stock reaches $75, we will buy back the call at a loss. We will make up for that by selling another July call at $90 for an approximate premium of $3000. If the stock hit $90, we will let it be called and keep the premium as well as the

profit from the stock and 75% of the premium from the two puts for a total profit of: $45000 (stock profit) + $3000 ($90 covered call premium) + $2625 (75% of puts profit) = $50,625. Notice that we did not count the premium from the $75 covered call since we had to buy it back. In addition, the $50,625 is not an exact number since the price of buying the $75 call will depend on how close we are to expiration date.

(3) If the stock drops we will buy back the call when it is worth 25% of the original premium. This is expected to occur if the stock drops below $60.

If we have already executed step (1), we will sell $40 July puts on 2000 shares to replace the position we closed at an estimated premium of $3500.

In this case we will keep 0.75 x $3500 (75% of the original put premium) + 0.75 x $3000 (75% of the call premium) + $3500 (the premium from the last two puts) if the option expires for an estimated total profit of $8375 or 18% in two months (110% /year) without selling the stock. We get to keep the stock to sell at a later date and at a higher profit.

On May 21,2001, QCOM closed at $70.95 and the puts on the 2000 shares were at $0.30, so we bought them back for a profit of ($1.75 − $0.30) x 2000 = $2900 in one week. Furthermore, our choice of $75 rather than $70 for the strike on the call was a wise one since we avoided having to buy the call back.

ALERT: Do not be greedy. Always buy back any puts or calls that are worth 25% of the premium you received. This way you can lock your profit and be able to repeat the process.

Review: We own 1000 shares of QCOM purchased at $45 /share for a total cost of $45,000. On April 27, 2001, we sold a $70 strike May call for $1500 and purchased it back for $150 for a profit of $1350. On May 14,2001, we sold 2 July puts for a premium of $3500 and purchased them back on May 21st for $600, netting a profit of

41

$2900. Our total profit is $4250 in one month or 120%/year.

We also sold 10 contracts (1000 shares) July $75 calls for a premium of $3/share or a total of $3000.

After reaching $70.95 on May 21st, 2001, QCOM started trending down and closed at $60 on June 12, 2001. The $75 calls we sold on May 21st are now worth $0.50, so we bought them back for a profit of ($3 – $0.5) x 1000 = $2500. Our total profit is now $4250 + $2500 = $6750 in 45 days or 122%/year.

We took advantage of the stock moving toward the $40 support and on June 15, 2001, with the stock at $49 we sold two July $40 strike puts or 20 contracts (2000 shares) for $1.40/share or a total premium of $2800.

ALERT: Notice how we are using support and resistance to sell puts and calls to raise cash on the stock. As the stock moves toward resistance, we sell calls and buy back any puts we previously sold for a profit. As it moves toward support, we sell puts and buy any calls we previously sold for a profit. We will continue playing this cat and mouse game until the stock breaks resistance to the upside or support to the down side.

On July 1st, 2001, QCOM started moving towards the intermediate support of $60. The puts we sold on June 15th are now at $0.10, and we now have a paper profit of ($1.40 – $0.10) x 2000 = $2600. However, since there is less than three weeks left to expiration and our strike price is $20 below the market price, we will let the option expire.

With the stock moving up toward the $70 resistance, we will be on the lookout to raise more cash by selling calls. On July 3rd, news came out on QCOM concerning extension of their CDMA contract with Nokia. The stock was up $6 to $63.80. Since the stock closed near its high, we anticipate that there will be further upward momentum the next trading day and wait further to sell the calls.

ALERT: Do not be hasty and sell calls as soon as the stock moves higher, especially if there is news behind the move. The ideal time to sell calls is when the stock is moving higher but the upward momentum is fading. You can gauge that in three ways:

(1) Look for a drop in volume as the stock is moving higher
(2) Use the 102030 test on page **27** and wait until the MA (10) starts curving downward.
(3) Look for a failure to penetrate the previous day's high. In other words the formation of a double top.

You do not have to be very accurate in picking your timing on selling the calls since we will have at least a 10% safety factor when you pick the strike. However, by using the above rules you can maximize your premium.

On Thursday, July 5, QCOM failed to penetrate the high of $63.80 established on Tuesday, thus forming a short term double top. So by using rule (3) we sold 10 contracts (1000 shares) August $70 strike covered call at $3.00/share for a premium of $3000.

Due to earnings warnings from Advanced Micro Devices and EMC after the close on Thursday, July 5, QCOM drops to $58.5 on Friday, and the calls we sold are now worth $1.60/share. We thus have a profit of ($3.00 – $1.60) x 1000 = $1400 in two days. With the market showing signs of weakness we will keep the position open.

IMPORTANT ALERT: Notice how we now have two open positions on QCOM. Two (2000 share) July $40 strike puts and one (1000 share) August $70 strike call. What we have in effect done is **boxed** the stock between the $70 resistance and $40 support. We will make money no matter which way the stock moves by buying back whichever option is at 25% of the premium we received. We will also look to replace any option that expires or is closed out by a new one as soon as the time is right.

On July 20, 2001, option expiration day, QCOM closed at around $64, and our July $40 strike puts on 2000 shares have expired so we get to keep the premium of $2800.

We now still have one open position for $70 strike August covered calls on 1000 shares of QCOM. We will look for an opportunity to close this position at a profit and replace the put positions with new ones as the stock moves to the $40 support. We are in effect continuing the cat and mouse game between the $40 support and $70 resistance.

What have we accomplished:

We purchased 1000 shares of QCOM at a price of $45/share. We have raised a total of $6750 + $2800 = $9550 between April 27 and July 20,2001 for a 21% return in 80 days (97%/year). We also reduced the cost basis of our stock from $45/share to $35.45.

We can thus achieve 100% profit on the stock by selling at close to $70/share which is the next resistance of the stock. Originally we would have had to sell at $90/share to achieve our 100% target profit.

In fact, we can allow the covered call position we now hold for August $70 strike to be exercised and achieve our 100% profit goal. In this case our profit will be over 100% since we get to keep the $3/share or $3000 premium, effectively reducing our cost basis to $32.45/share.

On July 24,2001, QCOM dropped to $58 and the call we sold for $3.00 is now worth $.80, so we bought it back and locked in a profit of ($3.00 − $0.8) x 1000 = $2200. We decided to lock in our profit since QCOM earnings were coming out after market close. We did not want to risk a positive earnings surprise that may result in a jump in the stock and an increase in the value of the option. If the stock jumps after earnings, we will look to cash in again by selling more covered calls.

Our total cash is now $9550 + $2200 = $11750 for a return of 26% in about 3 months or 104%/year. Our cost basis on the stock is down from $45 to $33.25.

On July 26,2001, QCOM came out with positive earnings after the close. Next day the stock moved up 4 points on heavy volume.

We will be looking for the right opportunity to sell covered calls as soon as positive momentum starts fading. On Monday, July 30, we notice a 30% drop in trading volume in addition to a downward curvature of the MA(10). Furthermore, QCOM had trouble penetrating through the $65 resistance forming a short term double top. We took this opportunity to sell 10 contracts (1000 shares) September $70 strike calls for a premium of $3.40/share or a total of $3400. If this option expires, our cost /share is down to $33.25 − $3.40 = $29.85, and our target selling price for 100% profit is reduced to $59.70.

We are now in a good position, since we can sell the stock at $60 and achieve our 100% target profit once we buy the call we sold back or let it expire.

ALERT: Do not sell your shares in a stock before closing any call positions open on the stock. Otherwise you will be open to the possibility of the option being exercised and having no stock to sell. This is why we will have to wait to close the position to sell our stock if we wish to do so.

Unbelievable! If the last option we sold expires, in three months we will have reduced our cost basis from $45 to below $30 and raised a total of $11750 + $3400 = $15150 in cash during the process. At this rate we will own QCOM at zero cost within less than a year's time.

Case History (CHK continued)

As you may recall, we left out one possibility when we discussed CHK on page **26.** What if the stock never reaches $10 and stalls between $9 and $9.50 and then starts trending down?

We studied the charts and found that CHK has strong support at $7.50. In fact, it tried to break below that three times and failed. We thus concluded that there is little risk of it breaking below $7.50.

Even though we are betting on a price increase to make maximum profit, we will devise a plan that will limit our down risk and come out ahead even in a bad situation:

(1) As soon as we see a double top form between $9 and $10 we will plan to sell 25 contracts (2500 shares) October $10 calls at an approximate premium of $1.30/share or a total of $3250. This was based on the price on 5/23/01 when the stock was at $9.40.

(2) When the stock starts trending down from the double top, we will plan to sell 50 contracts (5000 shares) October $7.5 puts at an estimated premium of $0.70/share or $3500. The price was $0.70/share on 5/23/01 when the stock was at $8.82. We will execute this step as soon as the stock stops dropping and finds support.

(3) We will buy either the puts or call back when they are valued at 25% of the premium we received.

ALERT 1: We picked October options since the premium on July was too low and there were no option quotes for August and September.

ALERT 2: I will repeat this; do not get greedy. Always buy back your puts and calls if they are worth less than 25% of what you received in premium, and always sell calls at strike prices near resistance and puts at strike prices near support.

Review: We purchased 2500 shares of CHK at $20,000 and July $12.5 call options on 20,000 shares for $3000. If we execute steps (1) and (2) above and the options expire, we will have received premiums of $3500 + $3250 = $6750.

What will we achieve:

If the stock breaks $10 before October, we will buy the 5000 share puts at 25% of their value, let the stock be called and pocket the call premium and sell the calls on the 20,000 shares for a profit of $9000 as we discussed on page **25**. Our total profit is: $5000 (stock profit) + $3250 (2500 share call premium) + $9000 (20,000 share call profit) + $2625 (75% of put premiums) for a total of $19875 or 86% in three months.

If the stock drops down to $7.50, we will buy the $10 call back at 25% of its value or less. We will then sell 50 contracts (5000 shares) of $5 strike puts and use the proceeds to buy back the $7.5 puts. We will pick the expiration date to get a premium high enough to purchase back the $7.5 strike puts. Our situation is now as follows: ($7.5 − $8) x 2500 = -$1250 (stock loss) + (0.05 − 0.15) x 20,000 = − $2000 (loss on 20,000 share call assuming $0.05 price) + $3500 ($5 put premiums) + 0.75 x $3250 = $2437.50 (75% of $10 call premium) for a total of $2687.50 or 11.5% profit. We did not count the $7.5 strike put premium of $3500 since these were bought back. We expect this to be the least likely situation.

ALERT 1: You need to sell the new option at an expiration date far enough into the future to give you sufficient premium to pay for the option you are buying back. This will depend on the stock price as well as the time left on the option you are buying. Generally if little time is left to option expiration you will not have to go too far into the future and may be able to make a profit. By picking your strike prices carefully this situation should rarely occur.

ALERT 2: If the stock drops to $7.50, we could have purchased additional shares if they were assigned to us and avoided buying the puts back. We opted not to do that since with our original price at $8, this will tie up cash without reducing our cost basis by much.

ALERT 3: Notice that in the case where CHK dropped to $7.5, we were able to counteract the $2000 loss on the calls we bought by selling covered calls at $2437 profit. As you recall, we paid $0.15/share for buying the calls which is below our $0.20/share target. If we would have paid $0.30/share, our loss would have been (($0.05

– $0.30) x 20,000 = $5000 and our position would have ended in a cumulative loss.

Having laid out our plan, we now wait to see what step to implement based on the activity of the stock.

On May 24,2001, CHK failed to break through $9.40 for the second time confirming a double top formation. The first failed attempt on this level was on 5/15/01. We hence implemented step (1) of our strategy and sold 25 contracts (2500 shares) October $10 call at $1.30/share for a total premium of $3250.

As expected, the stock traded down from the double top and closed at $8.20 on 5/31/2001. On 6/1/2001 our call was worth $0.40, so we bought it back for a profit of ($1.30-$0.40) x 2500 = $2250. CHK reversed at the end of the day on June 1, 2001, indicating that a possible uptrend is starting. We then implemented step (2) of our strategy on page 46 and sold 50 contracts (5000 shares) of October $7.5 put at a premium of $0.70/share for a total of $3500.

On Monday, 6/4/01, CHK moved up to $9 on heavy volume and our puts were worth $0.50/share. Our profit at this point is: $2250 (from covered calls) + ($0.70 – $0.50) x 5000 = $1000 (from puts) for a total of $3250 which is a 14% profit in one month (170%/year). Reviewing the price pattern of CHK we notice that the stock is stuck in a trading range approximately between $8.10 and $9.40. In fact, it has visited both levels twice between May 3,2001 and June 4,2001.

We will use the following strategy to come out ahead whether the stock stays in a trading range or breaks out to the upside or downside.

(1) As CHK moves to the $9.40 resistance, we will sell $10 strike October covered calls in the amount of shares we have.

(2) As CHK moves to the $8.10 support, we will buy back the calls at a profit and sell $7.50 October puts in twice the amount of shares we own.

(3) We will repeat the process as long as the stock is confined within the trading range. This is what we have done on the previous page.

(4) If CHK moves above the $10 strike, we will buy back the $10 call at a loss. We will pay for this by selling an October $12.5 call. We will buy back any puts we sold at the support level for a profit.

(5) If CHK breaks below $7.50, we will buy back any $7.50 puts we sold at a loss. We will pay for that by selling October $5 strike puts. We will buy back any calls sold at the resistance level for a profit.

ALERT 1: Selling puts in twice the amount of shares you have is a powerful cash generating technique. This is not risky since you already own the stock and you can replace your shares by any other ones that are assigned to you. Your strategy will be to buy one of the puts back and avoid the loss on buying the other put by replacing the shares you presently own by the new shares assigned to you.

ALERT 2: Selling calls in more than the amount of shares you have is highly discouraged unless you are sure that the stock is unlikely to hit the strike price and be called. You will have to be ready to buy both calls back or risk having to sell a stock you do not own at lower than the market price.

REVIEW: We purchased 2500 shares of CHK on May 3, 2001, at $8/share for a total cost of $20,000. We supplemented the position with a 20,000 share July 2001 $12.5 strike call at $0.15/share at a cost of $3000. Our total cost is $23,000.

We have already sold October $10 strike calls on 5/24/2001 and closed the position for a profit of $2250 or 10% in one month (120%/year). We also sold October $7.5 puts on 5000 shares for a premium of $0.70/share or a total of $3500. We still have this position open.

On June 19, 2001, CHK broke below $7.50 and closed at $7.30. We will now have to decide if and when to buy the $7.50 October put we previously sold.

Our strategy is to check if CHK establishes a new resistance at $7.50. Looking at the charts we see that CHK attempted to break $7.50 on 6/19/2001 and failed. A second attempt was made on 6/21/2001, and the stock could not break through $7.30 forming a double top. We thus applied a similar strategy to the one described on page **46** and sold $7.5 strike October call on 2500 shares for a premium of $1.10/share (price on 6/21/2001) for $2750 premium. We also decided to cut our losses by selling our 20,000 share July calls for $0.10 for a loss of $.05/share or $1000. This decision was made since the stock broke the $7.50 support

ALERT 1: We have not changed our approach; however, with the stock going down a new resistance level has been established. We are again raising cash by selling covered calls at a strike price close to resistance.

ALERT 2: We are also raising cash in case we have to buy back the October $7.5 puts we sold. When you are deciding to buy any option back to prevent it from being exercised, remember the following:
   (1) Options are seldom exercised unless they are at least 3/4 of a point in the money.
   (2) Options are seldom exercised more than two weeks before expiration.
So if your option reaches the strike price, do not make a hasty decision and be sure to keep the above considerations in mind before acting. In most cases **both** conditions must occur for an option to be exercised.

CLARIFICATION: When an option is 3/4 point in the money, that implies the market price of the stock is 3/4 above the strike in case of a call option and 3/4 below the strike in case of a put option
   On 6/26/2001 the stock broke below $6.50 and reached an intraday low of $6.30. The calls we sold at $1.10/share are now at $0.30/share, so we buy them back and lock a profit of ($1.10 −

$0.30) \times 2500 = \$2000$.

Our 5000 share put position is now over $1.00 in the money. We will watch the stock and decide on whether to buy the put back. We will do this keeping in mind that our expiration date is not until October. We will also keep an eye on the premium for the $5 strike put, since in case we decide to buy the $7.5 strike put we will make up for our loss by selling a $5 strike put.

Review: Our total cash raised to this point is $2250 ($10 calls on 6/4/2001) + $2000 ($7.5 calls on 6/26/2001) − $1000 (July 20,000 share calls) for a total of $3250 or 14% in one month or (170 %/year). We did this even though the stock went down in price. Our per share cost on the stock is at $8 − $3250/2500 = $6.70/share.

IMPORTANT ALERT: Make being proactive a habit. Start raising cash on *any* stock above $5 as soon as you buy it. If the stock goes higher this will enhance your profit, and if it goes lower you will be immediately reducing your cost basis. Notice that our cost on CHK is no longer $8 and is at $6.70 because we started implementing this cash generating system as soon as the opportunity presented itself after we purchased the stock.

You are probably wondering why I picked this example and not cherry-picked another one that turned more favorable. The reason is that I firmly believe that it is how you handle losses and trades that go against you that ultimately determine your overall level of success in raising cash on your stocks.

If you can handle such setbacks well, situations that go your way will be easy.

CHAPTER 6

Generate Cash on Stocks
Before Buying Them

WE HAVE, in fact, used this approach previously as a way to average down on stocks we already own. I am talking here about selling puts.

As you may recall, selling a put option gives the holder (buyer) the right to sell 100 shares of stock (contract) at a specified price (strike) by a certain date (expiration date). You as the seller of the option will get a premium. In return for that premium, you agree to buy the shares if the market price drops below the strike price and they are assigned to you.

From the above definition, it is thus preferred that you use this approach on stocks that you ultimately intend to buy. Although this is not necessary, it is advisable for risk reduction purposes.

You may be wondering why not just buy the stock outright and not have to go through the process of selling puts. In fact, there are several advantages to this approach.

(1) You will be raising cash on a stock before you even buy it. This will lower your cost basis on the stock whenever the purchase is completed.

(2) You control the price you are willing to buy at and only buy at that price.

(3) How many times you have bought a stock thinking it cannot go lower and it did. By selling puts you can easily buy the put

back at a small loss. You can sell a new put at a lower strike to make up that loss and at the same time buy the stock at a cheaper price. This is an excellent way to buy a stock close to its bottom, thus limiting losses.

The effectiveness of this system will be more evident once you study the following real life example.

Case History: JDS Uniphase (JDSU)

I have been waiting for the right opportunity to buy JDSU (JDS Uniphase) for a while. The reason for that is I do believe that this company has a potential equivalent to Intel in the next decade. It has even been called the Intel of the Telecosm.

Since I cannot predict where the actual bottom will be, I have decided to use selling puts to purchase the stock. My intention is to purchase a total of 12,000 shares at a price of $12.5 or lower. The reason I have picked the $12.5 price is because it is close to the support for the stock established on 4/4/2001 at $13.

My Plan is as follows:

(1) I will wait until the stock gets close to $12.5 and sell puts on 60 contracts (6000 shares) at $12.5 strike.

(2) If the stock moves lower, I will sell additional puts on 60 more contracts (6000 shares) at a lower strike corresponding to next support. I will let the first 6000 shares be exercised and buy the stock.

(3) If the stock moves higher, I will get to keep the premium and wait for another opportunity to repeat the process.

ALERT 1: Why did we want to wait until the stock price gets close to the strike before selling the puts ? Remember that our aim is to buy the stock, so we would like to get a high premium to reduce our cost basis just in case the stock goes lower.

ALERT 2: Why did we just sell puts on one-half the shares we intend to buy? The reason is you can never pinpoint the exact bottom and this will allow you to raise a high premium a second time at a lower stock price. In addition, you will end with a lower average price for the total shares.

On June 15, 2001, JDSU hit $12.40, so I sold 60 contracts (6000 share) $12.5 strike July puts at $1.50/share for a premium of $9000. Notice that if the option is exercised my actual cost for the stock is $12.5 − $1.5 = $11/share.

On June 20, 2001, JDSU traded between $9.50 and $10.50. The chart showed evidence of strong buying at $9.50, so I decided to sell $10 strike July puts on the remaining 6000 shares at a premium of $1.30/share for a total of $7800. If this option were to be exercised, my actual cost will be $10 − $1.3 = $8.7/share.

If both options were exercised, my average cost will be 1/2 ($8.7 + $11) = $9.85/share.

On June 29, 2001, JDSU was above $12.50 and on July 13, 2001, one week before option expiration, it traded between $11.60 and $12.59.

ALERT: Remember what we said before, an option is rarely exercised unless it is 3/4 point or more in the money **and** there is two weeks or less left to expiration. This explains why our $12.5 strike option has not been exercised even though the stock dropped to $9.50 on 6/20/2001.

By assessing the situation, it looks that it is unlikely that our $10 strike option will be exercised by July 20, option expiration date. It is possible, however, that our $12.5 strike option will be exercised. If this situation were to occur, our actual cost for the 6000 shares will be $12.50 (price /share) − $1.50 ($12.5 strike premium) − $1.30 ($10 strike premium) = $9.70/share.

If both options are not exercised, we will keep the premiums and look for another opportunity to repeat the process. If this happens, we in effect have locked in a discount of $2.80 on the whatever price we purchase JDSU at in the future.

Personal Note: This system is so effective that I rarely buy stocks outright. I always use half/half split put selling as I showed in this example to buy stocks at my determined price. I do hope you will start doing this, too.

Finally, July option expiration date has arrived and JDSU closed on Friday, July 20,2001 at around $10. Our $12.5 option was exercised and we ended up buying 6000 shares at JDSU at $12.5/share. Our $10 strike option on the other 6000 shares expired and we ended up keeping the premium. Thus our actual cost for the 6000 shares we bought is $9.70/share. As you can see, we are still ahead even though the stock is 2-1/2 points below the exercised strike of $12.5.

Now, we start immediately looking for opportunities to raise cash on the 6000 shares we own by selling calls at resistance levels. In addition, we will raise cash while attempting to buy the other 6000 shares. We will use a similar technique to the one I described above by splitting the purchase into 3000 share lots and using the half/half put selling approach.

IMPORTANT ALERT:

Make it a habit to start raising cash on any stock you intend to buy by selling puts before buying. After buying the stock, be sure you start looking for opportunities to sell covered calls on the stock using the techniques described in this book. Do this consistently and within a year or less, your cost basis on any stock you own will be below $5 and in many cases close to zero.

On June 19,2001, JDSU released their earnings, announcing a wider than expected loss and a layoff of 6000 workers. The stock dropped to $7.70 the next day. Since we are still intending to purchase 6000 more shares, we will implement the half/half put selling strategy to do that.

We took advantage of the market price being at $7.75 close to the $7.50 strike and we sold 30 contracts (3000 share) $7.5 August puts at $1.10/share for a total premium of $3300. One of two possibilities can occur by option expiration on August 18 based on the movement of the stock.

(1) The option expires and we get to keep the premium. In this case we will own 6000 shares of JDSU at $9.70 − $1.10/2 = $9.15. Note that the premium applies to only 3000 of the 6000 shares.

(2) The option gets exercised and we end up buying an additional 3000 JDSU shares at $7.50 with an actual cost of $7.50 − $1.10 = $6.40 since we get to keep the premium. In this case we will own 9000 shares at an average price of ($9.70 x 2 + $ 7.50 − $1.10)/3 = $8.60/share. We will still have 3000 more shares to buy.

ALERT: Notice how effective the strategy of selling puts on half the shares is when you intend to buy a stock. This in effect allows you to reduce your cost basis on the stock as you are in the process of buying it. This approach is very useful in a falling market since you can never tell where the bottom is. This is certainly a much better situation than if we went ahead and purchased all the 12,000 shares of JDSU at the perceived support of $12.5.

On August 17, 2001, JDSU closed at $7.75 and the option expired so we get to keep the premium on the $7.5 strike puts we sold. Scenario (1) above applies and we now own 6000 shares of JDSU at a price of $9.15/share. We will continue to raise cash while attempting to purchase the additional 6000 shares by selling half/half puts. In addition, we will use any rise in the stock towards $12.5 resistance to raise cash by selling covered calls on the 6000 shares we own.

On Tuesday, August 21, 2001, the Federal Reserve is meeting to decide on interest rates. There is a high level of expectation for a 1/4 point rate cut. If there was to be a 1/2 point rate cut we expect that the market will experience a temporary rally. We will plan to sell additional puts on JDSU before the meeting takes place.

On Monday, August 20, with JDSU trading at $7.37 we decide

to sell $7.5 strike September 2001 puts on 30 contracts (3000) shares for a premium of $0.90/share or a total of $2700. One of two possibilities can occur by option expiration on September 21,2001.

(1) JDSU closes above $7.50 and the option expires in which case we get to keep the premium. We thus still own 6000 shares at a price of $9.15 − $0.90 /2 = $8.70

(2) The option gets exercised and we end up buying an additional 3000 JDSU shares at $7.50 with an actual cost of $7.50 − $0.90 = $6.60 since we get to keep the premium. In this case we will own 9000 shares at an average price of ($9.15 x 2 + $6.60)/3 = $8.30. We still have 3000 more shares to buy.

Unbelievable: Our initial goal was to purchase 12,000 shares of JDSU at a price of $12.5/share or less. While in the process of buying the stock, we used selling half/half puts to reduce our cost basis on JDSU from $12.5 to $8.70 or $8.30, dependent on which of the above scenarios plays out. We bought 6000 shares at an actual price of $9.15 and have raised $ $9000 + $7800 + $3300 = $20,100 in cash in the process. If the last option expires, our cash total will be $20,100 + $2700 = $22800 for a gain of 30% in three months or 120%/year.

CHAPTER 7

Time Saving Tips

IN THIS SECTION, I will show you how to implement this system with little time investment on your part. In fact, all you need is 15-30 minutes a day to achieve the goals described in this book.

To successfully implement this system with minimum time, you need to keep track of the following:

(1) Market news that could potentially affect the stock you are looking to raise cash on.

(2) Close your positions whenever you have a 75% profit.

Every day after the market closes, you should spend 15-30 minutes checking on the following potential news:

(a) News directly related to the stock you want to raise cash on.

(b) News related to any major stock belonging to the same sector as the stock you are intending to raise cash on.

(c) Earnings expectations.

(d) Federal Open Market Committee (FOMC) meetings and decisions on interest rates.

I will now show you what to look for in each of these cases to manage your cash generation efforts effectively with little time.

(1) Any news relating to the stock you own, good or bad, will certainly result in a move one way or the other on heavy volume. If the news is good, the stock will move up on heavy volume. In this case you will wait for signs of fading momen-

59

tum recognized by a volume drop as the stock is moving higher and sell the calls. In case of bad news, the opposite applies and you will look to sell puts as the stock downward momentum fades.

(2) Any news, good or bad, on a major stock in a related sector could move the stock you own. The effect in this case is similar to having news on the stock itself but less pronounced. Follow the same guidelines described in (1).

(3) Earnings expectations. As you are probably aware, earnings come out four times per year: January, April, July and October. How you use this to your advantage depends on the kind of economic climate prevalent at the time.

In a **Weak Economy,** earnings expectations are low, and earnings are preceded by an earnings warning period. In this case you want to sell calls before the earnings warning season. When the stock drops due to either a warning from the company itself or other companies in a related industry, you buy back the calls at a profit and sell puts. With earnings expectations being low, it is expected that the stock will experience a temporary bounce right after earnings are released. The puts are then purchased back after earnings for a profit and calls are sold. This was the situation in most of 2001.

In a **Strong Economy**, earnings expectations are high and stocks tend to run up in anticipation of good earnings. In this case earnings warning season is not a major factor since most companies are not expected to warn.

The most effective strategy in this case is to sell calls during the run-up prior to earnings. After earnings come out, a temporary sell-off usually occurs that will allow you to buy back the calls for a profit and sell puts.

Remember that in a strong economy best cases are usually factored into earnings, and no matter how good the earnings are a temporary sell-off will occur after they are released. This is, in fact, what happened in 2000.

(4) FOMC interest rate decisions

The FOMC meets every couple of months to decide on interest rates. These decisions usually have an immediate effect on the market if they are significantly different than what is expected by economists.

In a **Weak Economy, if** a higher than expected rate cut is implemented, a temporary upmove in the market occurs. You should use that opportunity to sell calls and raise cash. Plan to buy the calls back and sell puts when the rally starts weakening. This occurred several times in 2001

In a **Strong Economy** where inflation worries are prevalent, a higher than expected interest rate increase may result in a temporary surge in the market. If that occurs, use this opportunity to raise cash by selling calls. Plan to buy calls at a profit and sell puts as the rally weakens.

In cases where interest rate adjustments are as expected, market moves are usually muted and do not represent much of an opportunity to raise cash.

CHAPTER 8

How to Accurately Time Your Moves for Maximum Cash

THE PURPOSE of this chapter is to show you how to use simple charts to maximize your cash returns. As you may recall, we have learned in this book that to raise maximum cash on a stock you should be selling calls as the stock is moving toward resistance and puts as it is moving toward support. Accurate timing of these moves depends on the ability to recognize signs of fading momentum.

We have previously stated the signs of **fading momentum** and they are:

(1) Decrease in volume as the stock is moving toward resistance when selling calls or towards support when selling puts.

(2) Double top formation when moving toward resistance or double bottom formation when moving towards support.

(3) The 10-day simple moving average MA(10) is curving downward when selling calls or upward when selling puts and converging toward the 20-day exponential EMA(20) and the 30-day exponential EMA(30) moving averages. The trend is confirmed when the MA(10) crosses the EMA(20) and EMA(30).

In the following examples, I will show you how to easily recognize the above signs to maximize your cash generation.

Example 1: QUALCOMM (QCOM)

Note that each number or letter below refers to a location on the chart.

1. MA(10) curving upward with a steep slope. **Sell put at $40 (support) strike**
2. MA(10) converging towards and crossing EMA (20) and EMA (30) confirming upward trend. **Hold position**.
3. MA(10) is curving downward with steep slope. **Buy put back for a profit and sell call at $70 (resistance) strike.**
4. MA(10) converging towards and crossing EMA(20) and EMA(30) confirming downward trend. **Hold position.**
5. This point corresponds to low point of the stock price and the highest premium you can obtain if you sold puts. **DO NOT sell puts here** since you do not know where the bottom is. Remember that we now have the benefit of hindsight. We have sold the put at a stock price of $52.5-$53 instead of $50, giving up a potential 10% profit on the put. This is better than having to buy the put back and take a potential loss.
6. MA(10) curving upward with a steep slope. **Buy calls back for a profit and sell Puts at $40 (support) strike.**
7. MA(10) converging and crossing the EMA(20) and EMA(30) confirming the upward trend. **Hold position**.

R = resistance   **S** = support

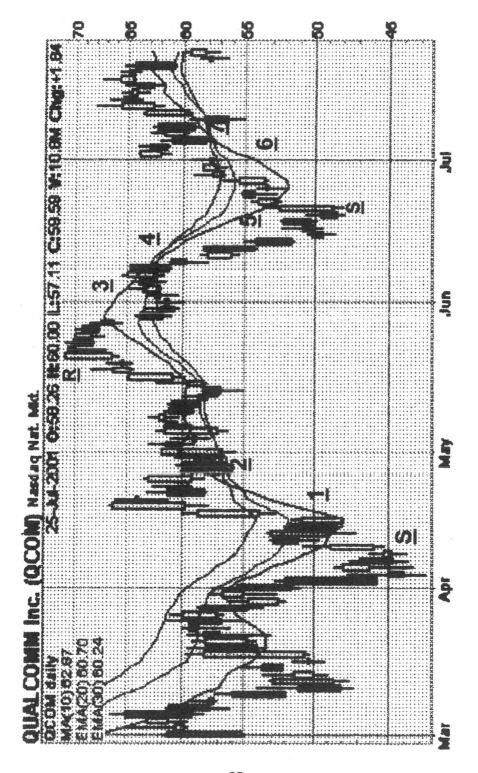

EXAMPLE 2: Chesapeake Energy (CHK)

Note that each number or letter below refers to a position on the chart.

1. MA(10) curving downward and crossing the EMA(20) and EMA(30) confirming downward tend. **Sell calls at $10 (resistance) strike.**
2. MA(10) curving upward. **Buy calls back for a profit and sell puts at $7.5 (support) strike**.
3. MA(10) Crossing the EMA (20) and EMA(30) confirming upward trend. **Hold position.**
4. MA(10) curving downward with steep slope in addition to a double top formation and failure to break resistance. **Buy puts back for a profit and sell $10 (resistance) strike calls.**
5. MA(10) Crossing the EMA(20) and EMA(30) confirming downward trend. **Hold position.** Notice the steep decline after point 5 which would have resulted in a significant profit.

R = resistance   **S** = Support

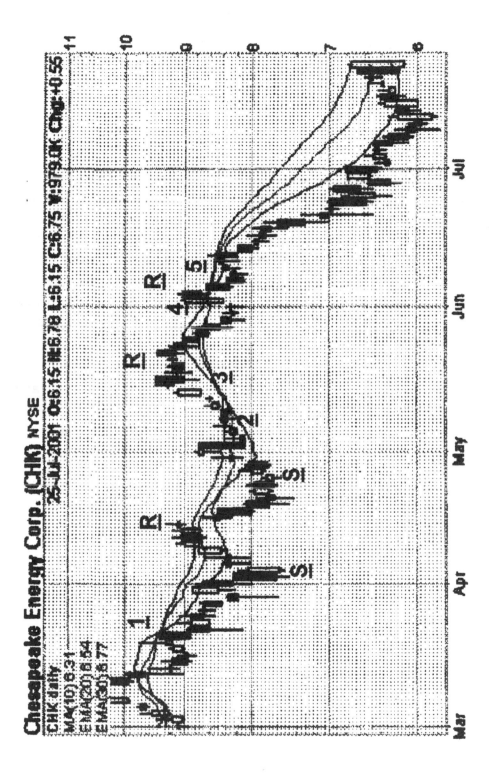

EXAMPLE 3: Applied Micro Circuits (AMCC)

Note that each number or letter below refers to a position on the chart.

1. MA(10) is curving upward with a steep slope. **Sell puts at $12.5 (close to support) strike.**
2. MA(10) is converging onto EMA(20) and EMA(30) and crossing them. Upward trend is confirmed. **Hold position.**
3. MA(10) is converging downward and crossing the EMA(20) and EMA(30) lines confirming the downward trend. **Buy back the puts for a profit and sell $30 (near resistance) strike calls.** Note also the appearance of a double top between May first, and June first confirming the downtrend. In this case a steep downtrend ensued which would have resulted in a significant profit.
4. The MA(10) is curving slightly upward. **Buy the calls back for a profit, but do not sell puts yet since the upward MA(10) slope is flat**. In this case it is wise to close the call position even if we are not planning to sell a put due to the large profit.

S = Support   **R** = Resistance

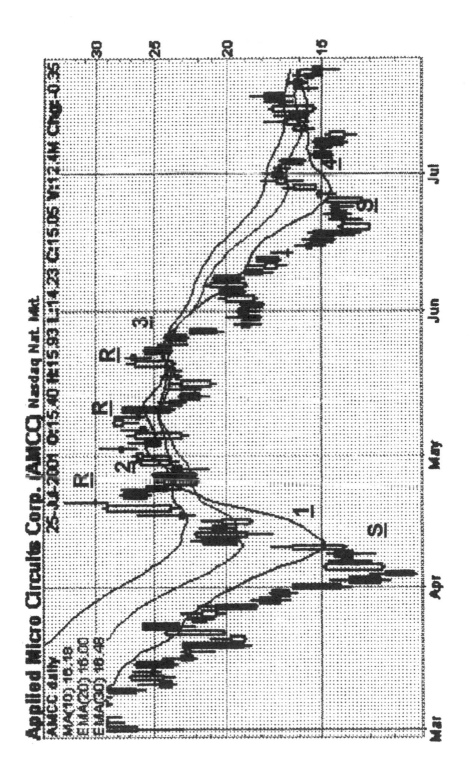

EXAMPLE 4: Global Crossings

Note that each number or letter below refers to a position on the chart.

1. MA(10) curving upward with a steep slope. **Sell puts at $7.5 (close to support) strike .**
2. MA(10) is crossing the EMA(20) and EMA(30) confirming the upward trend. **Hold position.**
3. The MA(10) is curving downward with a steep slope and crossing the EMA(20) and EMA(30) confirming the downward trend. **Buy puts back for a profit and sell calls at $17.5 (Near resistance) strike.**
4. The MA(10) is curving upward, but the slope is quite shallow. **Buy the calls for a profit, but do not sell any puts until the trend is confirmed.** In cases where you have a 75% or better profit, it is recommended you close the position no matter what the MA(10) is doing.
5. MA(10) fails to cross the EMA(20) and EMA(30) signaling that the upward trend is not confirmed. **No action necessary**.

S = Support   **R** = Resistance

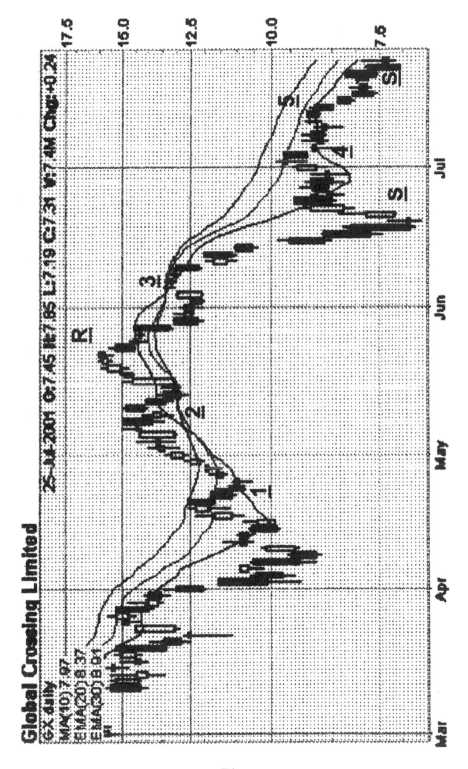

Global Crossing Limited

6X July
MA(10) 7.97
E MA(20) 8.37
E MA(30) 8.01

25-Jul-2001 O:7.45 H:7.85 L:7.19 C:7.31 V:7.4M Chg:-0.24

EXAMPLE 5: LSI LOGIC (LSI)

Note that each number or letter below refer to a position on the chart.

1. MA(10) is curving upward with a steep slope. **Sell puts at $12.5 or $15 (close to support) strike.** Note that we did not sell puts on LSI in our case history since we owned the stock at a lower price and had no reason to average down.
2. MA(10) is crossing the EMA(20) and EMA(30) confirming the upward trend. **Hold position.**
3. MA(10) is curving downward and converging on the EMA(20) and EMA(30). **Buy the puts back for a profit and sell $22.5 (resistance) strike calls.**
4. MA(10) does not decisively break through EMA(20) and EMA(30) and, in fact, reverses upward with a positive slope. **Hold position since there is no clear trend based on MA(10).**
5. MA(10) is curving downward and crossing the EMA(20) and EMA(30) confirming a downward trend. **Hold position.**
6. MA(10) is curving upward with a shallow slope. **Buy the calls back for a profit, but do not sell puts until the upward direction is confirmed.**

R = Resistance   S = Support

Note that between points 2 and 5 on the graph we could have raised cash multiple times. We could not do that using the 102030 test since the MA(10) is essentially flat in that range. In this case we should have used volume and double top, double bottom formations as an indication of when to sell puts and calls. Note also the fact that the MA(10) has a flat slope is indicating that any move upward or downward will be limited in size.

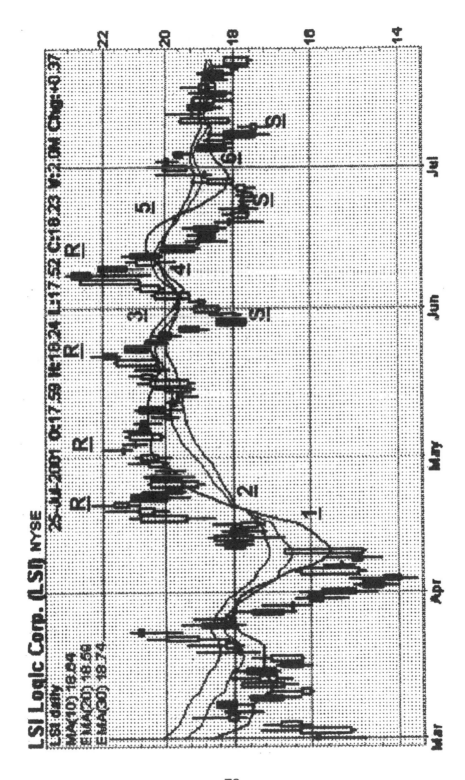

Below are dates, volumes and prices for LSI between support and resistance levels recorded between 4/16 and 4/23/2001:

Date	Volume (Millions of shares)	Price ($)
4/1 6	2.72	17.68
4/17	3.25	17.80
4/18	10.76	20.72
4/19 (sell calls here)	8.17	20.77
4/20 (sell calls here)	8.15	21.64
4/23	4.41	19.90

As you can see from the above table, LSI reached peak volume of 10 million shares on 4/18/2001. A 20% drop in trading volume on 4/19 and 4/20 occurred, indicating that upward momentum is fading even though the price was higher on 4/20 than on 4/18. As was indicated numerous times in this book, the time to sell calls should be when the stock is moving higher but the momentum is fading. The right time to sell calls was on 4/19 or 4/20. Do not get fooled that the price was higher on 4/20 and pay attention to the volume.

A similar pattern occurred between 5/30 /2001 and 6/11/2001 as can be seen from the following table:

Date	Volume (Millions of shares)	Price ($)
5/30	3.73	17.70
5/31	2.66	18.31
6/1	3.00	19.10
6/4	2.38	18.99
6/5	3.74	20.30
6/6	6.44	20.75
6/7	6.01	22.76
6/8 (sell calls here)	2.38	22.16
6/11	2.41	21.20
6/12	3.48	20.87
6/13	2.72	20.20

6/14	2.70	19.11
6/15	4.78	18.98

As you can see from the above table, peak volume at 6.4 million shares was reached on 6/6/2001 which was followed by a steep drop on 6/11/2001 to 2.38 million shares even as the price was going higher. This was an indication that the upward momentum was quickly fading, warning of a coming reversal giving a clear sign to sell covered calls on 6/8/2001 before the stock dropped.

A secondary signal was also given by the fact that peak volume occurred at a price close to resistance at $22.5. This was also confirmed by the formation of a double top near $22. **These observations are clearly seen in the LSI Price Volume Relationship chart between 5/30 and 6/15 that follows.**

As you can see, the downward trend accelerated on June 15 with over 4 million shares traded and was confirmed by the MA(10) curving to the downside and converging towards the EMA(20) and EMA(30).

Whenever the MA(10) does not show a clear trend, it is advisable to use volume change as an indicator on when to sell calls or puts. In cases where the moving averages are flat, the stock is usually stuck in a trading range as seen in this case. If you use volume indications correctly, you can make cash multiple times during the recurring movement of the stock between support and resistance. Make it a habit to watch any unusual volume activity on stocks you intend to sell covered calls or puts on. This should only take few minutes a day and generally involves comparing the traded volume on a specific day to the previous day and the average volume on the stock.

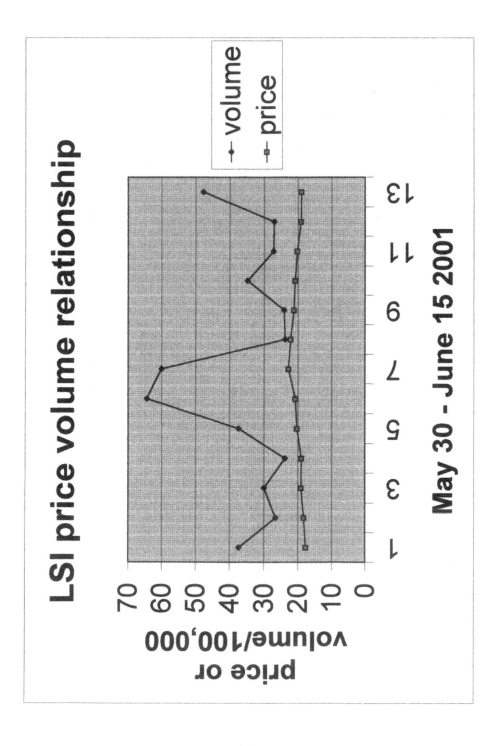

EXAMPLE 6: Scientific Atlanta (SFA)

Note that each number or letter below refers to a position on the chart.

1. MA(10) curving upward with a steep slope. **Sell puts at $30 (support) Strike.**
2. MA(10) curving downward and crossing the EMA(20) and EMA(30) lines. **Buy back puts for a profit and sell calls at $60 strike (near resistance).**
3. MA(10) curving upward with a steep slope. **Buy calls back for a profit and sell puts at $35 (intermediate support).**
4. MA(10) crossing the EMA(20) and EMA(30) lines confirming uptrend. **Hold position.**
5. MA(10) curving downward and crossing the EMA(20) and EMA(30) lines confirming downtrend. **Buy puts for a profit and sell calls at $60 (resistance) strike.**
6. MA(10) curving upward but with a shallow slope. **Hold position until you see the MA actually cross the EMA(20) and EMA(30).**
7. MA(10) fails to cross the EMA(20) and EMA(30) confirming further downtrend. **Hold position until you have at least 75% profit on your calls.**

R = Resistance   S = Support

What we did here is critical. **Do not try to second guess the direction of the stock when the MA(10) does not show a steep slope. Wait for either a confirmation by the MA(10) crossing the EMA(20) and EMA(30) lines or significant volume pick-up.**

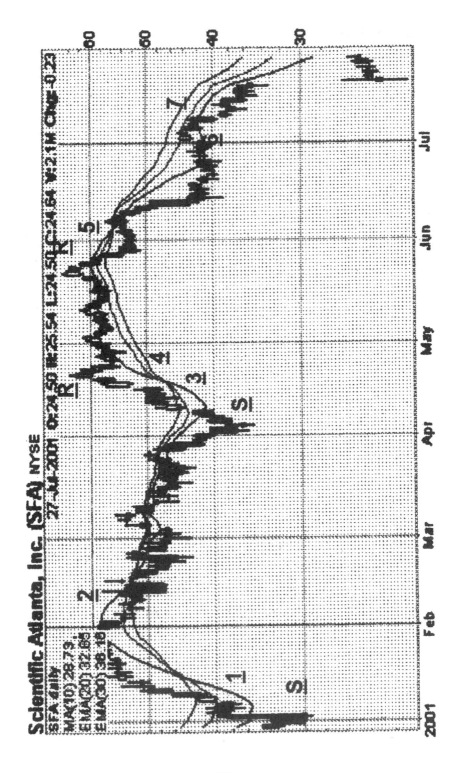

If we look at the price volume relationship for SFA between 6/15/2001 and 7/12/2001 we see from the chart that the volume was decreasing on up days and increasing on down days which indicates that there is no upward momentum.

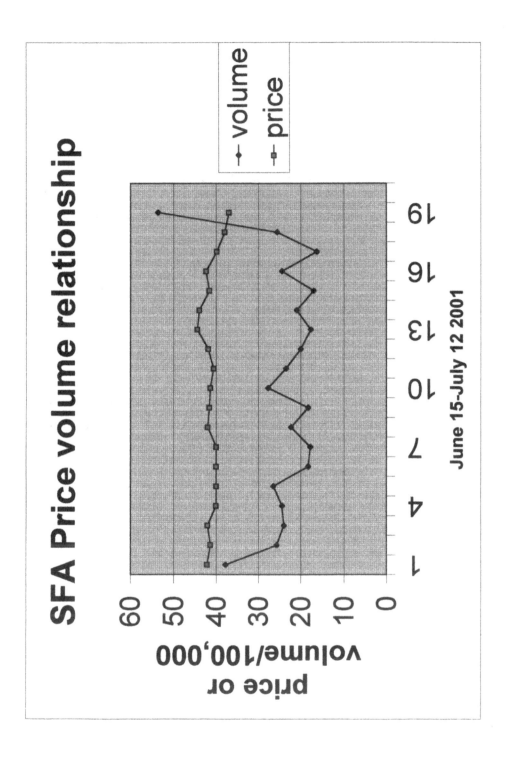

SFA Price volume relationship

price or volume/100,000

June 15-July 12 2001

→ volume
→ price

CHAPTER 9

Cash Generation Strategies

Selling covered calls:
(1) Sell covered calls when the stock is moving higher toward resistance.
(2) If you intend to sell the stock, follow these steps:
   (a) Pick the strike price you are willing to sell the stock at.
   (b) Sell the call when the market price is 1/2 point or less below the strike.
(3) If your objective is to generate cash and keep the stock, follow these steps:
   (a) Pick a price 10% above the market price of the stock. Then pick the resistance closest to that price and a strike price one step above that resistance.
   (b) Sell the call while the stock is still moving higher in price but when the upward momentum is fading.
   Fading upward momentum can be recognized when the following occur:
   (a) Decrease in volume as the stock is moving higher.
   (b) Use the 102030 test. If the MA(10) is starting to curve downward crossing the EMA(20) and EMA(30) lines.
   (c) Formation of a double top as the stock is moving higher.

Selling Puts:
(1) Sell puts as the stock price is moving down towards support.
(2) If you are intending to buy the stock, follow these steps:

(a) Pick a strike price at which you are comfortable buying the stock.

(b) Sell the put when the market price is less than 1/2 point above the strike price.

(3) If your objective is to generate cash without buying the stock, follow these steps:

(a) Pick a price 10% below the market price of the stock. Then pick the support closest to that price and the strike one step below the support.

(b) Sell the put when the stock is still moving lower but the downward momentum is fading.

Fading downward momentum can be recognized when the following occur:

(1) Decrease in volume as the price of the stock is moving lower.

(2) Use the 102030 test. If the MA(10) is starting to curve upward crossing the EMA(20) and EMA(30).

(3) Formation of a double bottom as the stock is moving lower.

Selling both puts and calls:

Remember that an option is rarely exercised unless both of the following conditions are in place:

(1) The option has less than two weeks left to expiration.

(2) The option is at least 3/4 point in the money.

Before you buy an option back at a loss, be sure to verify whether *both* conditions above are satisfied.

Use a combination of selling puts and calls simultaneously to speed up raising cash on stocks that have gone down in price. To reduce risk be sure to observe the following:

(1) DO NOT sell calls in more than the amount of shares you have.

(2) Be sure to close any open call positions already sold before selling new calls at a different strike or expiration date.

(3) Selling puts in twice the amount of shares you have is a highly effective cash raising strategy.

(4) If you have sold twice the puts you have, be ready to replace your existing shares with half the new shares that you buy.

(5) Be ready to buy back one of the puts if the conditions described above are in place if you do not want to own more than your original number of shares.

CHAPTER 10

Cash Generation Worksheet

USE THIS WORKSHEET to do your own analysis using this system on stocks you own.

Stock Symbol:

Step 1: Locate resistance and support zones for the stock:
    Resistance _____
    Support   _____

Step 2: Pick the strikes for selling options:
    Call Strike _____
    Put Strike _____

Step 3: Check if the volume traded is at least 10% over the average:
    Volume Today: _____
    Average Volume _____
    If this condition is not satisfied, wait or look for another stock

Step 4: Check which of the following conditions apply:
    (a) Stock moving towards resistance
    (b) Stock moving towards support
    (c) No clear direction
        If 4 (c) is in place wait or look for another stock.

Step 5: Decision Step Calls or Puts:

(a) If 4 (a) is in place, look to sell calls in the amount of shares you own while the stock is moving higher toward resistance but the momentum is fading.

(b) If 4 (b) is in place, look to sell puts on twice the amount of shares you own while the stock is moving lower toward support but the downward momentum is fading.

Signs of fading momentum:

(1) Double top as the stock is moving towards resistance (sell calls) or double bottom as it is moving towards support (sell puts).

(2) Decrease in volume as the stock is moving towards resistance (sell calls) or towards support (sell puts).

(3) The 10-day simple moving average MA(10) is curving downward (sell call) or upward (sell put) and crossing the 20-day exponential EMA(20) and the 30-day exponential EMA(30) moving averages.

Step 6: Generate cash as follows:

(1) As the stock moves towards resistance sell calls and buy the puts back for a profit.

(2) As the stock moves towards support sell puts and buy calls for a profit.

Step 7: Limit your risk and cut your losses as follows:

(1) If the stock is 3/4 point or more above the strike and the option has two weeks or less to expiration buy the call back and sell a call at a higher strike.

(2) If the stock is 3/4 point or more below the strike and the option has two weeks or less to expiration, buy the puts back and sell new puts at a lower strike.

CHAPTER 11

Use Other People's Money to Generate Thousands on Stocks Below $5

IF YOU WERE to research option strikes, you will find that the lowest strike price quoted for most stocks with few exceptions is $5. Consequently, if you own a stock trading 3/4 of a point or more below the minimum strike of $5, it will be difficult to use selling covered calls to raise cash.

In this chapter, I will show you an effective strategy that will allow you to raise cash on such stocks before even buying them. You can then use the cash to buy the stock at the right time and close your option position and keep part or all of the cash premium you received.

The strategy that is most effective in this situation is **selling in the money puts**.

REVIEW:

As we described on page 53, selling a put option gives the holder (buyer) the right to sell 100 shares of stock (contract) at a specified price (strike) by a certain date (expiration date). You as the seller of the option will get a premium. In return for that premium, you agree to buy the shares if the market price drops below the strike price and they are assigned to you.

In addition, we mentioned that when a put option is 3/4 of a point in the money, the market price of the stock is 3/4 of a point below the strike. On page 55 we learned that a put option is seldom exercised unless it is 3/4 point in the money AND two weeks or less are left to expiration.

All these factors are important in making the right decisions to maximize your cash generation on stocks below $5.

For the purpose of illustration, let us assume that you are interested in buying a stock trading at $3.00. You research the options on this stock and find that the lowest strike for which a premium is quoted is $5. The general strategy will be as follows:

(1) Sell Puts on the stock for an estimated premium of $2 (value premium) + ($0.10 to $0.60) time premium.

ALERT 1: The value of any in the money option is composed of two segments:

A value premium equal to the difference between the strike and the market price of the stock, which in this case is ($5-$3) = $2 ; and a time premium which is a reflection of the time left to expiration. The time premium usually ranges between 5% and 30% of the value premium dependent on the time left and volatility on the option. In the case of the above example that value is $0.10 to $0.60.

(2) Use the cash premium you obtained from selling the puts or part thereof to purchase the stock at the appropriate time.

(3) As the stock rises in price look for an opportunity to close the puts for a profit.

    The criteria used for when you should lock your profits on the puts is one of the following:

(a) Buy the puts back at the first signs of fading upward momentum as described on page 63.

(b) Buy the puts back as soon as the **stock price** closes at 50% above the price you bought it at.

    The criteria you use depends on your level of experience and comfort in recognizing fading momentum using the techniques in this book.

88

ALERT 2: Throughout this book, I have been recommending that you lock in your profit when you can buy the option back at 25% of the premium you obtained. Notice, however, that in previous cases the options we were selling were out of the money and had little chance of being exercised. In the present case the options we are selling are more than 3/4 point in the money, it is thus critical that you lock in your profit on the option as soon as signs of fading momentum occur. If you are a beginner in using this system, I would recommend you implement the 50% rule.

(4) You can sell the stock whenever you have achieved your profit target.

You may be wondering why not just buy the stock rather than selling in the money puts. In fact, there are several advantages to this approach:

(1) By selling in the money puts, you will get immediate cash and, in effect, be using other people's money to buy the stock.
(2) If the stock rises in price, you will make a profit on the stock. In addition, you will be able to keep part or all of the premium by buying your puts back at a lower price or letting them expire.
(3) If the option gets exercised and you end up buying the stock at the strike, your actual cost will be less than the present market price of the stock due to the time value premium.

As an example, for a stock trading at $3.00, you may get a premium of $2.50 for selling a $5 strike put, $2 of which is the value premium and $0.50 is the time premium. If the option gets exercised, you will have to buy the stock at $5. Your actual cost will be $5-$2.50 = $2.50 which is $0.50 less than the $3.00 market price. In effect, what we have done here is use other people's money to make a profit on the stock. After that we only had to return a small part of the money we used and kept the rest. Case histories later in this chapter will demonstrate the unbelievable amounts of cash you can generate with this approach.

As I mentioned previously, one critical difference between stocks below $5 and other stocks is that the puts we are selling are already more than 3/4 point in the money. This situation presents additional risk of the option being exercised as described before. Even though we are still better off than buying the stock outright, our objective is to minimize risk as much as possible. To do this we have to implement this system on carefully chosen stocks.

There are two types of stocks below $5 which are ideal candidates for selling in the money puts:

(1) Stocks that are exhibiting an upward reversal followed by a confirmed uptrend. Use the following signals to pick such stocks:

   (a) The 102030 test described on page 27. Wait to sell puts until you have a confirmed uptrend by the MA(10) crossing the EMA(20) and EMA(30).

   (b) Tell tale volume spike. Stocks below $5 usually do not attract much institutional interest or large fund investment. Any sudden change in the level of participation by such major players will be reflected in very noticeable volume increase. In the majority of cases a tell tale volume spike or spikes will occur before a price run up takes hold.

The characteristics of a **tell tale** volume spike are:

   (i) Volume increases of at least 20% over the average. In cases of stocks below $5 such increases are usually over 50%.

   (ii) A closing price between 0 and 20% higher than the price at the open. Pay special attention to situations where the price spikes up during the day at higher than normal volume but closes within a range of 0-20% above the open. This is a clear sign of accumulation by institutions.

IMPORTANT ALERT: If you see a stock closing down more than 5% on heavy volume, this may be a sign of impending sell-off or correction. Be sure that you pick stocks for which the **tell tale** volume spike is accompanied by **a closing price equal or higher than the open.** This will be clearer as you read the case histories in this chapter.

(2) Stocks where the risk reward ratio of implementing an in the money put selling strategy is extremely low.

To recognize such stocks, you do not even need to use charts. As a guideline you should look for stocks where the premium you will obtain on selling the puts results in at least a 25% discount on the market price of the stock if the puts were to be exercised. To do this subtract the premium from the strike, then divide the resulting number by the stock price, if the resulting fraction is 0.75 or less, the stock is a good candidate. This will become clearer as you read the case history later in this chapter.

Case History: Corvis (CORV)

I have been looking to purchase shares of Corvis for a period of time. With the stock in an established downtrend, I decided to wait for some signals of a reversal before acting. I also did not want to use out of pocket cash to buy the stock since this stock is not marginable as is the case with most stocks under $5. This implies that I am required to have 100% of the needed cash available to withdraw in my account. Furthermore using that cash will significantly reduce my buying power available for other stocks.

My strategy is to sell in the money puts to raise cash, then use part of the proceeds to buy the stock. I will then close my puts by buying them back at a profit and hold the stock to sell at the right time.

The first step is to look for **tell tale** volume spikes that indicate possible accumulation and a pending reversal. Below are the volumes and prices for Corvis between October 1 and October 16, 2001. This data is represented in the next chart with volumes shown as bars.

Date	Volume(millions of shares)	Price ($)
10/1	0.873	1.45
10/2	1.15	1.47
10/3	5.46	1.52
10/4	9.91	1.79
10/5	1.27	1.75
10/8	1.17	1.65
10/9	1.84	1.60
10/10	3.19	1.88
10/11	8.10	2.06
10/12	6.27	2.27
10/15	10.09	2.41
10/16	7.05	2.28

As you can see from the data, the first **tell tale** volume spike occurred on 10/4/2001 with 9.91 million shares traded. The stock opened at 1.62 and closed at 1.79 which falls between the 0 and 20% guideline described previously.

This volume spike was followed by a three-day pullback on low volume which Indicates lack of heavy selling interest. A second **tell tale** spike occurred on 10/11/2001 with 8 million shares traded which confirms the accumulation pattern. We will wait for a pullback and an uptrend confirmation using the 102030 test discussed on page 27 before implementing our put selling strategy.

ALERT 1: How do we know that volume spikes with small price movements are signs of accumulation? The easiest way to visualize this is by thinking of a large institution as a big whale jumping into a lake. If the whale jumps all at once he will create a big splash. In a similar manner, if an institution were to buy a large block of stock all at once, the price will run away from them. What an institution will do is sell a block of shares and then buy back a slightly larger block; the difference will be the accumulated stock. If they do this over a period of time, they are more likely to buy shares at

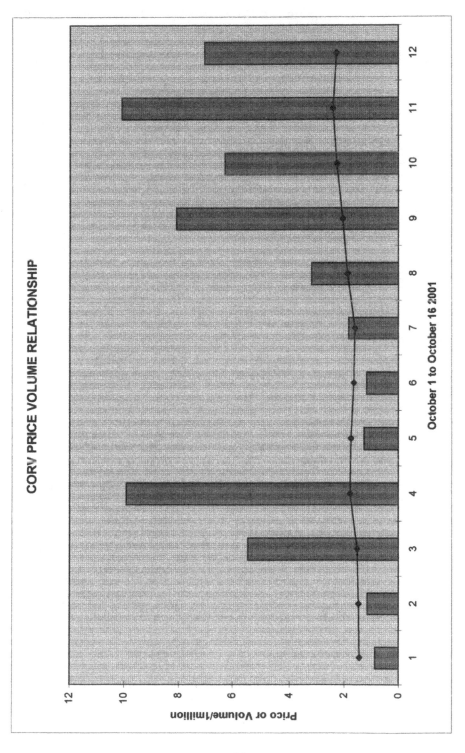

CORV PRICE VOLUME RELATIONSHIP

October 1 to October 16 2001

Price or Volume/1million

lower prices. This explains the large volume but small price movement. Think of this as the whale we talked about asking a large number of smaller fish to enter the lake in his place over a period of time so as not to create a splash and alert the fishermen.

Our first confirmation of a pullback came on 10/16/01 when the stock traded on heavy volume but it closed below the open. Subsequently the stock pulled back to $2 on October 22,2001.

We will now use the 102030 test to check whether the stock is still in an uptrend. Point 1 on the following chart shows that the MA(10) continued moving higher and crossed the EMA(20) and EMA(30) even as the stock corrected down to $2.

With this confirmation we now decide to sell 5000 share CORVIS $5 strike December 2001 puts at $3.30/share for a premium of $16,500. Since we are confident that the stock will continue its uptrend, we will use part of the proceeds to buy 5000 shares of stock at $2.10 a share at a total cost of $10,500.

Review: We have purchased 5000 shares of Corvis for $10,500 using $16,500 of other people's money at an effective price of $5-$3.30 = $1.70 and we still have $6000 in cash

We will now wait for the right time to close our positions. On November 19 CORV reached 3.75 (point 2 on the chart) and our puts were at $1.40. We now have a paper profit of $1.90/share on the puts for a total of $9500 and $1.75/share on the stock for a total of $8750. Our grand total profit on paper is $18250. With the stock having run up from 2.25 to 3.75 in 10 days, it is natural that a pullback is imminent. The stock pulled back to $3 and then went back up to $3.5 but failed to break through forming a double top (point 3 on the chart) which is a clear sign of fading momentum. Thus, On Monday, November 26, 2001, we decided to buy the puts back at $1.60 and sell the stock at $ $3.50. Our total profit is ($3.30-$1.60)x5000 = $8500 (puts profit) + ($3.50-$2.10) x5000=$7000 (stock profit) for a total of $ 15,500 in one month. To do this we did not use any out of pocket cash.

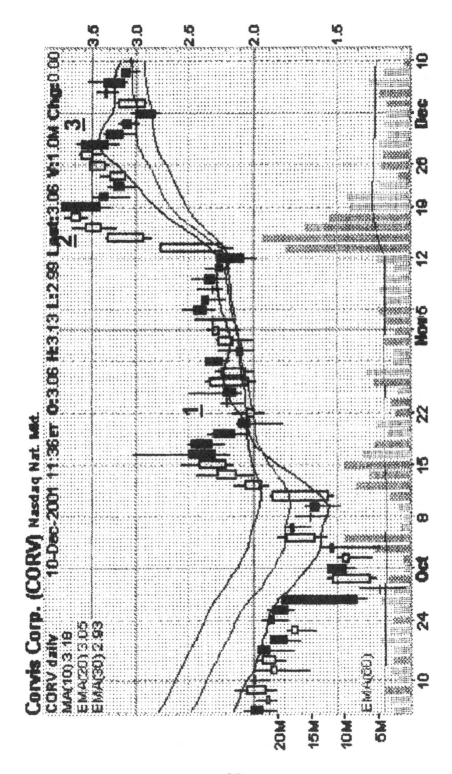

Unbelievable! Using the in the money put selling strategy we were able to use $16,500 of other peoples money to generate $15,500 profit in less than one month on a $2 stock. To do this we did not have to use any out of pocket cash and were able to keep $8500 of the $16,500 premium we obtained.

Case History: ENRON

I am sure that by this time you are familiar with the story of Enron, an energy trading and gas pipeline giant that saw its stock crash from over $80 to $0.25.

Many investors who owned the stock trusted the fundamental story and ignored the technical indicators and they certainly paid a heavy price.

As an Enron investor, you could have recovered all of your losses and come out ahead just by implementing a single concept in this book. In addition, with the strategies in this chapter you could have raised thousands of dollars when the stock was trading for pennies and at the verge of bankruptcy.

To avoid significant losses on the stock, all one had to do is use the 102030 test described on page 27. Between October 19 and 22, 2001 the MA(10) crossed the EMA(20) and EMA(30) to the downside as clearly seen on point 1 in the following chart. The strategy at that time would have been as follows:

(1) Sell $30 strike calls on the shares you own as soon as the MA(10) crossed the EMA(20) to the downside.
(2) Buy the calls back when they are worth 25% of the premium you obtained.
(3) Sell new covered calls at a lower strike, say $27.5
(4) Repeat steps (2) and (3) until a sign of reversal occurs. If you did this, you would have recovered all of your losses and more without selling the stock.

ALERT: You are probably wondering why not just sell the stock at $30. In fact, one should have sold when the CD chart signals de-

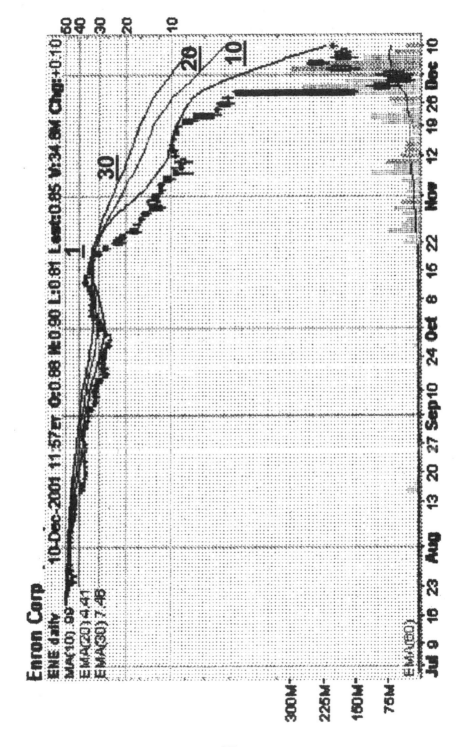

scribed in Chapter 14 turned negative, but if you did not sell, you can still recover your loss by following the trend. Recall what I said in the beginning of the book, "the trend is your friend," and all we did is follow the trend on the chart. As long as the downward trend is in place, we continued raising cash by selling covered calls.

I will now show you how you could have used the strategy discussed in this chapter, namely selling in the money puts, to raise thousands after the stock crashed.

On November 30,2001, there were rumors that Enron is about to file for bankruptcy and the stock dropped to $0.25. Checking the put options on the stock we found that the lowest strike was at $2.50 which is very rare and below the most common lowest strike of $5. The January 2002 $2.50 strike put had a premium of $2.35 a share.

ALERT: It is important to pay attention to what is happening here. Remember that options reflect the sentiment on the stock, and with most investors thinking the company is about to go bankrupt, put options are at a high premium. In fact, after getting $2.35 a share, your cost will be only $0.15 if the option was exercised.

By evaluating the situation it is evident that we have an extremely favorable situation for using the in the money put selling strategy. Let us consider the different possibilities:

(1) The stock goes bankrupt and the options stop trading. If the option expires you get to keep the cash. It is possible that an exception can be made and the option gets exercised after the stock emerges from bankruptcy and resumes trading. In this case, we expect that the stock will trade at a higher price and we will have a net profit on the puts.

(2) The stock moves up and we will have a profit on the puts and any stock that we may have bought.

(3) The stock does not go bankrupt but drops to $0.05 and our puts get exercised. This is the only situation where we would have a loss and since we obtained a $2.35 premium/share; our actual cost will be ($2.50 -$2.35)= $0.15. Thus in our

worst case scenario we are facing a loss of $0.10/share or a total of $500 for a 5000 share option.

To assess the likelihood of option 3 occurring, we look at other stocks that have faced similar situation. Exodus (EXDS) comes to mind since it has recently filed for bankruptcy. We find that the stock is still trading at $0.10, but no options are trading on it. We thus conclude that our loss on Enron is more likely to be below our estimated $0.10 /share worst case.

With these kinds of odds, we decide to sell 10,000 shares in the money January 2002 puts at $2.35/share for a total premium of $23,500. We also decide to use $15,000 of the proceeds to buy 60,000 shares of Enron at $0.25/share.

On Monday December 3,2001, Enron secures $2.5 billion in loans to continue operations and cuts 4000 positions to save money. On Wednesday December 5, the stock reaches $1.25 and our puts are now worth $1.35. We decide to buy back the puts for a profit of $1/share or a total of $10,000. With the opportunity to lock in 400% profit on the stock in three days we vote against greed and decide to sell the 60,000 shares we have at $1.20 a share for a profit of ($1.20- $0.25) x60,000 = $57,000. Our total profit on this $0.25 stock is $67,000 within four days, and to do this we had to use no out of pocket cash.

These types of opportunities occur rarely; however, you only need a couple each year to make large amounts of cash, so be sure to keep your eyes open.

Unbelievable! We used the selling in the money put strategy on an almost bankrupt $0.25 stock to generate $67,000 in profit in less than one week. To do this we used no out of pocket cash and were able to keep almost 50% of the put premium "other people's money" we obtained.

CHAPTER 12

Squeeze Thousands in Short Term Cash by Investing Against the Crowd

HAVE YOU EVER felt like the unluckiest investor on the face of the earth? It seems in most cases than not, a stock will go down right after you buy and up right after you sell. The reason for this is that you are investing with the majority, and the majority is always wrong. "If you follow the herd, you will get slaughtered with it."

In this chapter, I will show you how to effectively use reverse crowd psychology to identify stocks that can generate significant short term cash profits. You will also learn how to use the techniques described in this book to generate significant cash income without having to buy or sell any of these stocks.

To accomplish these goals, we will use a two-step process:

(1) Screen for stocks where there is an overwhelming crowd sentiment in either positive or negative direction. This will screen out more than 90% of available stocks.

(2) Out of the stocks obtained in Step 1, look for the ones that show relative performance opposite to the prevailing crowd sentiment. In other words, look for strong relative performance on stocks showing negative sentiment and weak relative performance on stocks showing positive sentiment. Screening using Step 2 will narrow the field to no more than 20 stocks.

Measuring Sentiment

To effectively measure crowd sentiment on a stock, pay attention to the following two indicators:

(1) Amount of short interest

As you probably know, when traders short a stock, they are making a commitment to buy the stock at a future date to close their positions.

Excessive short interest indicates that there is an overwhelming negative sentiment on the stock or, in other words, the crowd is betting that the stock will go lower. A low amount of short interest on a stock indicates that most investors are expecting the stock to go higher. In this case there is no commitment by investors to buy the stock at a later date.

(2) Option trading

Measure the call/put ratio traded. A high call/put ratio or a large volume of call buying indicates that the crowd is betting on higher prices and a high level of optimism. A high put/call ratio or a large volume of put buying indicates expectation of lower prices or a high level of pessimism.

Since options are time-sensitive expiring assets, they are a reflection of the short term sentiment of the crowd. For an option buyer to make a profit, the underlying stock must move in their direction quickly.

In summary, to buy, look for stocks with high level of short interest and high put/call ratio. To short or sell, look for stocks with a low level of short interest and low put/call ratio.

ALERT: The best way to effectively measure the short interest on a stock is to calculate the days needed to cover. This is done as follows:

Days to Cover = Number of shares short / Average Daily Volume

Using this ratio will give you a normalized number in case large variations occur in the average daily trading volume from one month to the next.

Many internet sites are available that give short interest information. The one you use will depend on your personal preference on how the data is presented.

By focusing on stocks with high level of short interest, you are assured that there is a pool of investors committed to purchase the stock at a future date. The question, however, is when will the buying begin?

The catalyst that will force the shorts to cover their positions is an upward move in the stock. We will thus focus on stocks with strong relative performance. This is an indication that the stock is under accumulation and is poised for an up move.

Measuring Strength

There are numerous technical indicators used for evaluating the relative strength of a stock. Some investors believe that the larger the number of technical indicators they use, the better the results. Unfortunately, however, many indicators give conflicting signals resulting in confusion and lack of confidence to act on the part of the investor.

For buying purposes, our objective is to assess whether a stock with high level of short interest is showing strong price action and vice versa. It is logical to assume that if a stock is under heavy accumulation, a price move should follow. Once the price starts moving, the shorts will have to cover their positions creating strong positive momentum and upward price acceleration.

A highly effective indicator to use for measuring relative strength is **Chaikin Money Flow (CMF).** This gives a quantitative measure of accumulation or distribution and a qualitative measure of the extent of money flow.

Combining Chaikin Money Flow as a strength indicator, with short interest as a sentiment indicator, results in a potent technical combination that allows you to raise quick cash on stocks using the concepts in this book.

In the next section I will give you a brief summary on how to effectively interpret the Chaikin Money Flow. Later in the chapter

CMF will be used in combination with short interest and techniques previously described in this book to raise significant cash on stocks.

Chaikin Money Flow

Chaikin Money flow uses price and volume measurements to give an indication of the existing supply demand situation on a stock. This is based on the premise that if a stock closes below its mid-point of the day there is distribution occurring. If, on the other hand, the stock closes above its midpoint, accumulation is taking place. The midpoint is calculated as:

(High price + Low price)/2

Chaikin money flow is a common technical indicator available on many internet stock analysis sites. The calculation period used depends on the time horizon of the investor. A period of 20 days is recommended when the objective is to raise short term cash as is in this chapter.

Chaikin Money Flow Signals

(1) If CMF is between zero and 0.1, this indicates weak buying. In this case the signal is positive if it occurs during a price correction.

(2) If CMF is above 0.1, it indicates heavy accumulation and predicts higher prices ahead. This signals a subsequent break of resistance if a stock is in an uptrend and a price breakout if the stock is stuck in a trading range.

In cases where the CMF is above 0.1 during a correction, it is a signal that the support is likely to hold.

(3) If CMF is between zero and -0.1, this indicates weak selling. In this case the signal is negative if it occurs during a price rise.

(4) If CMF is below -0.1, it indicates heavy distribution and predicts lower prices ahead. This signals a subsequent break of support if the stock is in a downtrend and a price breakdown if the stock is stuck in a trading range.

In cases where the CMF is below -0.1 in an uptrend, it is a signal that the resistance is likely to hold.

(5) The higher the CMF indicator stays above zero the more sustained the buying is, and the lower it stays below zero the more sustained the selling is.

(6) If CMF forms a lower peak, the buying pressure is diminishing, and if it shows a higher low, the selling pressure is diminishing.

(7) If the CMF is oscillating above and below 0.1 or -0.1, it is important to give more weight to readings corresponding to higher trading volumes.

Combining CMF and Moving Averages

As you recall, I have indicated in previous chapters that to raise cash on a stock you should sell calls as the stock is moving towards resistance and puts as it is moving towards support. To maximize your cash generation, action should be taken when signs of fading momentum as explained on page 63 can be clearly identified.

To effectively use a combination of the Chaikin Money Flow and moving averages to raise cash, observe the following rules:

(1) The moving average (102030,1030, or a modification thereof) should be used as the primary indicator. This implies that the curvature and lining up of moving averages should take precedent over money flow to dictate your immediate action.

(2) Chaikin Money Flow should be used as a secondary or reinforcing indicator to assess whether support will hold in a downturn or resistance will break in an upturn.

ALERT: Being able to predict the success of a breakout or failure of a breakdown with a large degree of accuracy is critical to maximize cash returns. The cash generation action to be taken depends on whether we expect support and resistance to hold.

This is best illustrated in the following examples.

Example 1: Chesapeake Energy (CHK)

Chart Interpretation: By studying the chart on page 107 you can see that up to point **1** the Chaikin Money Flow (CMF) was above 0.1, indicating sustained heavy accumulation. Between points **1** and **2** on the chart the stock dropped from $7.50 to $6.00. The CMF, however, remained between zero and -0.1, indicating weak selling. This is usually a sign of a shake-out rather than a sustained downtrend, indicating that the support will hold.

ALERT: Shake-outs are very common in the market and are designed to scare weak investors into selling at a low price. This allows institutions which control the majority of the trading volume to accumulate shares at lower prices. Before you panic and sell, be sure to check the money flow.

Between points **2** and **3** the CMF was consistently above 0.2, indicating heavy accumulation and expectation of higher prices ahead.

At point **3** the MA(10) is curving downward and crossing the EMA(20), signaling a confirmed downturn. Note that between points **3** and **4** the CMF remained between zero and -0.1, indicating weak selling. This is a sign that the support close to $5 will hold.

Notice that between points **4** and **5** the stock was under accumulation since the CMF was mostly above 0.1. Looking at the total picture, we can see that the CMF stayed mostly above 0.1 between November 2001 and April 2002, indicating that CHK was undergoing heavy accumulation during this period and it is just a matter of time before a breakout occurs.

At point **5** the MA(10) curves upward crossing the EMA(20), signaling a confirmed up trend. Since the stock has shown overwhelmingly positive CMF for almost six months, we expect that the price will quickly move to the next resistance at $7.5, which is what actually happens.

Cash Generation

Review: We purchased 2500 shares of CHK at $8 and used

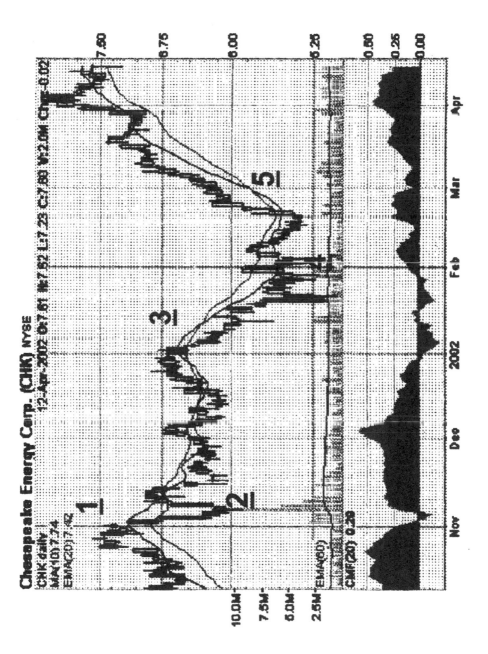

the put/call selling strategy described in previous chapters to reduce our cost basis to $6.70/share as described on page 51.

Note that we left the EMA(30) out of the chart for clarity purposes. If you use a combination of moving averages and CMF, the MA(10) and EMA(20) are sufficient.

Between points **1** and **3** on the chart the stock moved quickly between support and resistance with the moving average not showing a decisive trend. In this case the use of volume/price criteria and double top, double bottom formations are the best approach.

At point **3** a confirmed downtrend occurs with the MA(10) curving downward and crossing the EMA(20). As I mentioned previously, the CMF indicates weak selling, so it is expected that the price will hold support.

We will follow the moving averages as the primary signal and sell February 2002 $7.5 strike calls for a premium of $0.80/share for a total premium of $2000. At option expiration on February 16, 2002, the stock closes at $ 5.89 and the option expires and we get to keep the premium. Our effective cost on the stock is now at $6.70-$0.80 = $5.90/share.

After point **4** the stock forms a double bottom followed by an upward curvature of the MA(10) and crossing of the EMA(20) at point **5**. With CMF readings mostly above 0.1 for the past six months, this indicates a powerful advance in the making.

We expect the stock to quickly move to the $7.5 resistance, and thus with the stock at $5.50 we sell $7.50 strike April 2002 **in the money** puts for $2.50/share for a total of $6250. If this option expires, our cost/share will be $5.90 - $2.50 = $3.40 /share. The premium is high since we are selling in the money puts and $2 are due to price premium ($7.5-$5.5 = $2) while $0.50 is the time premium.

ALERT: Notice that we did something different in this example by selling in the money $7.5 strike puts rather than out of the money $5 strike puts.

This is an effective strategy if the moving averages primary signal indicator has been preceded by CMF readings overwhelmingly above 0.1 for a sustained time period. In this case, selling in the money puts is not risky and is, in fact, quite profitable since we could double our cash profit on the stock.

On April 19, 2002, CHK closes at $8.04, and the option expires, so we get to keep the premium of $6200, and our cost/share is now at $3.40.

Unbelievable, we now have a profit of ($8.04- $3.40) x 2500 = $11600 on an initial $20,000 investment for a return of 58% even though CHK is not much higher than our purchase price of $8. We still own the stock and can continue raising cash on it. We have accomplished this even without raising cash between points 1 and 3 on the chart.

By recognizing the existence of a **tell tale** volume spike at point **2** on the chart, we could have raised additional cash. As you may recall, a tell tale volume spike was defined on page 92. Volumes and prices for CHK between Nov. 1, 2001 and Nov. 14, 2001 are listed below.

Date	Volume (Millions of shares)	Price
11/1	0.712	7.35
11/2	2.97	6.78
11/5	2.42	6.29
11/6	2.42	6.11
11/7	11.73 (Tell tale spike, Sell puts here)	6.17
11/8	5.61	6.65
11/9	3.63	6.83
11/12	2.57	6.94
11/13	1.35	6.84
11/14	1.39	6.69

As you can see. the volume jumped up 500% on Nov. 7, 2001, but the price moved only slightly from the day before. In addition, the stock opened at $6.05 and closed at $6.17, which is within the zero to 20% guideline previously described signaling a tell tale volume spike. Based on this, we sold $5 January 2002 puts for $0.70/share for a cash premium of $1750.

We closed the position on Nov. 13 when the MA(10) started reversing course accompanied by a volume drop by buying back the puts for $0.25/share. Our net profit per share is $0.45 and our per share cost for CHK is now at $2.95. In this case, our profit is ($8.04 -$2.95) x 2500 = $12725 or 64%.

ALERT: If you are a beginner at using the system in this book, try to focus on clear signals when raising cash. As you can see from this example, you could have done quite well even if you missed the opportunity to raise cash between points **1** and **3** on the chart. Recognizing these types of cash raising opportunities will come with experience.

Example 2: JDS Uniphase (JDSU)
Chart interpretation: By examining the chart on page 113 we can see that the CMF was mostly above 0.1 up to point **1** on the chart. At point **1** the MA(10) never crossed the EMA(20) to the downside and starts curving upward indicating a confirmed move in the stock.

As the price moves between points **1** and **2,** the CMF is starting to form lower peaks, indicating that the buying pressure is diminishing and the resistance at $12.5 is likely to hold. At point **3,** the MA(10) is curving downward and crossing the EMA(20) confirming a downward move; in addition, the CMF moves below zero.

Even though the stock moves higher between points **4** and **5,** the CMF is below -0.1, indicating heavy selling and the resistance at $10 will hold. As soon as the stock reaches resistance, a reversal occurs and at point **5** the MA(10) curves down and crosses the EMA(20) indicating a confirmed down move. With the money flow in highly negative territory between points **3** and **5** indicating heavy selling, we expect that the stock will break support and move quickly to $8 or less. As the price moves closer to point **6,** the CMF starts forming higher lows and is mostly between 0 and -0.1, indicating that the selling pressure is diminishing. Between points **6** and **7** both the CMF and moving averages show no clear direction with the stock remaining in a trading range.

Cash Generation

Review: We have purchased 6000 shares of JDSU at an effective price of $9.15 and we still had a September 2001 put option open on 3000 shares of the stock at $7.5 strike.

On September 21, 2001, JDSU closed at $5.36 due to the significant drop in the market resulting from the September 11, 2001 incident. Our option gets exercised and we buy 3000 shares of JDSU at an effective price of $7.50 (strike) - $0.90 (premium) = $6.60. We now own 9000 shares of JDSU at an effective price of $8.30 as described on page 58.

At point **1** on the chart a confirmed uptrend occurs since the MA(10) fails to cross the EMA(20) to the downside and moves up with a steep slope. We will thus sell 90 contracts (9000 shares) $7.5 strike January 2002 puts at a premium of $0.50/share for a total of $4500. The stock eventually moves to $12 in November of 2001 and the option price drops to $0.05, so we close our position by buying back the option for a net profit of $0.45/share or a total of $4050. Our cost per share is now at $8.30-$0.45 = $7.95.

After reaching $12, JDSU drops to $10 and then moves to $11.5 in early December failing to break resistance at $12 forming a **double top** at point **2.** With the stock at $11.5 we sell 9000 shares February 2002 $12.5 strike calls for a premium of $0.80/share or a total of $7200. With a confirmed downtrend at point **3** and the MA(10) crossing the EMA(20) and CMF turning negative, we buy back the $12.5 call for $0.20/share, netting a profit of $0.60/share or a total of $5400. Our cost per share is now at $7.95-$0.60 = $7.35/share.

With a confirmed downtrend at point **3** and the CMF turning negative, we sell 9000 shares $10 strike February 2002 calls for $1.10/share (note that the premium is high since the stock price is close to the strike) for a total premium of $9900. The stock drops to $8.25 at point **4,** and our option is now worth $0.25/share, so we buy it back, locking a profit of $0.85/share or a total of $7650. Our cost per share is now $7.35-$0.65 = $6.50/share.

ALERT: We bought back the $12.5 strike and replaced it by a $10 strike call since we know due to the moving average and CMF signals the stock is going lower. This way we can lock our profit and get a higher premium by selling an option at a lower strike.

On its way between points **4** and **5** the stock moves up to $10 but fails to break out. This is what we have expected since the CMF is heavily negative in that range.

At point **5** the MA(10) is curving downward and crossing the EMA(20) accompanied by CMF readings below -0.2 between points **4** and **5,** indicating a pending steep decline. We expect the stock to break $8 support, so with the stock close to $9 we sell 9000 shares $7.5 strike **in the money calls** for a premium of $2.10/share ($9-$7.5 = $1.5 (price premium) + $0.60 (time premium)) or a total of $18,900. After point **5,** the stock continues going down and reaches $7 in early February. Our option is now worth $0.50, since the price premium is down to zero, so we buy it back for $4500 and lock in a profit of $1.60/share or a total of $14,400. Our cost per share of JDSU is now down to $6.50-$1.60 = $4.90/share.

ALERT: Notice that we did something different than our normal procedure by selling in the money calls. This is an effective strategy if the moving averages primary signal indicator has been preceded by CMF readings overwhelmingly below -0.1.

As I said in previous chapters, it is not advisable to sell calls on stocks you do not own. If you are inexperienced with this system, use selling in the money call strategy if:

(1) You have a profit you are willing to take if the stock is called away.

(2) You have mastered the concepts in this book to be confi-

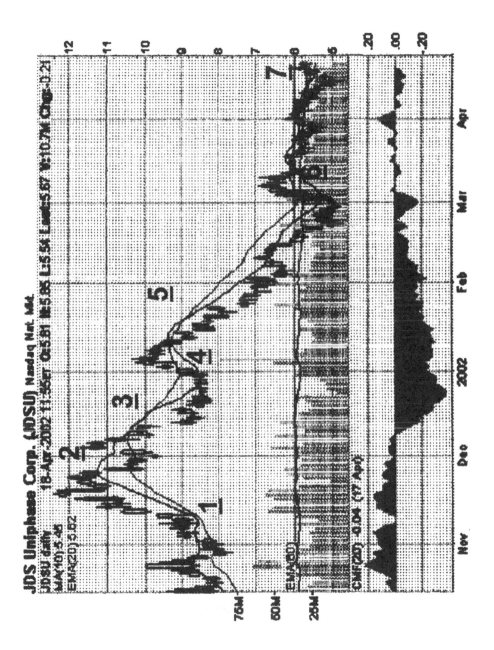

dent in your ability to assess the stock price direction by option expiration.

If you do not fall into any of the above scenarios and you are a beginner, it is advisable to sell **out of the money calls.** You will get lower premiums but will avoid risking losing the stock.

With JDSU at $7.00 in early February 2002, we notice that the money flow is below -0.1 and the moving averages still lined up in a downward spiral, indicating that a slide to the $5.00 support is imminent. With the stock at $7.00 we sell 9000 shares April 2002 $5 strike in the money calls for $2.50 ($7.00 - $5.00 = $2.00 (price premium) + $0.50 (time premium). In early March 2002 the stock drops to $5.00 and the option is at $0.45, so we buy the option back and lock in a profit of $2.05 or a total of $18450. Our cost is now at $4.90 - $2.05 = $2.85/share.

Between points **6** and **7,** there is no clear direction, so we do not take any action to raise cash.

What a difference! We now own 9000 shares of JDSU at an average price of $2.85/share. We have used the concepts in this book to raise a total of $22800 (from page 58) + $4050 + $7200 + $5400 +$7650 + $14,400 + $18450 = $79,950 in cash on an initial investment of $74,700 for a return of 107%. On April 19, 2002, JDSU closed at $5.50, and even though the stock dropped from $12.5 to $5.50, we have a profit of ($5.5 - $2.85) x 9000 = $23850.

If we went ahead and purchased 9000 shares at the perceived support of $12.5, we will have a loss of ($12.5-$5.5) x9000 = $63000.

Combining Strength and Sentiment for Explosive Profits

As I have discussed in the previous section, to identify stocks that are about to experience a sharp upward move, look for the following:

(1) Overwhelming negative sentiment as measured by an increase in the short Interest on the stock.

(2) Strong price action as measured by the combination of moving average and Chaikin Money Flow (CMF) indicators.

ALERT: Just because there is a large amount of short selling on a stock does not in itself imply that the price will move higher. It is critical that increasing short interest be accompanied by heavy accumulation. This will ultimately result in a short squeeze which will accelerate the upward momentum of the stock.

How to effectively combine these principles can best be demonstrated using real life examples.

Example 3: Cymer (CYMI)

By examining the short interest chart on page 116, it can be clearly seen that the **days to cover** have steadily increased from 1 to 3.5 between October 15, 2001 and March 15, 2002. This is an indication of a substantial increase in negative sentiment in that time period.

It can also be seen in the weekly price chart on page 117 depicting moving average and CMF indicators that the stock hit bottom in early October 2001 at $15. Starting the beginning of November, the CMF turned positive indicating the start of accumulation. At point **1,** the MA(10) crossed the EMA(20) confirming the upside move. Notice also that between January and March 2002, the CMF stayed above 0.1, indicating a high level of accumulation on the stock.

Notice the explosive move on the stock between October 2001 and March 2002. The negative sentiment depicted by a constant increase in the short position was accompanied by positive strength as shown by the moving averages and CMF creating a short squeeze. As the price moved higher, the shorts were thinking, "The price is moving up too fast and I will keep shorting more as the stock goes higher." This is the same deadly mistake that buyers make by averaging down in a weak price action.

The most effective cash generation strategy in this case is to start selling **in the money puts** as soon as the MA(10) is curving

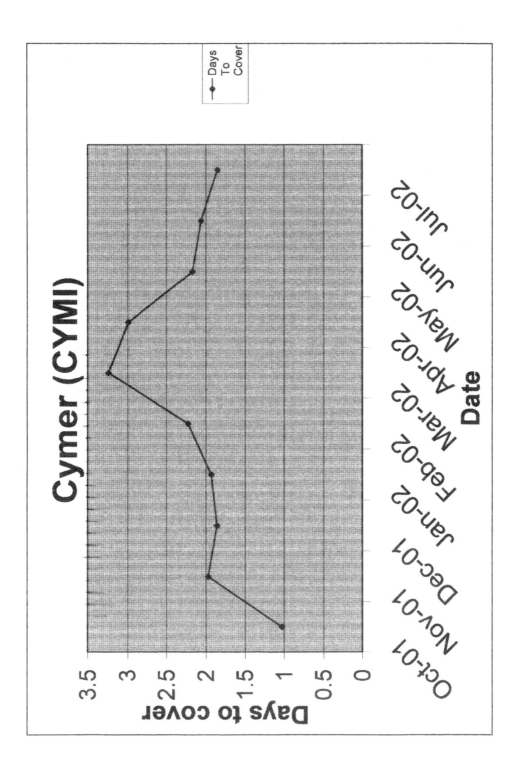

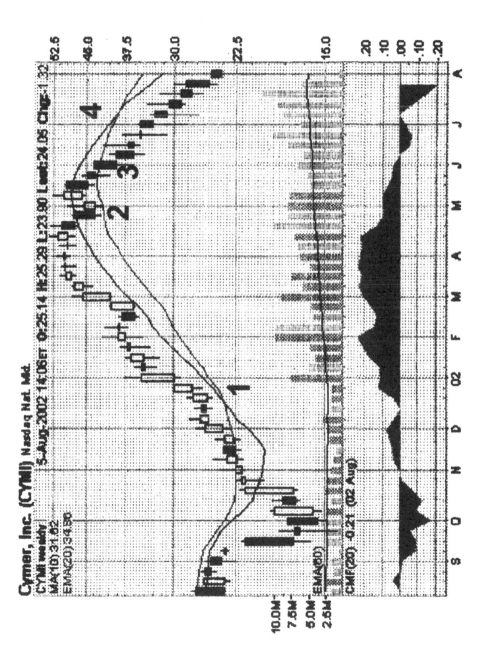

117

upward and crossing the EMA(20). With the stock at $20 you will sell $22.5 strike puts at a premium of ($2.50 + time premium). When the stock moves above $22.5, you will lock in the profit by buying the puts back and selling new in the money puts at $25 strike and so on.

Between March 15 and May 15, 2002 the short interest showed a significant drop. This was accompanied by lower CMF peaks corresponding to points **2** and **3** on the price chart. This is a clear indication that the shorts are giving up and covering their positions resulting in a reduction in buying pressure. At point **4** the MA(10) starts curving down and crossing the EMA(20), indicating a confirmed downtrend. This will be your signal to start using the strategies discussed in this book to raise cash by selling covered calls on the stock.

ALERT: Notice that a 350% price move on the stock occurred when increasing negative sentiment was accompanied by positive strength. A quick downward reversal happened as soon as the short interest decreased and the sentiment turned positive accompanied by negative strength indicators.

Quick Cash Using Short Squeezes

In this section, I will show you a simple stepwise process to identify stocks that are short squeeze candidates ready for explosive short term profits. To identify such stocks follow this procedure:

(1) Every month screen for the top 10 stocks that have experienced the highest short interest increase from the prior month. This is easily accessible on either http://www.viwes.com/invest/ or http://www.shortsqueeze.com/index.php.

(2) Eliminate the stocks that do not show strength as expressed by the Chaikin money flow and moving average indicators. To do this, use the following criteria:

(a) No clear trend indicated by the CMF/Moving Average Chart.

(b) Increase in price and/or upward curvature of the MA(10) not accompanied by strengthening money flow.

(c) Decrease in price and /or downward curvature of MA(10) accompanied by significantly weakening money flow.

(3) Of the remaining stocks, pick the ones that are at the start of their uptrend. To do this look for the following:

(a) Strong upward curvature of the MA(10) followed by a fresh cross of the MA(10), EMA(20) and EMA(30).

(b) CMF is moving from negative to positive and is forming higher peaks with increase in short interest.

(c) The stock is emerging from a base or moving up from a support, but is still close to the support price.

(d) Significant price drop accompanied by weak selling or buying as indicated by CMF reading above -0.1. Such stocks should be looked as candidates for the following month or two, but not for immediate action.

Our goal is to find one stock a month that is about to undergo a short squeeze resulting in explosive short-term profits.

Notice how these principles were applied in the CYMI example in the previous section on page 115. The CMF moved from negative to positive as the days to cover increased significantly. This was followed by a cross of the MA(10) and EMA(20) and higher positive CMF peaks which happened as the stock price was emerging from $15 support.

In the next section, I will take you step by step on how to use this process to generate significant profits.

Short squeezes. Your monthly ticket to explosive profits

In this section, I will take you step by step through the elimination process described previously to identify high profit potential stocks undergoing a short squeeze.

Important points to remember:
(1) Your goal is to pick just one stock each month that will gen-

erate explosive profits. You can thus eliminate stocks that diverge even slightly from the winning criteria described in the previous section.

(2) I will be using real life examples to demonstrate this strategy, so do not expect the chart to have perfect signals. However, with experience, you will be able to decipher these signals and pick a single winner every month.

Step1:

Using the web site http://www.viwes.com/invest or http://www.shortsqueeze.com/index.php, we will search for the first 20 stocks with the largest short interest increase from the previous month. On July 15, 2002, we look up the list for June shown on page 122, while on August 15th we search for the July list shown on page 123.

Using the June list we pick the first 10 stocks after eliminating QQQ since it is an index (Nasdaq 100) and Wcom since it is bankrupt. The 9 stocks left are

AMAT, AMZN,CMCSK,CSCO,JDSU,LVLT,MSFT,NXTL,ORCL

Step 2:

Eliminate the stocks that do not show strength as expressed by the CMF and moving average indicators. Note that point **X** on the charts indicates mid-July which is when the data is available for June. It is important to realize that when the decision is made at point **X** only prior data is available to us.

By applying this criterion to the 9 stocks at point **X** we can easily eliminate:

AMAT,AMZN,MSFT,CMCSK,INTC,CSCO, ORCL,LVLT,JDSU.

In case of *AMAT,AMZN,CMCSK,MSFT,INTC* and *CSCO,* both moving average and CMF indicators are clearly negative when considering the data up to point **X** in the charts on pages 124, 125, 126, 127, 128, 129.

In case of ORCL the moving average indicators are not accompanied by increasing money flow as seen with the chart on page 130.

JDSU and *LVLT* are eliminated since the upward curvature of the MA(10) is not accompanied by positive money flow as seen with the charts on pages 131 and 132.

This leaves *NXTL* which shows significant increase in CMF with heavy volume and a steep upward curvature of the MA(10) indicating that the stock is starting to undergo significant accumulation as seen with the chart on page 133. This is a clear short squeeze candidate and our choice for the month of July 2002.

Note that point **X1** appearing in some charts designates mid-August time frame which is when the July short interest data is available. It is apparent that some stocks that were eliminated from the June list reappeared in the July list. It is advisable to pay attention to such stocks in case a change in strength indicators have occurred that will make them a possible candidates.

Nextel Communications (NXTL), a classic short squeeze

By examining the short interest chart page 134, it is evident that a substantial increase in negative sentiment occurred between February and April 2002. The sentiment remained negative with days to cover ranging between from 4.5 to 5.5 between April and July 2002. In August 2002 a significant reduction in short interest occurred as seen by a decrease in the days to cover.

The significant increase in short interest between February and April 2002 indicates an increasing number of investors committing to purchase the stock at a later date. We expect that once the strength indicators turn positive, short covering will result in an explosive upturn in the stock price due to a short squeeze. It is thus important to keep an eye on the stock for indications of strength as represented by the CMF and moving averages.

By studying the moving average / CMF chart on page 137, between points **a** and **b** the CMF stayed mainly in a range below -0.1, indicating heavy distribution. It is thus our expectation that as soon as the negative CMF is accompanied by negative convergence of the MA(10) and MA(20), a fall in price will occur. This took place at point **1** where the MA(10) crossed the MA(20) to the downside.

Rank	Ticker	Company Name	Position
1	QQQ	Nasdaq-100 Trust Series I	160,607,936
2	WCOM	WorldCom Inc.	123,651,288
3	NXTL	Nextel Communications Inc.	86,036,896
4	CSCO	Cisco Systems Inc.	75,142,114
5	INTC	Intel Corporation	65,509,219
6	CMCSK	Comcast Corporation	63,192,923
7	JDSU	JDS Uniphase Corporation	50,554,077
8	AMAT	Applied Materials Inc.	50,346,736
9	MSFT	Microsoft Corporation	48,112,802
10	LVLT	Level 3 Communications, Inc.	47,602,315
11	ORCL	Oracle Corporation	43,572,229
12	AMZN	Amazon.com Inc.	42,279,808
13	JNPR	Juniper Networks Inc.	41,643,175
14	DELL	Dell Computer Corporation	40,725,734
14	SPY	Standard&Poor's Depositary Recpts	39,220,475
16	USAI	USA Interactive	33,417,720
17	CHTR	Charter Communications, Inc.	32,883,016
18	AMGN	Amgen Inc.	31,444,185
19	QCOM	QUALCOMM Incorporated	29,716,182
20	SUNW	Sun Microsystems Inc.	29,622,938

Source www.viwes.com   June 2002 top 20 short

Rank	Ticker	Company Name	Position
1	QQQ	Nasdaq-100 Trust Series I	163,553,414
2	WCOM	WorldCom Inc.	145,089,812
3	NXTL	Nextel Communications Inc.	89,324,949
4	CSCO	Cisco Systems Inc.	69,342,016
5	CMCSK	Comcast Corporation	60,200,950
6	INTC	Intel Corporation	57,626,754
7	MSFT	Microsoft Corporation	54,353,010
8	JDSU	JDS Uniphase Corporation	53,055,812
9	AMAT	Applied Materials Inc.	52,434,424
10	LVLT	Level 3 Communications, Inc.	50,621,164
11	ORCL	Oracle Corporation	49,841,543
12	SPY	Standard&Poor's Depositary Recpts	42,790,025
13	AMZN	Amazon.com Inc.	41,348,130
14	JNPR	Juniper Networks Inc.	40,181,149
14	DELL	Dell Computer Corporation	39,028,920
16	CHTR	Charter Communications Inc.	35,011,658
17	AMGN	Amgen Inc.	34,345,297
18	YHOO	Yahoo! Inc.	33,047,687
19	QCOM	QUALCOMM Incorporated	25,979,598
20	NTAP	Network Appliance Inc.	25,140,852

Source www.viwes.com   July 2002 top 20 short

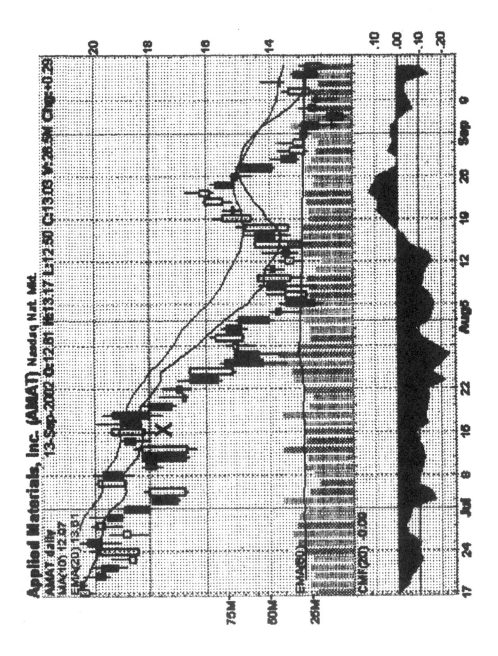

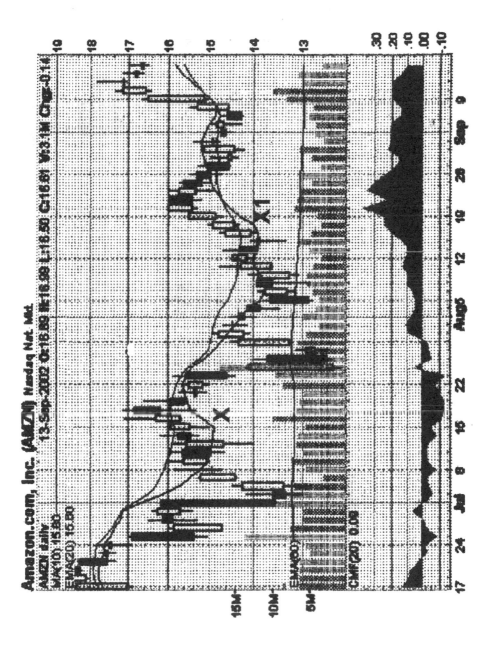

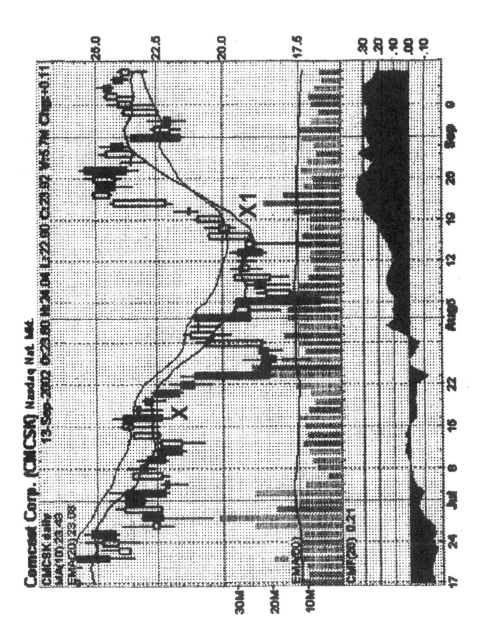

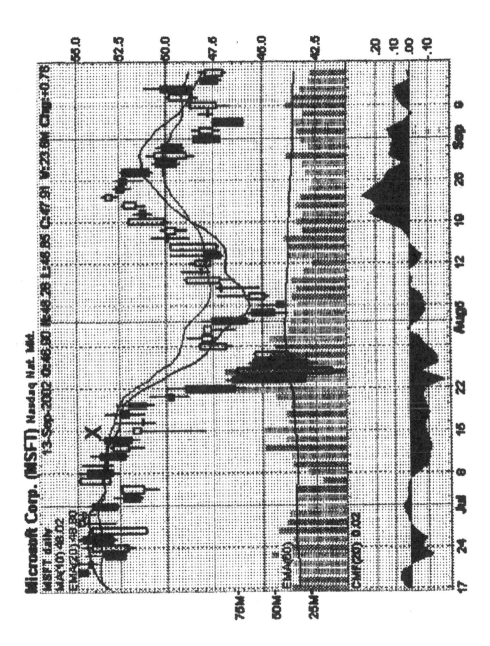

127

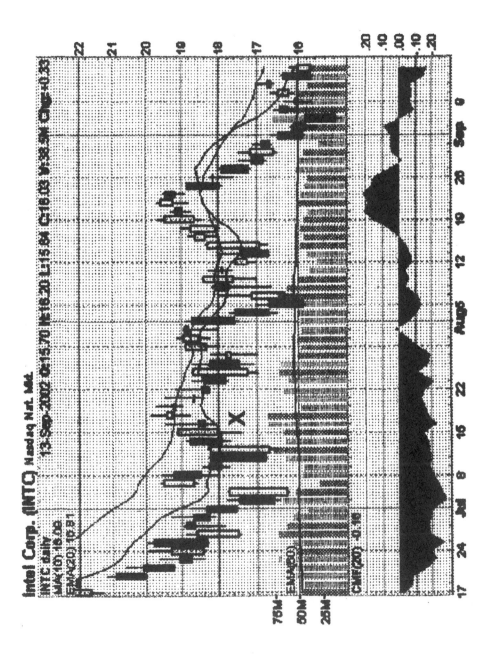

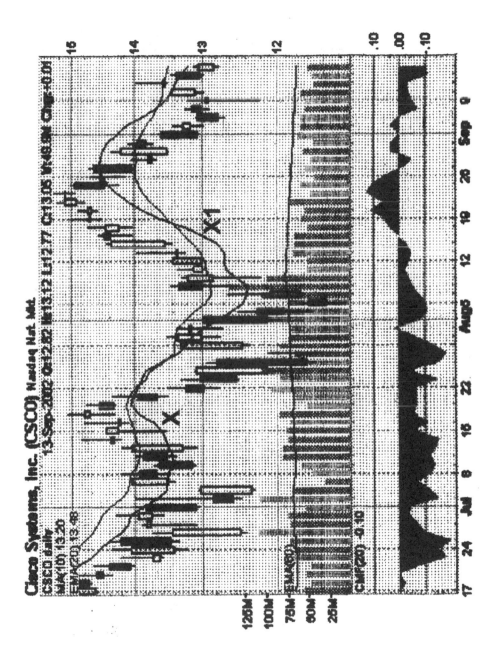

Cisco Systems, Inc. (CSCO) Nasdaq Nat Mkt

13-Sep-2002 O=12.82 H=13.12 L=12.77 C=13.05 V=5.9M Chg=+0.01

CSCO daily

MA(10) 13.20

EMA(20) 13.48

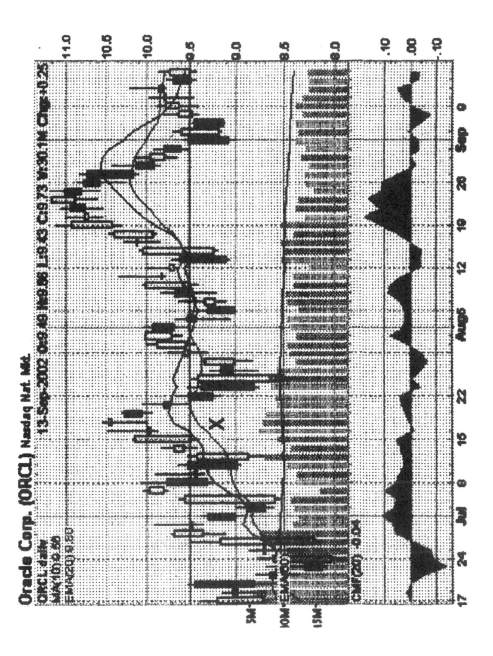

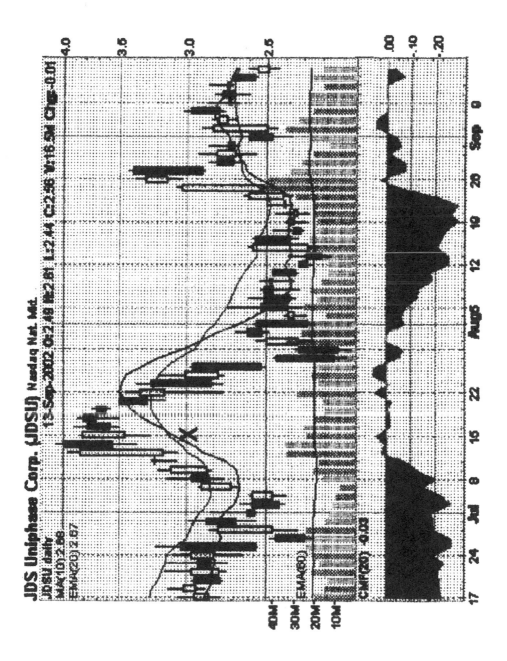

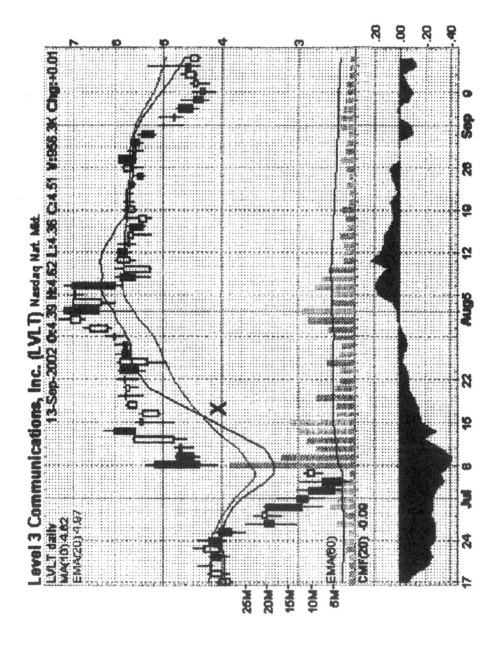

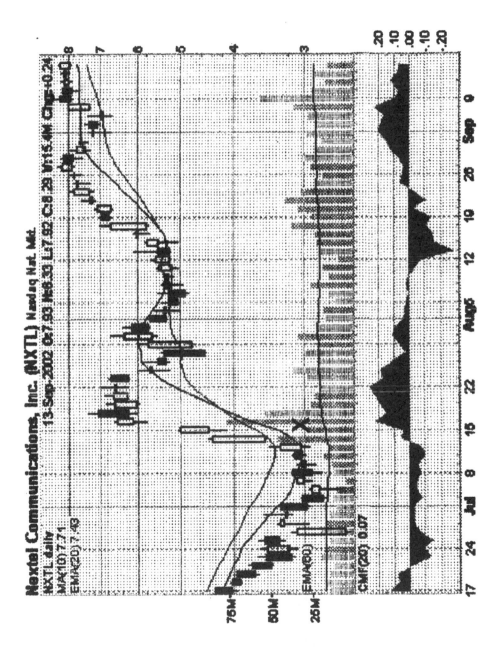

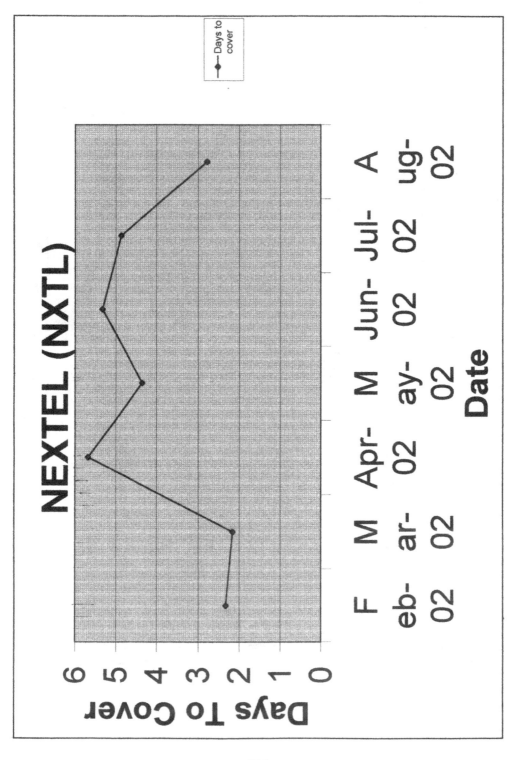

NEXTEL (NXTL)

Days to cover

Days To Cover

6 5 4 3 2 1 0

Feb-02 Mar-02 Apr-02 May-02 Jun-02 Jul-02 Aug-02

Date

ALERT: Notice that even though the level of short interest increased between February and May, this was not accompanied by price strength as detected by the CMF and moving averages. As I indicated previously, this is critical for a short squeeze to occur.

Between points **b** and **c** the CMF stayed mostly above -0.1, indicating weak selling. This is a signal that the steep drop from $5 to $3 was not accompanied by heavy distribution, indicating that the stock is likely to hold support and reverse direction.

At point **2,** the MA(10) curved upward accompanied by significant money flow increase between points **c** and **d.** Our buy signal would be around point **2** with the stock at $3.5. The positive MA(10) signal occurred with the short interest near its high, resulting in a possible short squeeze and an explosive upward move in the stock price.

Between points **d, e** and **f,** the money flow dropped significantly, but the MA(10) failed to cross the EMA(20) to the downside at point **3,** signalling a brief correction rather than a trend reversal. At point **3,** NXTL continued its upward move accompanied by significant money flow increase between **g** and **h,** indicating future strength.

ALERT: Even though the short interest dropped significantly in August, that in itself is not a reason to sell. A drop in short interest must be accompanied by weak price action as indicated by the CMF and moving average chart.

Maximizing cash on short squeezes

Having successfully identified a potential short squeeze, it is our objective at this point to determine the best way to profit. In effect, there are three ways to cash in on a short squeeze.

(1) Buy the stock outright.
(2) Sell in the money puts on the stock, then buy the puts at a lower price as the stock rises.
(3) Buy out of the money calls.

The method best used is dependent on the price of the stock and the time value of the underlying option.

Buying the stock outright: In situations where the stock does not trade options, this will be your only choice. Otherwise it is preferable that you only use this method in two cases: (1) The profit potential on the candidate stock is very high. To judge that, check where the stock price is at relative to the next resistance level; the further away it is the better. (2) The price of the stock is so low that the time premium on selling put options is negligible.

Keep in mind that buying a stock will reduce the cash you have, especially if it is high priced. I do not know about you, but I would rather receive cash than pay it out. It is thus advisable to adhere to the above situations.

Selling in the money puts: This is the most preferred strategy for cashing in on a short squeeze. By selling an in the money put, you will receive a premium equivalent to the difference between the strike and the market price of the stock. In addition, you get a time premium which will give you a cushion in case you were less than perfect in timing your move.

By applying this strategy to *NXTL,* we can see from the chart on page 137 that our short squeeze signal was at point **c** on the CMF and point **2** on the moving average chart.

With the stock at $3.50 we will sell $5 strike January 2003 puts for a premium of $2.10/share. Our price premium is $5 - $3.50 = $1.50, while our time premium is $0.60.

ALERT 1: Why did we pick January 2003 and not any of the months between August and December 2002? The reason is to reduce risk by taking advantage of the seasonal strength in the market. It is well known that November-March are strong months and April-October are weak months. We picked January because it is usually the strongest month of the year, especially for low-priced stocks.

ALERT 2: Remember that the price premium is fixed at $1.50 no matter which month we pick. The only difference is the value of the

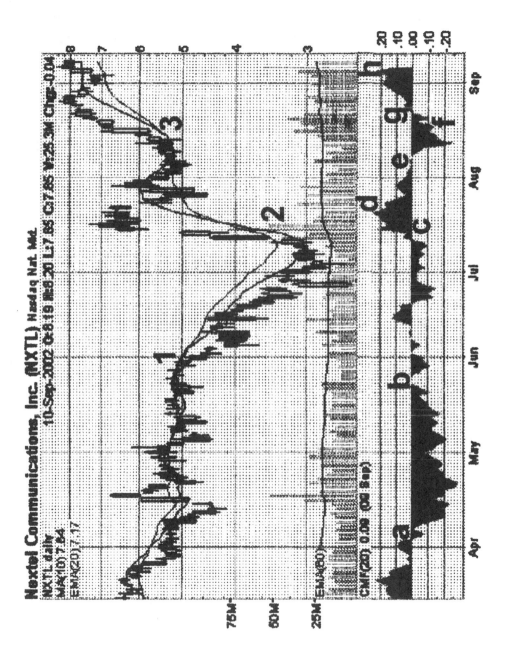

time premium, so why not be conservative and give ourselves the benefit of time.

Going back to the case of *NXTL,* we sell 5000 shares January 2003 $5 strike puts at $2.10/share for a total premium of $10,500. By early August with the short squeeze in full force, the stock moved above $5 and the price premium of the put is now at zero. We will thus lock our profit by buying the put for the time premium left ($0.5/share). Our profit is $10,500 - $2500 = $8000.

With the stock showing additional strength in mid-August as indicated by point **g** on the CMF chart and point **3** on the moving average chart we will raise additional cash by selling January 2003 $7.5 strike puts for a premium of $3/share[$2.50 (price premium) + $0.5 (time premium)]. For selling 5000 shares our premium will be $15,000.

By mid-September, the stock is already above $7.50, so we buy back the puts for the time premium left ($0.40/share) at a cost of $2000 and pocket $13,000 in profit.

Our total profit in three months is $21,000 with no out-of-pocket cash, and as long as the stock is showing strength, we will continue repeating the process. This is only part of the power of a short squeeze.

Buying out of the money calls

It is important to remember that when you buy an option, time works against you, so it is critical in this case to take risk reduction precautions. To accomplish this, we will observe the following rules:

(1) As I mentioned on page 23, we will not pay more than $0.20/share for any option we buy.

(2) To further reduce risk we will either sell covered calls if we own the stock or use part of the money (around 10%) from selling the puts as described in the previous section.

In the case of short squeeze stocks, it is best to employ the out of the money call buying strategy during an **earnings squeeze.**

Follow this procedure and you will be amazed by the amount of cash you can make by taking little risk.

An **earnings squeeze** occurs when a stock undergoing a short squeeze comes out with unexpectedly good earnings. The earnings squeeze can be played four times a year, January, April, July and October, so keep an eye for such candidates during these months.

The general strategy for profiting from an earnings squeeze is as follows:

(1) Just before earnings release, raise cash by selling in the money puts as described previously.

(2) You can either take a chance and buy the calls before earnings release or wait until after the release and buy the calls on a subsequent pullback in the stock price.

(3) When buying the calls, pick the option expiration date one month after the next earnings release. As an example, if this is January earnings, pick May for expiration date.

(4) Pick the lowest strike corresponding to an option price of $0.20/share or less.

I will now demonstrate how these steps are applied to a real life situation using the stock we identified as a short squeeze, namely *NXTL.*

Having identified *NXTL* as a short squeeze, based on the procedure described in this chapter, before implementing the stepwise process described in the previous section, we need to determine whether we are in an earnings release month. With short interest data for June available by mid-July and NXTL earnings coming out shortly after that, we are presented with an ideal situation for playing the earnings squeeze.

Our next step is to sell in the money put as we already have done on page 138, raising $10,500 in cash. We then plan to buy calls using approximately $1050 of the premium (10%) at an expiration date one month after next earnings release. With next earnings release scheduled for October 2002, our expiration date will be set for November 2002.

ALERT: Why are we picking expiration at one month after next earnings release? Usually when a company reports a turnaround in one quarter, the next quarter will tend to build momentum and show better results. In fact, the share price usually shows maximum appreciation within the first six months after an earnings turnaround.

We will now have to make a choice to either buy the calls before or after earnings. The dilemma in this case is that to make a significant profit on the calls we need the stock price to move above the strike by the expiration date, and the higher the strike, the less likely it is for that to occur. If we wait until after earnings and a short squeeze occurs, we will have to pick a higher strike to stay within the $0.20/share price limit we set previously for the calls.

With the stock at $2.50 before earnings, the November 2002 $5 strike calls are selling at $0.20/share, and using the $1000 we allocated we can buy an option on 5000 shares. Right after earnings the stock moves quickly above $3.50, and the November $5 calls move to $0.50 which is outside the $0.20/share limit. In this case we will have to buy 5000 shares $7.5 strike November calls for $0.20/share using our allocated $1000.

Note that by waiting for earnings we have reduced our risk because we know the earnings were good and the stock moved higher; however, our profit potential has been reduced since we had to pick a higher strike.

ALERT: To reduce risk, one possible option will be to take half a position before and the other half after earnings. In this case we will buy calls on 2500 shares $5 strike November 2002 earnings for $500 and use the other $500 to buy $7.5 calls on 2500 shares after earnings.

By studying the *NXTL* chart on page 142. The stock reached $13 by mid-November 2002, and our $5 strike option is now worth $8.00/share. Our calls on 5000 shares are worth $40,000 for a profit of $39,000.

If we picked the $7.5 strike, our calls will be worth $5.50/share for a total of $27,500 for 5000 shares and our profit is $26,500.

ALERT: Please pay attention to points **1,2** and **3** on the moving average chart and the corresponding points **a, b** and **c** on the CMF chart page 142. These are price surge points where the MA(10) crosses the EMA(20), and at the same time the Chaikin Money Flow (CMF) turns from negative to positive. This is an indication that the increase in money flow is starting to affect the longer term price of the stock as expressed by the MA(10), allowing it to overtake the short term price trend manifested by the EMA(20). Be sure to learn how to recognize such points since they usually signify the start of a new uptrend.

Unbelievable, by playing the earnings squeeze our total profit is: $13,000 ($5 strike in the money puts) + $8000 ($7.5 strike in the money puts) + 39,000 ($5 out of the money calls) = $61,000 in less than 4 months without spending any of our own cash. I am sure you can see the explosive potential of the earnings squeeze, even if you can identify one stock every earnings month or four stocks a year.

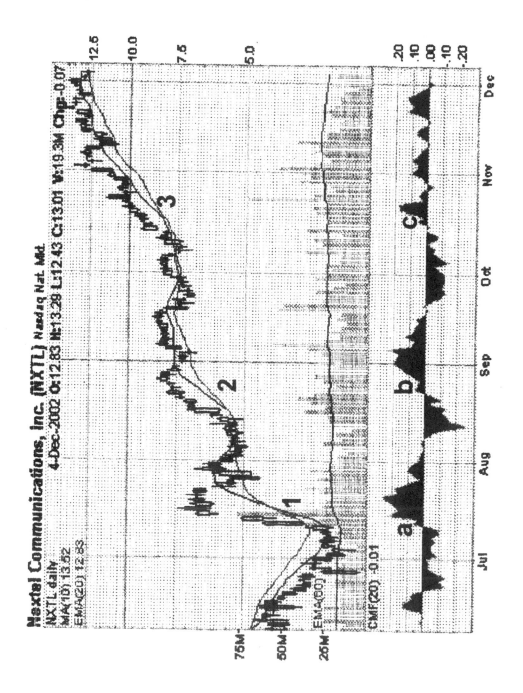

CHAPTER 13

Follow Smart Money on the Road to Explosive Profits

HAVE YOU EVER wondered why Enron and Worldcom stock collapsed way before bad news came out? In fact, by the time the problems were public the stock was already down by 90%.

There are always people who are more informed about a specific company's prospects than the average investor. These include insiders such as corporate officers and directors. In addition, there are professional traders who are continuously watching the price action on a stock who tend to be more alert to any sign of weakness than the average investor. These include the specialists on the floor of the exchange, market makers and some hedge fund managers.

These two types of investors reflect the smart money and tend to buy or sell before good or bad news is out.

It is true that corporate insiders have to file form 144 of their intention to sell with the SEC; unfortunately, by the time that is made public, the damage has already been done.

The use of the Chaikin money flow (CMF) in combination with the lining up of the simple moving average MA(10) and exponential moving average EMA(20) are excellent predictors of the smart money behavior. These indicators can capture the buying and selling by people in the know before it is significantly reflected in the stock price. In the first part of this chapter I will demonstrate to you the effectiveness of these tools using real life examples.

Applying Strength Indicators to Long Term Investing

Questions that are most difficult for the long term investor to answer are the following:

(1) I bought a stock and it is going down in price. Should I sell and take a loss or will the stock move up as soon as I sell?

(2) I bought a stock and it is going up. Should I sell and take my profit or will it continue going higher ?.

(3) I like the fundamentals on this stock, but how do you know when to buy?

The key to dealing with these issues of fear and greed is to remove emotion from the buying and selling decision process. To accomplish that, all you need to do is follow the moving averages and CMF indicators described in chapter 12. This will be clear when you see it applied to specific examples.

Example 1: Neoware Systems (NWRE)

By looking at the Price/CMF chart on page 145, you can see that the CMF moved from -0.2 to zero between points **a** and **b** on the chart even though the price did not move higher. This is an indication of a reduction in selling pressure during February-April 2001 time frame. Between April and September 2001 the CMF moved from zero to over 0.2, indicating several months of sustained heavy accumulation. This happened even though the stock remained in a trading range as seen between points **b** and **c** on the chart.

ALERT 1: A prolonged period of strong CMF signals without a significant price increase indicate heavy accumulation and is a sign that a strong price move will follow. When you see such a scenario, be on the alert for a buying opportunity.

Between September and November of 2001, the price dropped but was accompanied by a CMF reading above -0.1, indicating little selling pressure. This is a criteria of a shake-out to scare weak investors into selling. This type of action usually takes place just before a run-up as seen previously on page 107 with CHK.

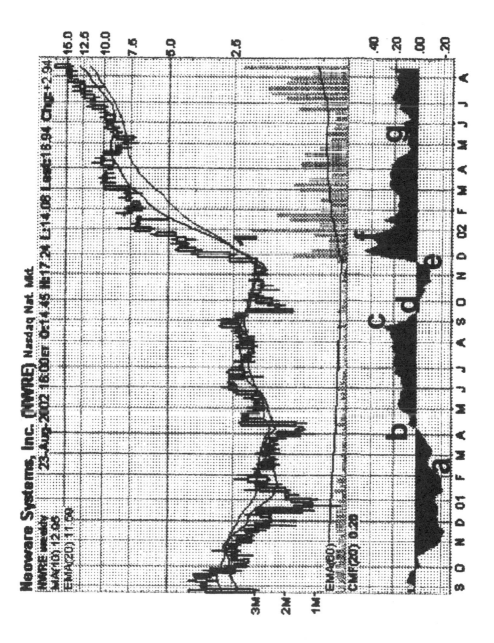

145

ALERT 2: Be on the lookout for a shake-out after a sustained period of accumulation for a buying opportunity.

Notice the explosive money flow increase between points **e** and **f** on the CMF chart. This was accompanied by a strong, almost vertical move of the MA(10) quickly crossing the EMA(20) as seen at point **1** which is a clear signal of an impending strong price appreciation. The best time to buy the stock is between mid-November to December of 2001, when the MA(10) started curving up with a strong slope.

A price correction occurred between April and May 2002 but was accompanied by positive CMF indicating little selling pressure. This is a signal of a temporary minor correction and that the long term uptrend of the stock will continue.

ALERT 3: Important points to learn from this example:
   (1) Positive CMF with consistently higher peaks over an extended period of time indicates heavy accumulation and a likely future price run-up.
   (2) Shake-outs are common after a long periods of accumulation and before the anticipated price rise takes place. These are orchestrated to flush out weak hands and are characterized by a significant price drop but weak buying or selling. This is reflected in CMF readings mostly between 0.1 and -0.1
   (3) It is more likely for a price run-up to be sustainable if it is accompanied by strong money flow as seen between points **e** and **f** in this example.

Example 2: Alaris Medical (AMI)

Although this stock does not trade options, I am including this example to demonstrate that using moving averages combined with CMF indicators can be highly effective for long-term investors.

Notice that on the AMI one-year weekly price chart on page 147 the stock dropped from $1.5 to $0.38 between September 2000

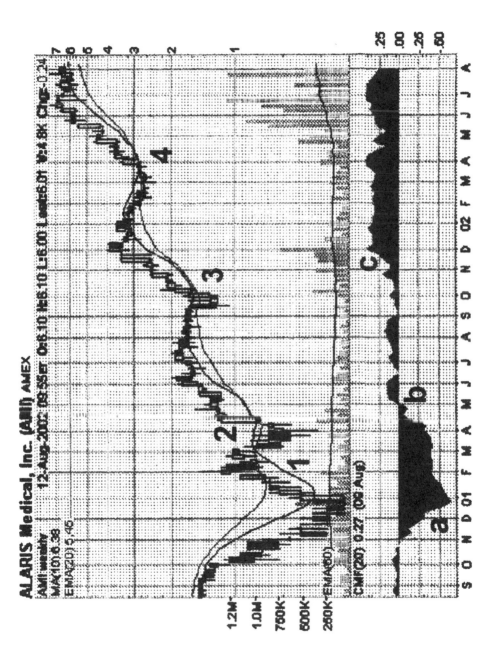

and January 2001. This was accompanied by a large drop in the CMF to -0.5, signaling heavy distribution as indicated by point **a.** This certainly is not a good time to buy the stock, even though the low $0.38 price may be tempting.

Between points **1** and **2** on the chart the MA(10) started curving upward and crossing the EMA(20). In addition, the CMF between points **a** and **b** started moving from -0.5 to around zero, indicating a reduction in selling pressure. Notice also that even though a significant correction occurred at point **2** the CMF did not trend lower, and the MA(10) stayed above the EMA(20). By following these indicators it is evident that the right time to buy was at point **2** when the stock was undergoing a pullback but the indicators were positive.

ALERT 1: At this point you are probably thinking you made a mistake not buying at the bottom, don't. The idea is not to guess where the bottom is, but to buy when you have solid signals that the stock is trending up. In addition, we now have the benefit of hindsight, and when the stock was at its low we could not have predicted it would not go lower.

As the stock continued moving higher, there were intermediate corrections at points **3** and **4,** but the MA(10) never crossed decisively below the EMA(20). In addition, the CMF accelerated to the upside at point **c,** indicating heavy accumulation during the correction phase. This is a signal that the stock has strong upside momentum and it is not time to sell yet.

ALERT 2: The lessons to be learned from this example are:
(1) What is important is not how complicated and impressive the indicators you use are, but how effective they can be in signaling buy and sell points. Use the KISS principle (Keep It Simple & Smart).
(2) Remove the emotions of greed and fear from the buying and selling decisions. We bought at $0.65 because, based on our simple indicators, it was the right time to do that. Our greed would have pushed us to buy at the bottom of $0.38,

which in this case was a better decision; however, most often than not such a decision will backfire. Our fear of losing our profits would have tempted us to sell at points **3** and **4**, but we stuck to our system and were rewarded with over 1000% profit. AMI was ultimately bought out by Cardinal Health at $22.5/share.

Example 3: Terayon Communications (TERN)

Looking back at the previous two examples, one may be tempted to rely on the Money Flow (CMF) without paying attention to the moving averages. I have deliberately picked this example to show that combining these two indicators together is critical, especially in highly volatile stocks.

On page 28, I have presented both formulas for the simple and exponential moving averages. I also indicated that the simple moving average (MA) gives equal weighting to all data in the period of interest; on the other hand, the exponential moving average (EMA) allocates a significantly higher weighting to the most recent data points.

To better understand this distinction, think of the Simple Moving Average as a reflection of the longer term trend of the stock, while the exponential moving average can be thought of as a short-term trend indicator. As money flows into a specific stock, the short term direction of the stock starts getting affected. With continued money flows a more pronounced impact is made on the longer term direction of the stock. The upward curvature of the MA is a visual manifestation of that trend which is further confirmed by the MA crossing the EMA to the upside. Crossing over is, in effect, a clear message that money flow is strong enough that the longer term trend of the stock has overtaken the short-term trend to the upside.

The ideal time to enter a position is when the longer term trend (MA) is starting to show strength and is supported by significant positive money flows. Conversely, the best time to exit a position is when the longer term trend (MA) is starting to show weakness and is supported by negative money flow.

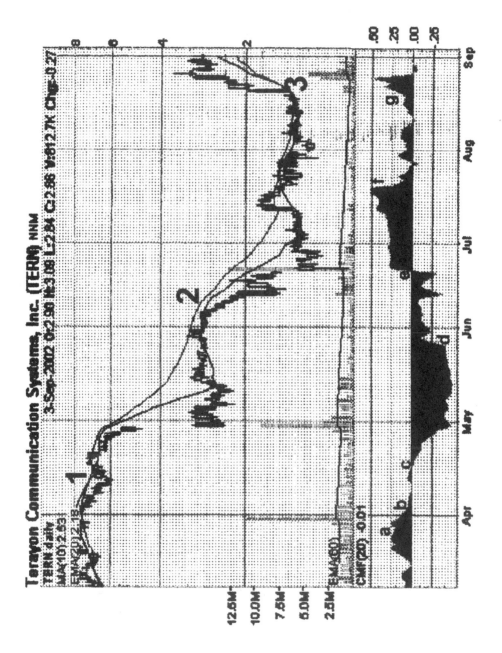

TERN Chart Interpretation

By studying the price/CMF chart on page 150, it can be seen that the money flow dropped from 0.2 to almost zero between point **a** and **b**. Between point **b** and **c** the money flow remained neutral. If we waited for the money flow to turn negative as seen between point **c** and **d** to take action, we would have suffered a 50% loss on the stock.

The drop in money flow between points **a** and **b** was accompanied by the MA(10) crossing the EMA(20) to the downside at point **1**. This is an indication that the money flow is starting to negatively affect the long-term trend of the stock. By listening to the combined money flow and moving average indicators, we could have taken action to sell or raise cash by selling calls at point **1** and avoided a significant loss. Between points **c** and **d** the CMF chart shows significant distribution occurring. Note that at point **2**, the MA(10) fails to cross the EMA(20), indicating that the longer time price trend of the stock was still negative.

Between point **d** and **e**, even though the price dropped significantly, the selling pressure was slowing down. This is an indication that the stock is about to find support. At point **e**, the money flow started turning positive and further strengthened until point **f**, clearly indicating that an upward reversal is about to occur.

As frequently happens before a strong up move, a shake-out occurs between point **e** and **f**. This is demonstrated by positive money flow as the stock is dropping, indicating buying on weakness.

At point **3**, the MA(10) curves upward crossing the EMA(20) accompanied by strong CMF at point **g**. This is a clear indication of strong sustainable upward momentum and an ideal time to enter a long position in the stock.

Example 4: Avanex (AVNX)

This example further illustrates that paying attention to both moving averages and Chaikin Money Flow (CMF) indicators can alert to an impending disaster before it happens.

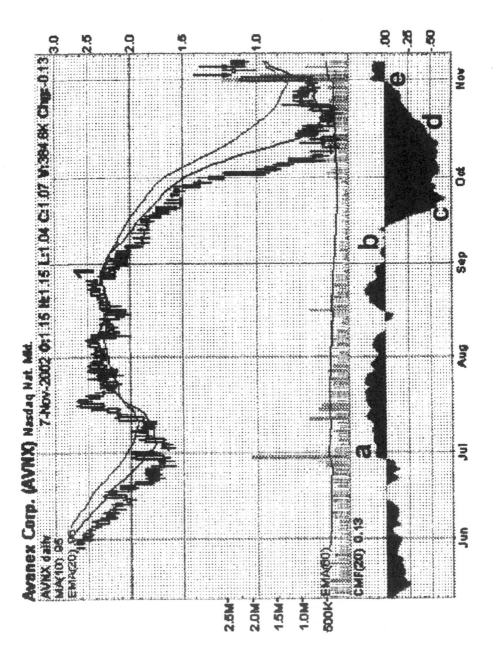

Avanex Corp. (AVNX) Nasdaq Nat. Mkt.
AVNX daily   7-Nov-2002 O:1.15 H:1.15 L:1.04 C:1.07 V:384.8K Chg:-0.13
MA(10): .95
EMA(20):

CMF(20) 0.13

By studying the chart of AVNX page 152, it can be clearly seen that the CMF was mostly above 0.1 between points **a** and **b**. It is thus our expectation that the stock eventually should move higher. What actually happens is the stock takes a steep plunge!

Our first warning came just before point **b** when the money flow starts dropping to zero. This may not be of much concern under normal circumstances, but in this case it was accompanied by a cross of the MA(10) and EMA(20) to the downside. This indicates that the drop in the money flow was significant enough to affect the longer term trend of the stock as expressed by the MA(10). When the MA(10) crossed the EMA(20) to the downside, this implies that the negative long-term effect of the money flow has eclipsed the short-term effect as manifested by the EMA(20). This is a warning that the long-term trend has turned negative.

ALERT 1: Remember what I mentioned in the beginning of this book. After the emergence of the internet, information travels quickly and a stock's price reflects all the information already known about it. To be profitable in this market, you need to use tools that will anticipate news not already reflected in the stock price.

As can be seen, the money flow dropped precipitously between points **b** and **c** and remained very negative until point **d**. As it turns out, the reason for the drop is that earnings were going to be below expectations. If, on the other hand, you waited until the news was out, you would already have lost 80% of the stock value at point **1**.

Between points **d** and **e**, the money flow started becoming less negative, probably due to short covering rather than actual buying interest. The money flow increased after point **e** with a steep increase in the stock price.

Once you have successfully picked a winning stock, one of the most difficult decisions to make is when to sell and take profits. As you are probably aware, most stocks do not go straight up but experience pullbacks along the way. It is thus important to be able to differentiate between a temporary pullback and a trend reversal.

The answer to this question lies in the ability to tell whether smart money is selling. If that is the case, you will expect sequential increase in volume as the price drops. On the other hand, if the price drop is accompanied by sequential decrease in volume, it is an indication that weak hands are selling and the correction is temporary. In this case the long-term positive trend of the stock is expected to continue. The next example shows how paying attention to these signals can prevent exiting a profitable position too early.

Example 5: Corning (GLW)

By studying the chart on page 155, it is clear that a buy signal was given at point **1** on the moving average chart and **a** on the CMF chart. As indicated in the example on *NXTL* in the previous chapter, points where a crossover of the MA(10) and EMA(20) to the upside accompanied by CMF reversal from negative to positive indicate price surge points and the start of a new uptrend on a stock.

As you are well aware, no stock moves straight up, and corrections during an uptrend are expected. Between points **2** and **3** on the moving average chart a significant price drop occurs accompanied by a drop in the money flow. The question to be answered is whether this is just a temporary correction or a trend reversal. To decide whether to sell or hold, we will look for two important signals:

(1) A temporary correction is accompanied by a decrease in the daily trading volume as the price falls.

(2) During a temporary correction, the longer term positive trend of the stock as expressed by the MA(10) is not affected. In such situations the MA(10) should maintain an upward trend, and any flattening should be a cause for concern.

As you can see, daily trading volume designated by **v1**, **v2**, and **v3** on the volume bars on the chart page 155 dropped as the price was falling between points **2** and **3**. In addition, the MA(10) sustained its upward trend signaling a temporary correction.

At point **4**, a different situation emerges and a pick-up in volume occurred on down days accompanied by flattening of the MA(10).

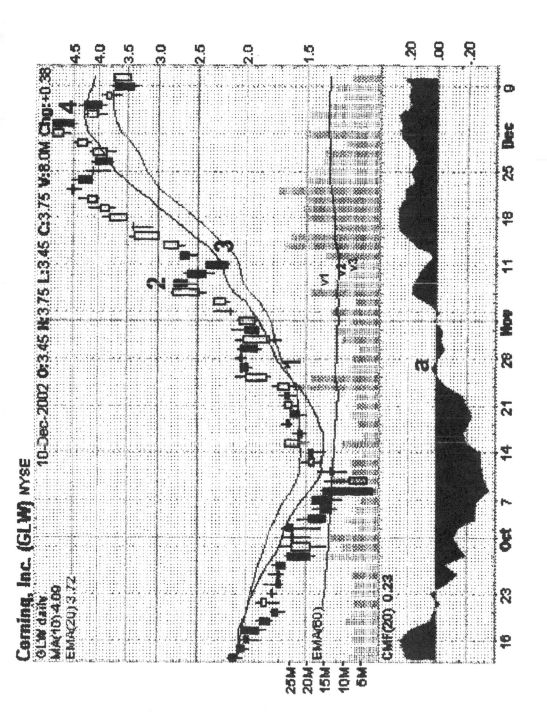

Corning, Inc. (GLW) NYSE
10-Dec-2002 O:3.45 H:3.75 L:3.45 C:3.75 V:8.0M Chg:+0.38
(GLW daily)
MA(10) 4.09
EMA(20) 3.72

155

This indicates that the drop in price is starting to affect the longer term trend of the stock.

Reminder: As indicated on page 105, we should follow the moving averages signal as a primary indicator and the CMF as a reinforcing indicator. Even though the CMF was still positive at point **4,** the flattening of the MA(10) should have prompted us to take action.

If you own the stock, the best action to take is to sell covered calls at point **4.** This way you can keep the stock and buy the calls back at a profit when the stock price stabilizes and stops dropping. If the CMF was turning negative at point **4,** it would have been advisable to cash out of the stock and reinvest the money in a better choice.

Comparison to other common indicators

In this section, I will illustrate why the Chaikin Money Flow (CMF) combined with moving average crossover are better indicators of smart money than other more common overbought/oversold indicators.

The two most popular overbought / oversold indicators are Relative Strength Index (RSI) and full Stochastics (STO). Detailed information on them can be easily obtained through technical analysis books or sources on the internet. For purposes of this discussion, it is sufficient to remember that an RSI reading over 75 indicates overbought, while a reading below 25 indicates oversold conditions. A Stochastics downward crossover with a reading above 75 indicates overbought, while an upward crossover with a reading below 25 indicates oversold conditions.

The main issue with these indicators is that they are static rather than dynamic in nature. In effect, we are picking a constant number to indicate buy and sell signal and are assuming that the smart money will act the way we expect when those numbers are hit. The problem is that a stock can remain overbought and continue its uptrend for a while even after these indicators flash a sell signal.

By using the CMF and moving average crossovers, we have in effect a dynamic system which is triggered as a result of money flow signals rather than the other way around. In this case our buy signal is triggered when the money flow has continued long enough to materially affect the long-term trend of the stock as expressed by the simple moving average MA(10). In addition, we can tell how far the stock is in its uptrend by checking how close we are to the MA(10) crossing over the EMA(20), and the CMF moving from negative to positive territory. These facts will be illustrated in the following example:

Example 6: Citrix Systems (CTXS)

By studying the chart on page 158, it can be seen that the MA(10) crossed the EMA(20) at point **1**. If we have used the RSI and stochastics as our primary indicators, we would have had an over-bought signal at points **a1** and **a** on the chart. Notice that between points **a** and **b** and **a1** and **b1**, both Stochastics and RSI indicators were overbought, giving a sell signal on the stock even though it kept rising in price.

This false signal could have been avoided by using the CMF, moving average crossover signal. Looking at the chart on page 159, we can see that the moving average crossover at point **1** was accompanied by CMF reversal from negative to positive with substantial increase in money flow as seen by the CMF moving above 0.1. Money flow continued strong until point **b** where it experienced a significant drop. This is the time to sell covered calls or sell the stock to raise cash. It is informative to note that between points **a** and **b** there were many false sell signals given by the Stochastics indicator as evidenced by many downward crossovers above 75. The only reliable signal was the one given at point **b**, which was accompanied by decrease in CMF and flattening of the MA(10).

From personal experience, what I found most useful is to look at overbought/ oversold signals as secondary reinforcing indicators to the CMF moving average combination discussed in this chapter.

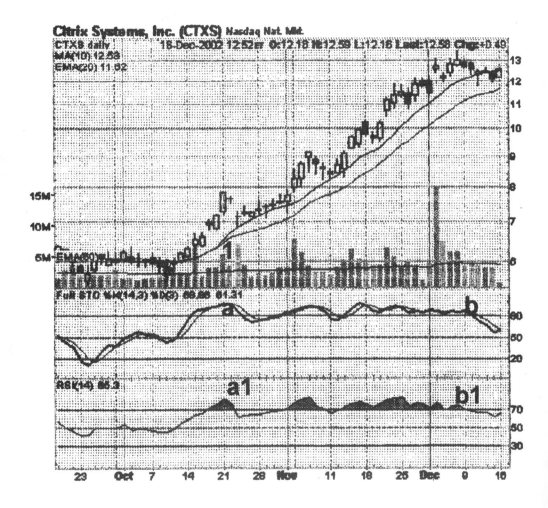

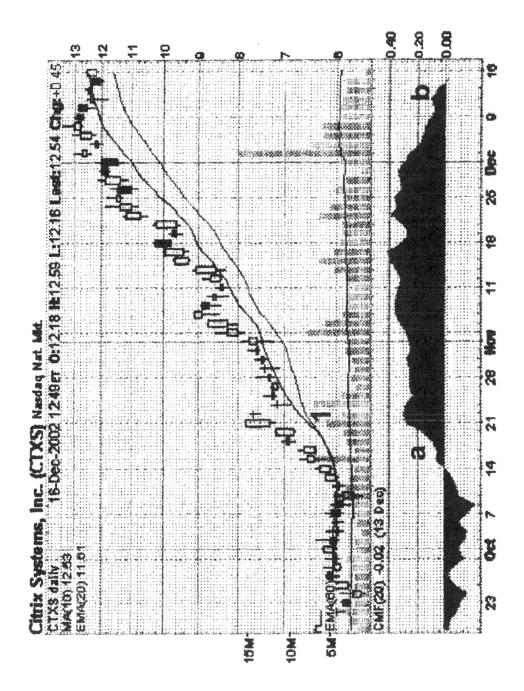

For most effective results, please follow the guidelines below:

(1) If a stock shows an oversold condition as indicated by the RSI and STO, do not take a long position unless the CMF and moving average indicators are showing strong signs of accumulation.

(2) If a stock shows an overbought condition as indicated by the RSI and STO, do not take a short position or sell unless the CMF and moving average indicators show signs of distribution.

ALERT: I am not suggesting that you abandon the system you are using right now, especially if it works for you; however, incorporating these techniques will give you more reliable indicators. I recommend you compare this system with the one you are using and decide for yourself whether complementing or replacing it with this technique will be most helpful in your case.

Another popular oscillator used as a buy/sell indicator is the MACD or moving average convergence/divergence. This oscillator consists of two exponential moving averages that generate buy and sell signals when they cross. These signals are considered especially strong when they are at extreme levels.

Although this indicator is quite useful for intraday and short-term trading, false signals are sometimes given when an intermediate daily or weekly time frame is considered. The reason for this is that both moving averages used are exponential and thus reflective of the short-term trend in the stock. This oscillator tends to give buy and sell signals even when the longer term trend of the stock has not changed.

The following example clearly illustrates this fact

Example 7: Stillwater Mining Company (SWC)

As you can see from the moving average chart on page 161, the MA(10) is in a downward trend at point **1** having already crossed below the EMA(20). Between points **1** and **2** the MA(10) started

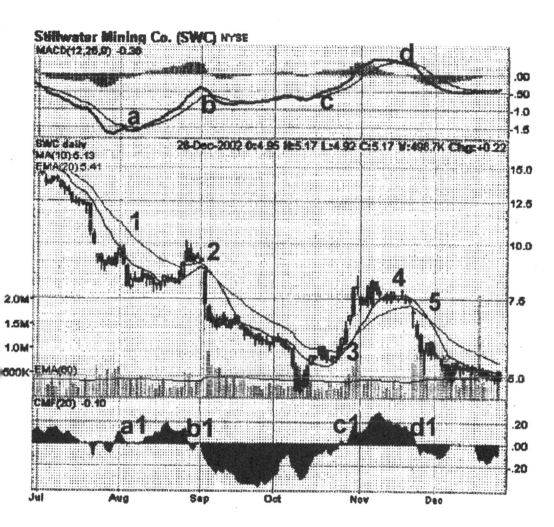

Stillwater Mining Co. (SWC) NYSE
MACD(12,26,9) -0.36

a b c d

SWC daily   26-Dec-2002 O:4.95 H:5.17 L:4.92 C:5.17 V:498.7K Chg:+0.22
MA(10) 5.13
EMA(20) 5.41

1 2 4 5 3

2.0M
1.5M
1.0M
600K EMA(60)

CMF(20) -0.10

a1 b1 c1 d1

.00
-.50
-1.0
-1.5

15.0
12.5
10.0
7.5
5.0

.20
.00
-.20

Jul   Aug   Sep   Oct   Nov   Dec

curving upward but failed to cross the EMA(20) at point **2,** indicating lack of confirmation of the price strength. Even though the CMF was slightly positive between points **a1** and **b1**, the lack of confirmation from the primary indicator, the moving averages, would have prevented us from buying the stock.

Note that at point **a** on the MACD chart a strong buy signal was given as indicated by the upward crossover at an extremely low value which continued to point **b**. Between points **b** and **c** the MACD remained flat, indicating a hold signal. As can be seen from the price chart, following the MACD by buying at point **a** would have resulted in a 50% loss on the stock. On the other hand, by using the CMF/ Moving average signals, it would have been clear to us that the failure of the moving averages to confirm the uptrend at point **2** accompanied by a change from positive to negative CMF indicated significant weakness in the stock.

By following the CMF/moving average indicators, the first clear buy signal occurred at point **3** when the CMF moved from negative to positive territory as seen at point **c1** accompanied by the MA(10) crossing over the EMA(20). In this case it just happens that the buy signal given by the MACD at point **c** is accurate.

At point **4** the MA(10) flattens out and crosses the EMA(20) at point **5** accompanied by the CMF moving to negative territory at point **d1**, giving a clear signal to sell the stock or protect your profits by selling covered calls. In this case it also happens that the MACD was correct in giving a sell signal at point **d**.

ALERT: Although I am not suggesting that you give up on your present system, especially if it is working for you, I strongly encourage incorporating these concepts into it. This is especially important when you are buying options and time is working against you. In this case you need to pick criteria that will ensure a sustained stock movement in your direction. You can clearly see by studying the numerous examples given that a positive Chaikin money flow accompanied by moving average crossovers is a strong signal of a sustained uptrend. This is especially true in the case of a stock undergoing a short squeeze.

Price congestion: Where smart money moves under the radar

A seemingly easy way to achieve significant profits in a stock is to anticipate breakouts before they occur. The problem lies in being able to identify which stock is getting ready to break out and when that will take place.

A very useful strategy is to identify stocks that are in a price congestion pattern. When a stock has been non trending for too long, it is likely to break out of the trading range and establish a new trend. The trend could be to the upside or downside, depending on whether there is accumulation or distribution by smart money.

To objectively decide whether a stock is in a tight daily consolidation range, we will use a common technical signal that measures the strength of a trend. Our indicator of choice is the average directional movement or **ADX** which uses a scale between zero and 100 to rate the "trendiness" of a stock.

The ADX identifies whether a stock is in a trend but does not reveal the direction of the trend. A rising ADX value indicates that the present trend is gaining strength, while a falling value indicates that the present trend is losing strength. For a stock to be trending, an ADX value of 30 and rising is required.

The longer a stock is in a narrow consolidation range, the less trending it exhibits. A common observation is that when the ADX falls below 20 and particularly below 15, the stock has been in a non trend for too long and is poised to breakout from its trading range and initiate a new trend.

To identify stocks that are poised for a breakout, look for low ADX values. The lower the ADX value, the greater the likelihood that when a breakout comes it will happen quickly, handing us a significant profit provided we can determine the direction correctly. To do this, we will use directional technical indicators.

ALERT: To identify stocks ready for a breakout, look for ones that are confined to a tight trading range as manifested by ADX valued below 20 and preferably below 15.

Having found candidate stocks in a price congestion pattern, we will now have to use directional indicators to determine the direction of the anticipated breakout. Our goal is to get into a position as close to a strong move as possible; consequently we will have to consider both long and short-term signals. This can be best accomplished as follows:

(1) For a long-term directional indicator we will use the CMF/ moving average indicator described in this chapter. For stocks in a congestion pattern we will require that the following conditions hold to go long on a stock:

(a) The simple 10 period moving average should be trending upward. However, we do not require that the slope be steep or that the MA(10) have crossed the EMA(20).

(b) The Chaikin money flow should have readings above zero during the congestion period indicating accumulation. Although it is preferable, we do not require that the CMF has readings above 0.1.

ALERT 1: Notice that our CMF and moving average requirements are not as stringent as in other "Normal" situations. The reason is that when a stock is non trending for a long period of time, we know a breakout is coming. Our task is reduced to determining the direction of the breakout and entering a position before it occurs.

(2) For a short-term directional indicator we will use the full Stochastics or STO explained previously in this chapter. For a stock to be a short-term breakout candidate, the Stochastics indicator should be rising with the slow and fast components converging or crossing each other.

ALERT 2: It is important to use both indicators at the same time. The long-term indicator (CMF and moving averages)will assure us that the longer term trend is positive while the shorter term STO indicator will indicate the timeliness of the breakout. If you find that the longer term criteria is satisfied but the short term criteria has not yet been fulfilled, wait until that occurs before taking action.

EXAMPLE 8: Biomarin Pharmaceutical (BMRN)

By examining the chart on page 167, it can be clearly seen that BMRN was in a price congestion around $10 between points **1** and **2**. To assess whether this period of congestion has gone for a long enough period to indicate a possible trend change, we will examine the ADX indicator. The chart shows an ADX value below 20 at point **c**, subsequently dropping to 15 at point **d**. This indicates that the stock has been non trending too long between points **c** and **d** and is likely to establish a new trend.

Our next step is to examine the long-term indicators, i.e., the money flow/moving average combination. During the congestion period the money flow was above zero with periods of heavy accumulation above 0.1. In addition, the MA(10) and EMA(20) showed upward convergence at point **2**. This is a sign that the longer term trend is expected to be to the upside.

We then examine the short term indicator to establish the timing of our move. By studying the stochastics indicator on page 166, we can clearly see a rising indicator with a crossover at point **e** corresponding to the low point **d** on the ADX chart and point **2** on the price chart.

We can enter the position at point **2** or alternatively wait for a breakout from the range right after point **2**. The choice will depend on the investor's experience in accurately determining the direction of the breakout.

ALERT: I recommend that you initially wait for a breakout to take action. After you have gained some experience, you can then enter your position once the long and short-term indicators give the trigger signal.

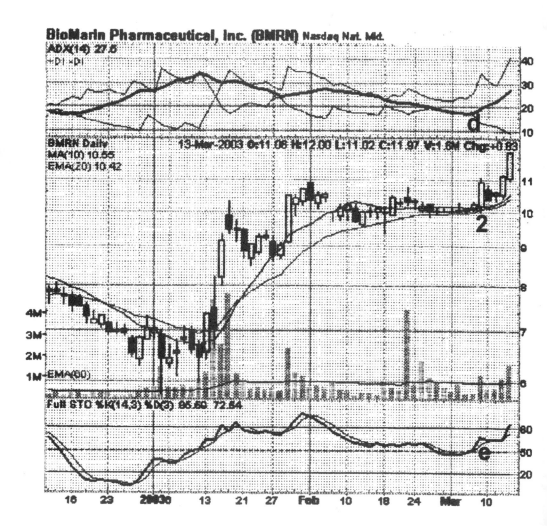

BioMarin Pharmaceutical, Inc. (BMRN) Nasdaq Nat. Mkt.

ADX(14) 27.5
+DI -DI

BMRN Daily   13-Mar-2003 O:11.06 H:12.00 L:11.02 C:11.97 V:1.8M Chg:+0.83
MA(10) 10.55
EMA(20) 10.42

EMA(60)

Full STO %K(14,3) %D(3) 85.60 72.64

d

2

e

16   23   2003 30   13   21   27   Feb   10   18   24   Mar   10

166

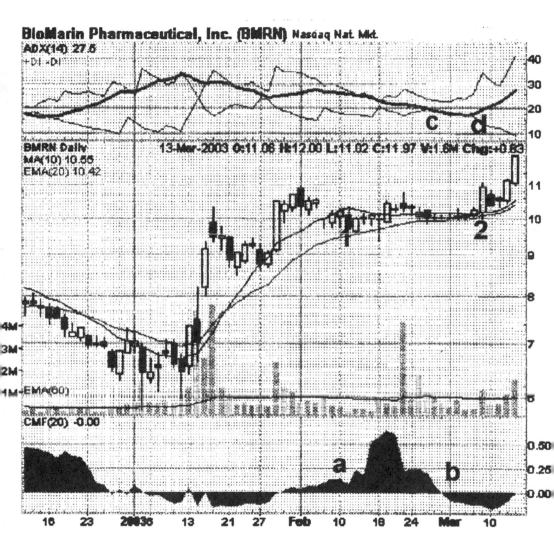

BioMarin Pharmaceutical, Inc. (BMRN) Nasdaq Nat. Mkt.

ADX(14) 27.5
+DI -DI

BMRN Daily   13-Mar-2003 O:11.06 H:12.00 L:11.02 C:11.97 V:1.8M Chg:+0.83
MA(10) 10.55
EMA(20) 10.42

EMA(50)

CMF(20) -0.00

Personal Note: In addition to short squeezes, I actively seek stocks in a congestion period with low ADX value for short term profits. To go long, I usually either purchase the stock outright or sell puts on the stock at the congestion pivot price ($10) in case of BMRN.

After purchasing the stock, I usually sell in the money covered calls when the uptrend starts weakening. The reason for this is such stocks move up quickly when they break out of the congestion range, resulting in a high implied volatility for the stock and hence a hefty call premium.

Divergent Signals, Your crystal ball to trend reversals

How would you like to have a crystal ball that can spot a stock reversal to the upside or downside before it actually occurs? Does such a magic ball exist?

My experience in the past few years has convinced me that trend reversals can be predicted beforehand when divergent signals are spotted. The problem is that these divergences do not occur very often, but when they do it is as good as a crystal ball into the future of a stock.

A divergent signal occurs when a specific technical indicator fails to confirm a new price high or low within an established trend. During the past few years of trading, I have experimented with different indicators and found the **MACD Histogram** to be the most powerful divergent signal indicator.

The **MACD Histogram** is shown as bars identical to volume bars, except that there is a zero line in the middle. The MACD oscillates above and below the zero line. The histogram measures the difference between the MACD line and the signal line with positive results represented by bars above the zero line and negative results represented by bars below the zero line.

If a stock is in an established uptrend, the MACD Histogram must show new highs corresponding to new price highs; conversely, if a stock is in a downtrend, a new low in the MACD histogram should correspond to a new price low. In cases where a new price high or low is not accompanied by a similar trend in the histogram, a divergent signal is given.

ALERT: A stock is considered in an established uptrend if the MA(10) has already crossed the EMA(20) to the upside and remains higher. A downtrend is established when the MA(10) has crossed the EMA(20) to the downside and remains lower.

In an uptrend, the failure of the MACD histogram to make a new high corresponding to a new price high indicates that buyers are losing momentum and the stock is due for a downward reversal. In a downtrend, if the MACD histogram fails to make a new low corresponding to a new price low, the sellers are losing momentum and the stock is due for an upward reversal.

The following examples demonstrate the power of the MACD Histogram divergence in predicting reversals.

Example 9: Abgenix (ABGX)

By examining the chart on page 170, it can be seen that ABGX is in an established downtrend between points **1** and **2** since the MA(10) has crossed the EMA(20) and remains below it. The downturn at point **1** was accompanied by a change from positive to negative in the Chaikin money flow as seen at point **a** and a new MACD histogram low at point **a1**. Notice, however, that point **b1** on the histogram is higher than **a1** even though the stock established a new price support low at point **2**. This is a divergent signal and the indication of a coming trend reversal.

ALERT 1: The time to take action is when another signal confirming the uptrend occurs. In this case action could have been taken when the slope of the histogram turned positive after point **b1**. Alternatively, one can wait for the MA(10) to have a positive slope or until it crosses the EMA(20) at point **3** if further confirmation is needed. The confirmation you need will depend on your level of experience using this technique.

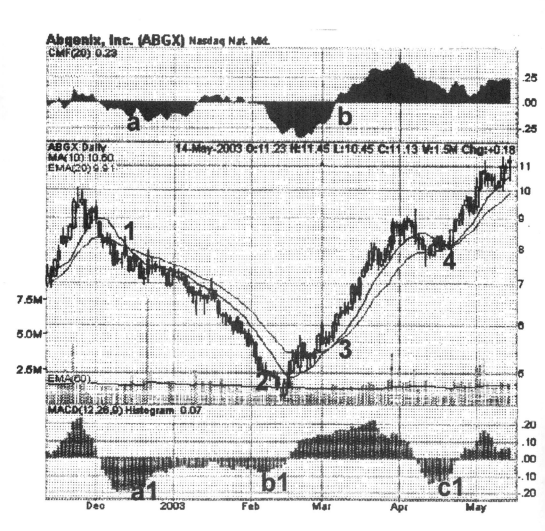

ALERT 2: Notice that even though the price at point **4** is higher than that at point **2**, the corresponding MACD histogram at point **c1** is lower than at point **b1**. Be sure to compare the histogram within a specific trend; otherwise the comparison will not be valid. Notice that point **4** is part of a new uptrend while point **2** is part of a downtrend, so in this case comparison of these two points is not valid since they do not belong to the same trend.

Example 10: Orthodontic Centers of America (OCA)

By examining the chart on page 172, it can be clearly seen that between points **1** and **3** the stock is in an established downtrend. Notice that as the price drops between points **1** and **2**, the slope of the MACD histogram is negative and a new low is established. On the other hand, between points **2** and **3** a new low in price is not accompanied by a new low in the histogram. In fact, the histogram value at point **c1** is not only higher than that at **b1,** but is above the zero line. In addition, even as the price dropped between points **2** and **3**, the histogram slope is positive, indicating a pending reversal. These signals are even more powerful than in the previous example and will justify an earlier entry point. The earliest entry signal is the appearance of a candlestick **doji** right after point **3**. Alternatively, one can wait for the MA(10) to show positive slope or for further confirmation by the MA(10) crossing the EMA(20) at point **4**.

ALERT: A **doji** is a Japanese candlestick whereby the opening and closing prices of the stock are almost identical and is a reversal sign. Going into details on Japanese candlesticks is beyond the scope of this book and is a book in itself. If you are interested in learning more about this subject, please refer to books by Steve Nisson. An introduction to candlestick charts and their use to spot sudden reversals is discussed in Chapter 17.

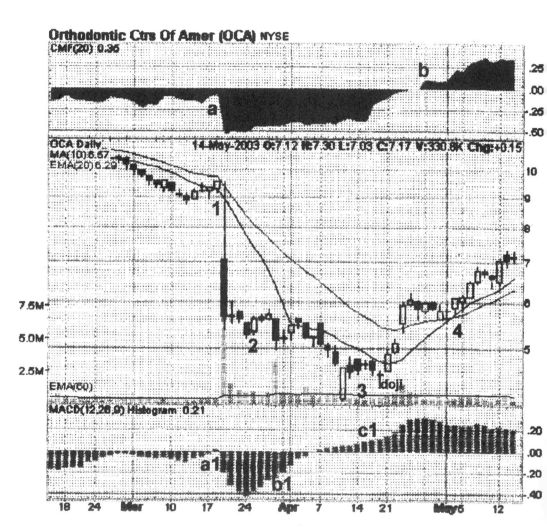

Example 11: Ask Jeeves (ASKJ)

Divergent signals are also effective in anticipating long-term reversals as seen by the weekly chart in this example.

By now you should be able to easily recognize the obvious entry point **3** on the chart on page 174 where the MA(10) crosses the EMA(20) to the upside accompanied by the Chaikin money flow moving from negative to positive at point **a**.

Even though the entry point at **3** will have resulted in significant profits, you could have done even better if you were paying attention to MACD histogram divergences. Notice that even though the price at point **2** is comparable to that at point **1**, the MACD histogram is higher at point **b1** than **a1**. In addition, the reading at **b1** is above zero while that at **a1** is below the zero line, indicating significant divergence and a strong upward reversal ahead. By recognizing this fact, action could have been taken at point **2** while the price was still below $1.

Comment: One of the most important points to remember is that the stock market is without human feelings, rationality or logic. Many investors let their emotions get in the way even when entry and exit signals are very clear. In the case of buying ASKJ, I could easily see anyone saying: are you nuts! Ask Jeeves was a hyped junk internet stock now below $1 and is definitely going bankrupt just like many other stocks in the same industry. What is happening here is human rationalization, which is a dangerous practice in the market.

Several investors who came to me for help in recovering their losses the past couple of years refused to take action on such stocks even when the signals were clear to them. Few of them were inclined to take action but were talked out of it by their brokers and financial advisors who, in fact, were making the same deadly mistake of incorporating human logic into the market.

If you look back one year from today (today's date is 5/30/2003), many so-called junk stocks have made spectacular gains, check out ABGX, AMI, AMZN, AMT, CTXS, EELN, JNPR, NTES and many others.

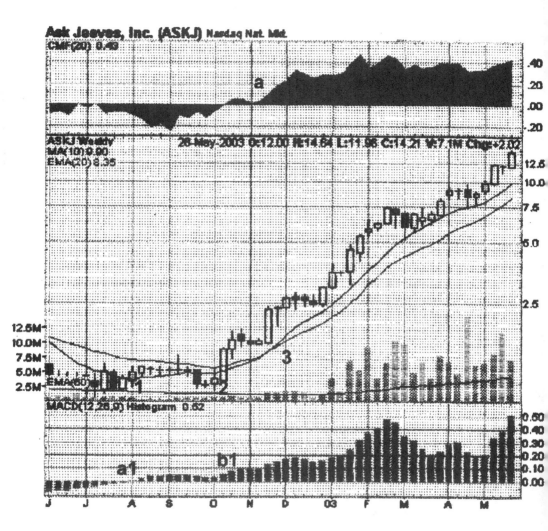

To be successful in trading and investing, you need to have confidence in a system devoid of emotions to talk to the market in a no-feeling language it can understand. Then and only then you can beat the market at its own game.

Multiple Time frames. Your key to avoiding shake-outs.
Your ability to lock in significant profits in the market is highly dependent on letting your winners run and cutting your losses short. To do this, you need to hold onto winning stocks and not let your emotions take control and scare you into selling on corrections or shake-outs.

Unfortunately, this is easier said than done; sometimes shake-outs are severe with drops of 20-30% or even more and are enough to scare most into selling.

The key to avoiding this trap is to look at more than one time frame when making a decision on whether you should sell a stock. If the trend is still intact in the longer time frame, then you should hold the position; otherwise you should consider selling.

To capture the lion's share of profits, you need to use the shorter time frame to trigger your entry point. Once you are in the position, you will look at both shorter and longer time frames to determine your exit strategy. This is important since entry point signals are evident earlier in a shorter time frame. If you use the longer time frame to take action, you will most likely miss a significant part of the profits.

ALERT: Unless you are a day trader, the two most commonly used time frames are daily for the shorter time frame and weekly for the longer time frame.

The importance of multiple time frames in avoiding shake-outs will be evident in the following example.

Example 12: E* Trade (ET)
Look at the daily chart page 176. Can you spot the initial entry point? If you have grasped the main concepts in this book, you

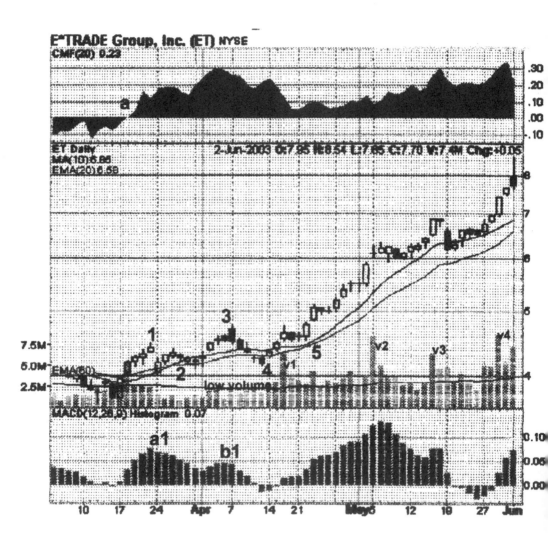

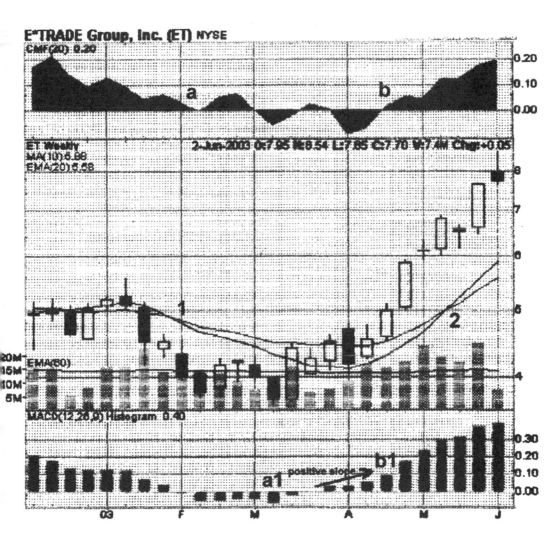

E*TRADE Group, Inc. (ET) NYSE

CMF(20) 0.20

a b

ET Weekly   2-Jun-2003 O:7.95 H:8.54 L:7.85 C:7.70 V:7.4M Chg+0.05
MA(10) 5.96
EMA(20) 5.58

EMA(50)

MACD(12,26,9) Histogram 0.40

a1 positive slope b1

03   F   M   A   M   J

should be able to immediately locate the initial entry point at **2**. This is where the MA(10) crosses the EMA (20) to the upside accompanied by the Chaikin money flow (CMF) moving from negative to positive at point **a**.

Based on this signal, say you go ahead and purchase E trade at $4.25/share. The stock moves to $4.75 at point **3,** but a warning signal is given by the lack of confirmation from the MACD histogram. Notice that even though the stock price at point **3** is higher than point **2**, the MACD histogram is lower at point **b1** than **a1**. This divergent signal within the established uptrend is an indication that a correction is coming. The question is, should you sell or ride out the correction?

ALERT 1: When an MACD histogram divergent signal is given, a good strategy will be selling covered calls to take advantage of the price drop to raise cash if the correction is assessed as temporary.

To determine the nature of the coming correction, we will study the weekly chart on page 177. Notice that the slope of the MACD histogram stayed positive between March and May, or points **a1** and **b1** on the chart. This contradicts the direction of the histogram between March 24 and April 7 on the daily chart page 176. This is telling us that the correction is temporary in the daily or shorter time frame, but the trend of the stock is still positive in the longer or weekly time frame.

ALERT 2: At this point you may be questioning why we entered the position at point **2** on the daily chart and not waited for an entry signal on the weekly chart. If we did that, the first entry signal will be point **2** on page 177 at a price of $5. As you can see, the signal in this case is at a 20 % higher price than the daily chart signal which stresses the importance of using the daily chart for the initial entry point.

As predicted by the MACD histogram divergence, a 20% correction takes place between points **3** and **4**. The low volume during the sell-off further confirms the temporary nature of the correction.

After the correction is complete at point **4**, a tell tale volume spike **v1** takes place and the stock starts moving higher. Notice that at point **5**, the MA(10) never crosses the EMA (20) to the downside, and both the Chaikin money flow as well as the slope of the MACD histogram remain positive. This is a clear indication that the stock is about to start a strong uptrend.

ALERT: If you have missed the initial entry point, look for other entry points by recognizing continuation volume spikes during the uptrend. Notice that in this example we have four such spikes, **v1**, **v2**, **v3** and **v4,** as seen on the daily chart.

Such spikes are characterized by a closing price above the high of the previous day. Be sure to enter the position a day or two after the spike since in most, but not all, cases a small correction follows.

As you can see with this example, we were able to practice several concepts discussed in this book. Our ability to recognize Moving average/CMF signals dictated our initial entry point. The MACD histogram divergence permitted us to predict a coming correction. Paying attention to the positive slope of the MACD histogram on the weekly chart indicated the correction was temporary. Continuation volume spikes signaled four other possible entry points in case we missed the initial trigger.

Using general market trends to multiply your profits

In the beginning of this book, I have stressed the importance of investing with the trend of the general market. In effect, an investor should be buying when the market is at a start of an uptrend and selling at a start of a downtrend. The question at this point becomes as to whether there are simple tools available to assess the intermediate term direction of the market.

If you ask most financial advisors, they always stress that timing the market is a losing strategy and no one can do that accurately. While this statement may be true in relation to daily fluctuations, which I agree are highly unpredictable, assessing the intermediate week-to-week trend of the market is possible using appropriate charting and mathematical tools.

Personal Note: Having been trained as an engineer and written a doctorate dissertation on computer modeling, I can say from personal experience that appropriate use of mathematical equations and algorithms to simulate real life system behavior is a powerful tool and is the basis of most design work. Using such techniques, spacecrafts can land on the moon or Mars within few hundred yards of a designated area, behavior of mixtures of liquids and gases can be virtually modeled and used to design distillation towers, and aircraft can be designed and tested before actual flight. Hence, it should not be a surprise that by defining appropriate parameters intermediate market turns can be predicted.

It is my assessment that since most financial advisors are not trained in the areas of mathematical modeling and design, they lack the capability to use such tools in their analysis of the markets. It is thus not a surprise that they recommend you hold for the long term no matter what the market does.

As in the case with individual stocks, the principles of fear and greed can be used to assess the intermediate trend of the market with a good degree of accuracy.

Measuring fear in the market

To measure fear in the general market, we will pick an index such as the Dow, S&P 500 or the Nasdaq and evaluate parameters that are reflective of the amount of fear in that index.

There are two main parameters that are reflective of the level of fear in a certain index:

(1) Short interest as measured by the days to cover discussed on page 102. An increase in short interest reflects a bet by the majority that the market will go lower. The majority is usually wrong, and the market keeps moving higher until

most give up and cover their short positions. As soon as that happens, the short interest starts dropping and the market goes down with it.

EXAMPLE 13: Diamonds (DIA)

The Diamonds (DIA) are a proxy for the Dow index and are represented by the value of the Dow/100.

As can be clearly seen from the chart on page 182, a significant increase in the short interest occurred between points **A** and **B** as well as **C** and **D** on the Days To Cover chart, indicating that the majority is betting on a drop in the index. What happens is the index rises as seen between points **1** and **2** as well as **3** and **4** until most of the shorts start giving up and covering since they are holding losing positions and are convinced the market rise will continue. This occurred at points **B** and **D** which correspond to points **2** and **4** on the index chart. With the majority having given up on continuing to short the market, the Dow does the exact opposite and starts going down as seen between points **2** and **3** in addition to **4** and **5** on the chart.

Point to remember: What we learn from the above discussion is that the market moves against the majority at risk. Thus, for an index to have a sustained upward move, a healthy amount of short interest must be present.

(2) Volatility index: This is a very good predictor of fear in the market and is represented by the symbol VIX for the S&P 500 and VXN for the Nasdaq. In most situations volatility rises with a drop in the underlying index and declines when the underlying index moves higher. As the level of fear increases with significant drops in the market, the volatility rises to highly unsustainable levels. It is usually at such points when a market reversal from a downtrend to an uptrend occurs.

The difficulty with using the volatility index to predict market turn-around is that there is no magic number at which the index could be

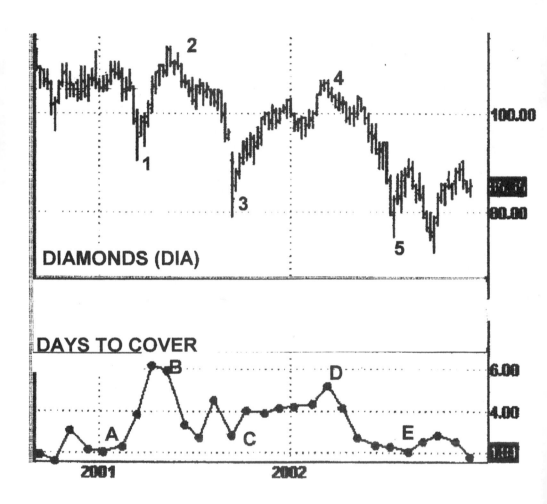

DIAMONDS (DIA)

DAYS TO COVER

deemed too high or low. As an example, the volatility index for the S&P 500 (VIX) could signal a high level of fear anywhere between a reading of 40 and 50 and a high level of complacency or lack of fear between readings of 20 and 30. The Nasdaq is inherently more volatile in nature; thus the VXN usually signals high levels of fear between readings of 60 and 70 and low levels of fear between 40 and 50.

It is also important to keep in mind that the volatility index is not a stock, so using money flow indicators will be of no value. Furthermore, our objective in using the volatility index is to spot market reversals as soon as possible after they take place. This requires a technique that emphasizes short-term changes in volatility to successfully signal a turnaround.

This is one situation where the moving average convergence divergence or **MACD** can be used as an excellent predictor of market turnaround points occurring at extreme levels of fear. This technique will be easier to understand after studying the example below.

EXAMPLE 14: S& P 500

A chart of the S&P 500 and its volatility index is represented on page 184. The timing indicator is none other than the MACD of the VIX in an inverted scale.

ALERT: We need to use an inverted scale since our buy points are at high VIX readings and our sell points are at low VIX readings. This is the opposite of what happens with an index or a stock, in which case our buy points are usually at lower price values and sell points at higher price values.

We can see clearly from the chart on page 184 that in early April the VIX was at 20 with the S&P 500 just below 1200. As the market experienced a steep drop from 1200 to 800 between April and July of 2002, the volatility index (VIX) climbed to 60, indicating a high level of fear. At this point the S&P 500 climbed back to 940 while the VIX dropped back to 30 in late August. This was followed by an-

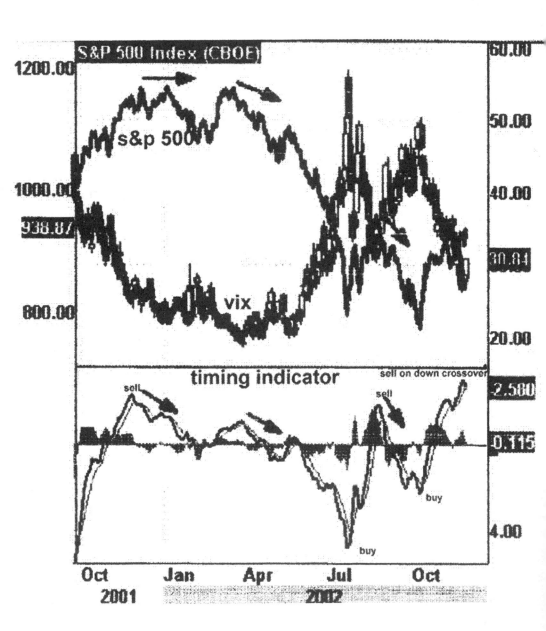

other drop in the S&P 500 to below 800 with an increase in the VIX to 50, indicating a healthy level of fear. This resulted in an S&P reversal back to 940 with the VIX dropping below 30.

Notice the MACD downward crossover occurring on the timing indicator chart giving sell signals when the VIX was around 30 or lower. This took place in late 2001, April 2002 and August 2002. Major buy signals were given when an MACD upward crossover occurred in July and October of 2002, both of which corresponded to VIX readings of 50 or higher.

ALERT 1: It is important not to use the VIX and VXN absolute values as triggers to buy and sell. As you can see from the chart, one buy signal was given at a VIX of 50 while the other was at a VIX close to 60. It is thus important to use the MACD timing indicator to time index reversals.

ALERT 2: The MACD parameters used on the chart are MACD (12,26,9) which are most common. This implies that the 12 and 26 period exponential moving averages are used with the 9 period moving average as a crossover indicator. The period can be minutes, hours or days, dependent on your time horizon. We have used days as our period for the chart in this chapter.

Point to remember: For the market to move higher, a sufficient amount of fear as reflected by the volatility indices must be present. To determine whether a climactic amount of fear indicating a possible reversal is at hand, the MACD of the VIX or VXN on an inverted scale is best used as an indicator.

Look for a sustainable upward reversal in the general market when the majority is betting on a downtrend as reflected by the short interest, and a high level of fear is present as reflected by the volatility indices.

CHAPTER 14

Do This Every Week and
Never Lose Money in the Market

NO, I AM not talking about going out to your local bar for a few drinks to forget about your losses. What I am referring to is a simple fact that you probably are already familiar with. It is based on the following premise:

"If a stock is moving higher in a weak market, it is expected that It will show further upward momentum In a strong market. On the other hand, if a stock is moving lower in a strong market, it is expected to show further downward momentum in a weak market."

Let us assume you are holding shares of Cisco (CSCO). You notice that on a certain day while the Nasdaq (the index in which CSCO trades) was up 50 points, CSCO was down $0.50. This is an indication that Cisco is performing poorly in a strong market. Consequently, you will expect that if the Nasdaq were to drop in a few days, Cisco's downward price momentum will accelerate.

The major question to address here is whether this is just a short-term correction or a long-term downtrend and a cause for concern.

To address this, we will need to quantify the extent of strength or weakness of a stock relative to the market as expressed by the index it trades in.

To do this, we calculate the **Convergence/Divergence** or **(CD)** value on a stock as follows:

CD Value = Stock Price/ Index value

Where the index value is the value of the index in which the stock trades at the close. It could be the Nasdaq, Dow, Semiconductor index, Biotech index, etc. The stock price is the price at the close of trading on the chosen day.

As long as the CD chart is in an uptrend, the stock shows increased convergence in a strong market and increased divergence in a weak market. This is what we want to see in stocks we are holding or intending to buy.

On the other hand, if the CD chart is in a downtrend, this indicates increased convergence in a weak market and increased divergence in a strong market. This is a sign to sell the stock you are holding or to short if you do not own the stock.

Convergence Divergence (CD) Chart Signals

To decide the action to take, pay attention to the following signals exhibited in a CD chart:

(1) As long as the CD chart is trending upward with an increase in price, it is a signal to hold onto the stock if you own it.

(2) If the CD chart starts flattening out and trending downward after a prolonged uptrend, this is a warning sign of possible downward price reversal. In this case check for the following:

(a) Decrease in CD value even as the stock price is going higher.

(b) The CD value is lower at a specific price (whether extrapolated or actual) when the CD chart is in a downtrend than for the same price when the chart is in an uptrend.

If either one or both of these signals occur, you should be either looking to sell the stock or raise cash on it by selling calls.

These criteria will be much clearer when you study the examples later in this chapter.

Now you are probably wondering what kind of a computer program you need to do this? The answer is that you do not even need a computer. You will have to perform a simple calculation once a week on each of your stocks. You can then connect data points **by hand** to get the CD value chart for that stock.

Constructing a CD Value Chart

To construct a CD value chart, follow these steps:

Step 1: Every week divide the closing price of the stock by that of the index it trades in. Although you can use any day of the week, it is best to have the first data point on a Friday, the second on a following Monday and then each Monday thereafter.

Step 2: Normalize the value to a number that ranges between 1 and 10. You can do that by multiplying the above quotient by an appropriate factor.

Step 3: Plot the point on a semi logarithmic chart paper. You can get this paper from the free website: http://www.Printfreegraph-paper.com

Step 4: Connect the data points by a hand-drawn smoothed curve. Note that when you connect data points, the extrapolated CD values will not correspond to the actual values on a daily basis. This is not an issue since we are interested in the week-to-week trend rather than the actual values in between.

Understanding CD Values

As a stock trader and investor with an engineering background, I am always interested in understanding the logic behind any technical indicators I use. In this section, I will explain the significance of the CD value introduced at the start of this chapter and its usefulness in the decision making process.

We already defined the Convergence Divergence or:

CD Value = Stock Price/Index Value

In a strengthening market where the index is moving higher, it is essential for the stock price to move up if we are to get an increase in CD value. This is an indication that in a strong market a rise in CD value implies that the stock is behaving well relative to the index. In other words, it is showing an increased convergence in an up market. If the market were to experience a powerful move, the stock will have to show a high level of strength to maintain a higher CD value.

It is thus clear from this argument that it is necessary to see a higher CD value with increased stock price for an uptrend to continue.

In a weakening market where the value of the index is moving lower, a higher CD value can result from an increase or a flat stock price. It is also conceivable that a higher CD value can accompany a small drop in the stock price combined with a relatively large drop in the index. This kind of behavior indicates that the stock we are considering is showing considerable strength in a weakening market. In this case the stock is showing increased divergence in a weak market.

Based on the above arguments, an increase in CD value is an indication that the stock still has upward momentum. In addition, an increase in price should be accompanied by a rise in CD value for that momentum to be sustainable.

A decrease in CD value with an increase in price is an indication that even though the stock is moving higher, its upward momentum relative to the market is weakening. This usually occurs if the stock price rise is small relative to the rise in the index.

A decrease in CD value in concert with a decrease in price is a sign of a short-term correction if it occurs during the uptrend cycle of a stock. On the other hand, significant drops in CD values take place during an extended down cycle. This is expected and is an indication of the continued weakening of the stock relative to the market.

By recognizing the early signs of weakening CD values while the stock is trading near its high, you can sell or raise cash by selling covered calls and avoid significant losses. This process will be illustrated in the following examples.

EXAMPLE 1: JDS Uniphase (JDSU)

Below are the closing prices for JDSU and the Nasdaq on the specified dates. The CD Value in the last column is the normalized value calculated for each data point.

Date	JDSU (price $)	NASDAQ	CD Value
09/21/2001	5.36	1423	3.77
09/24/2001	6.32	1499	4.22
10/01/2001	6.92	1605	4.31
10/08/2001	9.04	1703	5.30
10/15/2001	8.12	1671	4.86
10/22/2001	8.77	1769	4.96
10/29/2001	8.41	1746	4.81
11/05/2001	9.17	1828	5.02
11/12/2001	11.6	1899	6.11
11/19/2001	11.71	1903	6.15
11/26/2001	10.08	1931	5.22
12/03/2001	10.53	2021	5.21
12/10/2001	8.53	1953	4.37
12/17/2001	8.45	1946	4.34
12/24/2001	8.46	1987	4.26
12/31/2001	10.02	2059	4.86
01/07/2002	9.02	2022	4.46
01/14/2002	8.18	1930	4.23
01/22/2002	7.16	1938	3.70
01/28/2002	6.99	1911	3.66
02/04/2002	6.6	1819	3.63
02/11/2002	6.07	1805	3.36
02/19/2002	4.98	1724	2.89
02/25/2002	4.98	1803	2.76
03/04/2002	6.37	1930	3.30
03/11/2002	6.10	1868	3.26
03/18/2002	5.85	1851	3.16
03/25/2002	5.89	1845	3.19
04/01/2002	5.58	1770	3.15
04/08/2002	5.06	1756	2.88
04/15/2002	5.48	1797	3.04

We Now follow the procedure outlined in the previous section to construct the CD value chart.

(1) Calculate the CD Value = Closing Price/Index Value

For the First point: 5.36/1423 = 0.003766.

(2) Multiply by a factor of 1000 to bring the CD value to a number between 1 and 10.

Normalized CD value = 0.003766 x 1000 = 3.77

(3) Plot the value on the Y axis of the semi logarithmic chart as shown on page 194.

(4) The above 3 steps are repeated for each of the data points. The actual data points are then connected by a hand-drawn smoothed curve.

For easy comparison the price data is also plotted and hand connected by a smoothed curve.

Reading Semi Logarithmic charts

The X axis on a semi logarithmic chart is linear and can be read in a normal manner as any charting paper.

The Y axis is a logarithmic scale read in cycles. The first cycle is read 1,2,3,4...10; The second cycle 10,20,30,40...100. And so on.

Plotting the Data

As indicated in the previous section, the first data point was chosen on Friday 9/21/2001, the next point on Monday 9/24/2001, with subsequent points representing one week intervals from this date.

Each large square on the X axis is divided into six small squares. Each two small squares represent a time interval of one week except for the first two squares that represent the transition from the first Friday to the following Monday. This will have no effect on the data since no trading occurs during the weekend.

You can use any day of the week as your reference day as long as you are consistent. The actual CD value will change, but the trend of the CD line will remain the same.

My preference for using Mondays is that any unexpected weekend occurrence will be reflected in Monday trading. On the other hand, Friday trading may be affected by unanticipated external weekend events as well as option expirations. It is preferable that the data reflects the behavior of the stock itself than external factors.

In this example the Y axis has two cycles, 1-10 and 10-100. The graph paper shows the first cycle and the 10-20 part of the second cycle since all our data of interest falls in this range. As an illustration to plot 3.77, the first value on the Y axis, you will place a data point three-fourths of the way between 3 and 4. To plot 11.7, you will place a data point between the 1 and 2 (10-20) on the second cycle. Note that between the points 1 and 2 on the second cycle there are 20 divisions, indicating that each two divisions are 1 point. As an example, the point 11 will be two small squares above the 1 or (10) in the second cycle.

Be sure you clearly understand the charting rules on semi logarithmic chart papers before you start plotting and interpreting your data.

JDSU CD Chart Interpretation

Between points **1** and **2** on the chart page 194 the Convergence/Divergence (CD) curve is in an uptrend in sync with the price. After reaching point **2** which is the CD value corresponding to the price maximum of $11.71, the CD chart started trending down. This is an indication that the upward momentum of the stock is weakening.

Notice that even though point **C** on the price chart corresponds to a higher price ($10.53) than point **A1** ($10.08), the corresponding CD value at point **c** (5.21) is slightly lower than that at point **a1** (5.22). This is another sign of possible pending downtrend.

ALERT 1: At the start of a serious price reversal, you will start seeing lower or flat CD values with higher prices. If this occurs, you will want to keep an eye on the stock as a potential candidate for selling calls on to generate cash if you intend to keep holding it.

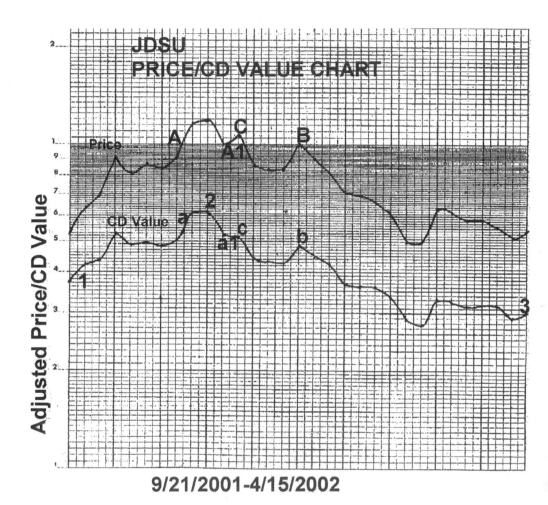

9/21/2001-4/15/2002

JDSU showed a flat weekly trend between 12/10/01 and 12/24/ 01 trading in the $8.5 area. On 12/31/01, it closed at $10.02 indicating a potential upward reversal. Note that on the CD chart point **b** corresponding to the price at point **B** ($10.02) is at a reading of 4.86 which is significantly lower than the reading of 5.22 at point **a1** corresponding to the price point **A1** ($10.08). This is a strong signal that the rise in price will not be sustainable.

In addition, the CD value at point **a** is higher than that at point **a1** even though both points correspond to a price of $10. This is an indication of a lower CD value at a certain price in a downtrend than a similar price in an uptrend pointing to weakness in the stock.

ALERT 2: It is important to realize that point **A** on the price chart as well as point **a** on the CD chart are extrapolated and not actual data points. Even though the daily readings may fluctuate, we are more interested in the weekly trend of the CD chart.

Point **b** on the CD chart was the last time you could have exited the stock at $10 before a significant price drop occurred. If you were paying attention to the weakening CD chart, you could have had up to one month warning to exit the position or sell calls to raise cash.

EXAMPLE 2: Genesis Microchip (GNSS)

Below are the closing prices for GNSS and the Nasdaq on the specified dates. The CD Value in the last column is the normalized value calculated for each data

Date	GNSS (price $)	NASDAQ	CD Value
09/21/2001	28.34	1423	1.99
09/24/2001	28.14	14.99	1.88
10/01/2001	32.70	1605	2.04
10/08/2001	34.85	1703	2.05
10/15/2001	39.18	1671	2.34
10/22/2001	46.14	1769	2.61
10/29/2001	47.85	1746	2.74
11/05/2001	45.09	1828	2.47
11/12/2001	43.69	1899	2.30
11/19/2001	47.28	1903	2.48
11/26/2001	56.93	1931	2.94
12/03/2001	59.65	2021	2.95
12/10/2001	69.81	1953	3.57
12/17/2001	65.84	1946	3.38
12/24/2001	67.10	1987	3.38
12/31/2001	68.75	2059	3.34
01/07/2002	72.11	2022	3.56
01/14/2002	66.18	1930	3.43
01/22/2002	56.17	1938	2.89
01/28/2002	59.8	1911	3.12
02/04/2002	49.24	1819	2.70
02/11/2002	44.76	1805	2.48
02/19/2002	39	1725	2.26
02/25/2002	25.5	1803	1.41
03/04/2002	29.08	1930	1.51
03/11/2002	29.65	1868	1.58
03/18/2002	27.93	1851	1.51
03/25/2002	26.00	1845	1.40
04/01/2002	23.07	1770	1.30
04/08/2002	22.00	1756	1.25
04/15/2002	22.05	1797	1.23

We now follow a similar procedure to the previous example to construct the CD chart.

(1) CD Value = Closing Price/Index Value
    For the first point: CD value = 28.34/1423 = 0.0199

(2) Multiply by a factor of 100 to bring the CD value to a number between 1 and 10
    Normalized CD value = 0.0199 x100 = 1.99

(3) Plot the value on the Y axis of the logarithmic chart as shown on page 198.

(4) The above 3 steps are repeated for each of the data points. The actual data points are then connected by a hand-drawn smoothed curve.

For easy comparison, the price chart is also plotted and hand connected by a smoothed curve. The price data is normalized by dividing by a factor of 10 to fit the range on the logarithmic chart paper.

GNSS CD Chart Interpretation

Between points **1** and **2** the CD chart is trending up with the price, and even though there was a price correction during the uptrend, the CD chart kept forming higher lows and higher highs.

The CD chart reached maximum value of 3.57 at point **2** corresponding to point **A** ($69.81) on the price chart. It then flattened out between points **2** and **B1**, indicating that the upward momentum of the stock is weakening.

This is further confirmed by the fact that the CD value stayed almost flat at point **2** (3.57) and point **B1** (3.56) even though the price showed an almost 5% increase from $69.81 at point **A** to $72.11 at point **B**.

At point **b1** the CD chart started forming lower highs and lower lows, indicating serious weakness in the stock. This was our last chance to sell at $60 before a serious price drop occurred.

ALERT 1: The most effective way to interpret CD charts is to first

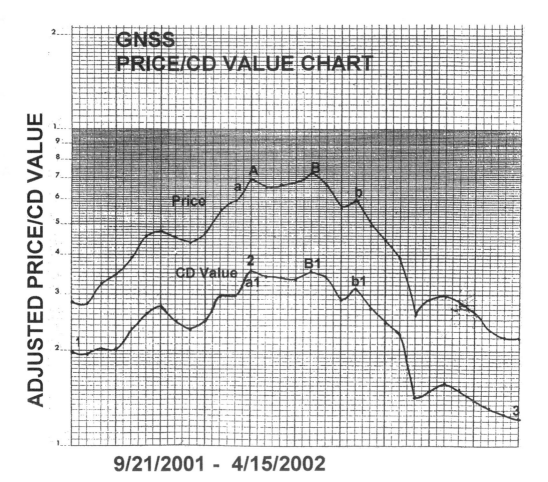

**GNSS
PRICE/CD VALUE CHART**

ADJUSTED PRICE/CD VALUE

Price

CD Value

9/21/2001 - 4/15/2002

look at the general trend. As long as the CD chart is moving up and forming higher highs and higher lows the stock should not be sold.

If the CD chart starts flattening or trending down without a measurable price drop in the stock, this is a call for concern. The best strategy will be to follow this procedure if you own the stock:

(1) At the first sign of weakening in the CD chart, sell covered calls on the stock at a strike close to the next price resistance below the current price. In the case of GNSS, with the stock at $72.11 (point B) we will sell $67.5 strike covered calls for a premium of at least $5/share.

(2) As the stock continues weakening, we will lock our profit by buying back the call at a profit and selling a new call at a lower strike. In this case as the stock approaches $67, we will buy back the $67.5 calls and sell $65 calls for a premium of no less than $2.5/share.

(3) As the stock shows significant weakening at point b1, you can sell the stock.

By using this procedure, even though we sold at $60 we have already cashed in $7+/share selling calls and our actual selling price is $67. This is a good technique to use until you gain experience using CD charts, since in case you are wrong, this will allow buying back the call at a small loss and keeping the stock.

Picking Strong Sectors Using CD values:

An important application of Convergence/Divergence or (CD) value charts is the ability to use them to evaluate the strength of a certain sector. In fact, one of the most important keys to investment success is recognizing strong sectors in the market and picking the strongest stocks within those sectors.

The example below shows how the CD value chart of the Gold Index (^GOX) reflected the continued strength of the gold sector in a down market. By recognizing the strength in the CD chart, an investor could have been able to tell that even sizable drops in the gold index were just temporary corrections on the road to higher values.

EXAMPLE 3: Gold Index (^GOX)

Below are the closing prices for the gold index and the Nasdaq closing prices on the specified dates. The CD value in the last column is the normalized CD value for each data point.

Date	Gold Index (price $)	NASDAQ	CD Value
03/01/2002	51.5	1803	2.86
03/04/2002	48.78	1930	2.53
03/11/2002	49.03	1868	2.62
03/18/2002	53.59	1851	2.89
03/25/2002	56.71	1845	3.07
04/01/2002	54.2	1770	3.06
04/08/2002	55.22	1756	3.14
04/15/2002	56.33	1797	3.13
04/22/2002	59.78	1664	3.59
04/29/2002	59.86	1613	3.71
05/06/2002	60.12	1601	3.76
05/13/2002	60.7	1741	3.49
05/20/2002	68.1	1662	4.09
05/28/2002	67.6	1616	4.18
06/03/2002	64.01	1535	4.17
06/10/2002	61.58	1505	4.09
06/17/2002	63.71	1441	4.42
06/24/2002	57.03	1463	3.89
07/01/2002	55.63	1448	3.84
07/08/2002	61.10	1374	4.45
07/15/2002	57.62	1319	4.36
07/22/2002	44.03	1262	3.49
07/29/2002	50.47	1248	4.04
08/05/2002	54.07	1306	4.13
08/12/2002	53.54	1361	3.93
08/19/2002	50.84	1381	3.68
08/26/2002	53.59	1315	4.08

We now follow the CD value calculation procedure described previously. Note, however, that in this case the gold index value replaces the stock price:

(1) CD value = GOX closing price/Nasdaq value = 51.5/1802.74
   = 0.0286

(2) Multiply by a factor of 100 to bring the CD value between 1
   and 10.

Normalized CD value = 0.0286x100 = 2.86

(3) Plot the value on the Y axis of the Logarithmic chart on page
   202.

(4) Repeat the above process for each data point and connect
   the points with a hand-drawn smoothed curve.

(5) We will also plot the gold index price chart for easy comparison. The gold index is divided by 10 to fit in the data
   range on the chart paper.

GOX Chart Interpretation

As you can see from the chart on page 202, the CD curve is in an
uptrend between points **1** and **2**, indicating relative strength of the
gold index in comparison to the market as represented by the Nasdaq.

Notice also that between points **a** and **b** on the CD chart there
was a noticeable flattening of the curve. It is interesting, however, that
occurred as the gold index dropped in value between points **A** and **B**.
This is, in fact, a sign of strength, telling us that even though the gold
index dropped in value, it is still performing well relative to the market.

ALERT: Remember that flattening of the CD chart is a concern only
if accompanied by a rise or a neutral stock price as seen in the two
previous examples. In this case the CD chart remained flat even
though the gold index dropped from around 68 to 60. The best way to
interpret this is that the Gold index is dropping at a much slower pace
than the Nasdaq, so it has a strong relative performance to the index.

By digging deeper into the CD chart, we also notice that the CD
value at point **b1** corresponding to a GOX value of 48 is almost
equivalent to the CD value at point **a1** corresponding to a CD value
of around 60. This is telling us that the drop in the GOX was accompanied by a much steeper drop in the general market, indicating

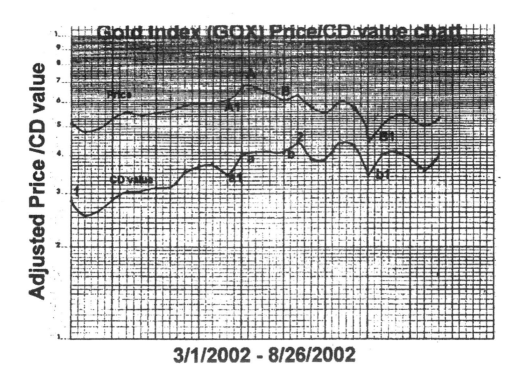

Adjusted Price /CD value

Gold Index (GOX) Price/CD value chart

price

CD value

3/1/2002 - 8/26/2002

exceptional strength. Furthermore, the flatness of the CD curve after point **2** accompanied by a more negative downward curvature of
the GOX index price curve confirms the resilience of the gold index.
These observations show that the Gold index showed convergence
in an up market and divergence in a down market.

ALERT 1: You may be questioning whether it is wise to put so much
faith in a one-point comparison between **a1** and **b1**. Remember that
each data point on the CD curve is a culmination of one week of trading and the movement week to week is an important trend indicator.

ALERT 2: I want to emphasize again that this is real life data, so do
not expect a straight smooth curve up or down. The most effective
way to look at the data is to study the general trend of the CD curve
relative to price movement to form your initial interpretation. After
that, look at data points that show significant convergence or divergence to confirm your observations further.

ALERT 3: When studying the CD chart, you must focus on the general trend first. Notice that as the CD chart was moving higher there
was one data point that showed an aberration. On 5/6/2002, the
GOX = 60.12 with CD = 3.76, while on 5/13/2002 the GOX = 60.70
with CD = 3.49. This is a cause for concern only if the trend of lower
CD values continue with higher prices resulting in a flattening of the
CD chart. As it turns out, the next data point came in line with the
trend. These situations occur when a shake-out or short-term correction takes place but is not enough to influence the overall trend.

Long Term Holders ... Listen up!

If you are a long term holder of what you consider safe, non-
volatile stocks in a retirement or regular account either managed by
you or your broker, I recommend you use this section to make edu-
cated decisions in concert with your financial advisor on when to
exit positions to avoid serious losses.

As I mentioned in the beginning of this book, I am not against using full-time brokers in principle. It is important, however, that you have a plan on when to sell to take profit or limit losses.

From personal experience, I found that most financial advisors still use mostly fundamental analysis to enter or exit a position. While this may have been a good approach in the past, it is no longer effective due to the proliferation of the internet.

Before the advent of the internet, your only choice to get up-to-date news or research on a company was through a licensed broker giving him or her an inherent advantage to get his clients in or out in a timely manner. Presently such information is available on line to anyone, and their reaction to news can be instantaneous. This is why you should remember that *"the price of any stock reflects all information already known about that stock."*

This means that unless you know something that no one else knows (illegal insider information) or you can somehow tell whether buying or selling interest will dominate the future price trend of the stock, it is unlikely that you will be able to pick long-term winners or exit long-term losers.

Convergence/ Divergence charts are extremely useful tools in predicting the future relative performance of a stock to the market as expressed by an index of choice. If you are a long-term holder of lower volatility stocks, you can calculate monthly CD values and construct CD charts as explained in the previous examples in this chapter to determine the best time to exit a position.

ALERT: In all previous examples in this chapter, I have used weekly CD values to construct the CD charts. The reason for this is that the stocks chosen were volatile, and waiting a whole month between CD calculation would have missed significant moves.

Although my preference is to use weekly CD charts, you can use weekly, biweekly or monthly calculations dependent on the volatility of your stocks and your holding period.

EXAMPLE 4: General Electric (GE)

General Electric is considered a safe stock held by many mutual funds as well as individual investors. How could anyone have predicted that this stock would lose 50% of its value since February 2000? In fact, by using Convergence/Divergence charts an investor could have anticipated the weak performance of the stock and sold within 10% of its price high.

Below are the closing prices for GE and the Dow on the specified dates. The CD value in the last column is the normalized value calculated for each data point.

Date	GE (price $)	DOW	CD Value
Feb 2000	44.12	10128	4.36
Mar 2000	51.87	10922	4.75
Apr 2000	52.41	10734	4.88
May 2000	52.63	10522	5.00
Jun 2000	53	10448	5.07
Jul 2000	51.69	10522	4.91
Aug 2000	58.63	11215	5.23
Sep 2000	57.81	10651	5.43
Oct 2000	54.81	10971	5.00
Nov 2000	49.56	10414	4.76
Dec 2000	47.94	10788	4.44
Jan 2001	45.98	10887	4.22
Feb 2001	46.5	10495	4.43
Mar 2001	41.86	9879	4.24
Apr 2001	48.53	10735	4.52
May 2001	49	10812	4.49
Jun 2001	49	10502	4.67
Jul 2001	43.5	10523	4.13
Aug 2001	40.9	9950	4.11
Sep 2001	37.2	8848	4.20
Oct 2001	36.41	9075	4.012
Nov 2001	38.5	9852	3.91
Dec 2001	40.08	10022	4.00
Jan 2002	37.15	9920	3.74
Feb 2002	38.5	10106	3.81
Mar 2002	37.4	10404	3.59
Apr 2002	31.55	9946	3.17
May 2002	31.14	9925	3.14
Jun 2002	31.15	9706	3.21

We now follow the CD value calculation procedure described in the other examples in this chapter:

(1) CD value = GE closing Price/Dow value: 44.12/10128 = 0.004356

(2) Multiply by a factor of 1000 to bring the value between 1 and 10.

Normalized CD value = 0.004356 x1000 = 4.36.

(3) Plot the value on the Y axis of the Semi Log chart page 207.

(4) Repeat the above for each data point.

(5) We will also plot the GE price data on the second cycle of the Logarithmic chart paper. Please be aware that we did not divide the GE price by 10 since this will place the price values too close to the CD values, making the chart inter-pretation more difficult.

GE Chart Interpretation

By studying the general trend of the CD chart, it can be clearly seen that the CD readings are in an uptrend between points **1** and **2**. This indicates that General Electric is showing strong performance relative to that of the index.

ALERT: Notice that the curvature of the CD chart is much flatter than that of the chart for JDSU or GNSS. This is an indication of the lower volatility of GE, which in turn permits us to effectively use monthly rather than weekly CD values.

After point **2** the CD curve starts moving lower, indicating that the relative strength of GE to the general market as represented by the Dow is starting to weaken. At this stage we will start examining each Convergence/Divergence value in relation to price more care-fully. We do this by comparing prices and CD values during the ascending and descending parts of the CD chart.

Points **A** and **B** on the price chart represent the fourth and ninth data points in the table with prices of $52.63 and $54.81 respec-tively. The corresponding points on the CD chart designated by **a**

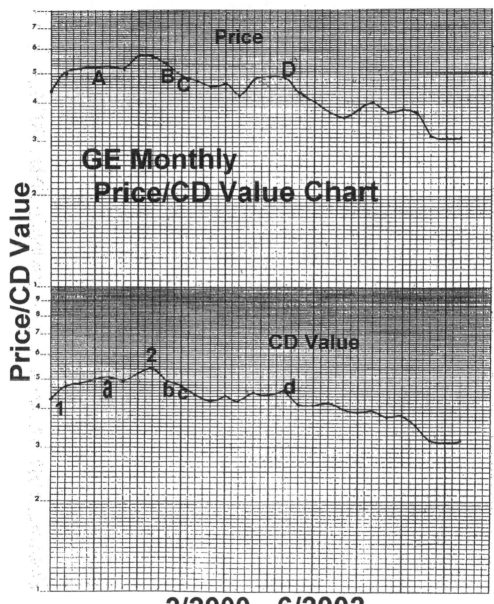

GE Monthly
Price/CD Value Chart

2/2000 - 6/2002

and **b** both have normalized CD values of 5.00.

This is a warning sign since the CD value failed to increase with an increase in price during the descending part of the CD chart as compared to a lower price during the ascending part of the CD chart. This should have prompted us to take action, especially when we consider that a 5% increase in the stock price did not result in any increase in the CD value.

A possible good strategy is to sell **in the money** covered calls on the stock with a strike price at the next support at $50. In this case you will still own the stock but can make up for a drop in price to below $50 using the option premium. If the stock shows further weakness and drops below $50, you can then buy the call back for a significant profit and sell the stock.

ALERT: Since we are dealing with a monthly chart, each point represents a full month of trading and has added significance. Any aberrations or warning signs in a monthly chart should be taken more seriously than weekly charts, since waiting an additional month for the next data point can result in missing precious exit chances. **Because of this, if you are a beginner, I do recommend that you plot CD charts for stocks you own on weekly basis to avoid missing important sell signals.**

Let us assume for the sake of argument that you decided not to take action at point **B** and sell either the stock or covered calls. It is critical in this case to keep a close eye on the stock for the next move up and study the strength of the CD chart during that phase and take action accordingly.

The movement of the stock and the CD chart demonstrated continued weakness until the March-June 2002 time frame where we see an increase in price accompanied by a rise in CD values. Notice, however, that the CD curve starts flattening between May and June and fails to make a new high as the stock moves to $49. Furthermore, a comparison between the CD values at points **c** and **d** show a 5 percent drop even though the stock price dropped only by 1 percent.

At this point we should make plans to exit the position if we have not done so at point **B**.

Convergence/Divergence charts are not only useful in deciding when to exit a position you are holding but are quite helpful in determining when to enter a new position. In fact, once you gain some experience in using these charts, you will be able to time your entry few weeks before a price surge occurs. This will be demonstrated in the next section.

CD Charts.... Your Ticket to Long Term Profits

Let me ask you a simple question. What do you do when your friend, broker or relative comes to you with a hot stock tip? Do you buy on impulse? Do you check the fundamentals of the company before you buy? Do you flip a coin or just ignore the tip?

If you decide to buy the stock, do you buy after a correction? Or do you buy when the stock makes a new high? Or do you use some magic technical indicators to time your entry?

By using Convergence/ Divergence charts you can time your entry point into a position with reasonable accuracy. The beauty of this approach is that you have to do one simple calculation per week. In addition, by learning how to interpret CD charts, you can enter a position either after a price correction or at a new price high and be confident of your decision.

ALERT: In this section, our objective is to use CD charts to decide whether to take a new position in a stock and when to time our entry. Since we do not already own the stock, our strategy is to make a commitment only if the stock's CD chart is extremely powerful, indicating a significant profit based on our entry price.

This is in a sense opposite to our decision on when to exit a position or take defensive action by selling covered calls. In such case our goal is take action as soon as the CD chart shows signs of weakness. Our logic is simple — we only enter new positions when the profit potential is high, and we will take protective measures or exit a position as soon as signs of weakness are evident to protect profits.

To recognize an exceptionally strong buy candidate look for the following CD chart Characteristics:

    (1) If a stock is confined to a trading range, check for an increase in CD values accompanied by flat or decreasing prices.

ALERT: This is a more stringent requirement than the one for holding a stock. In that case we stipulated that the CD chart shows an uptrend with a rising price.

    (2) A new low in the stock price is not accompanied by a new low in the corresponding CD value is a particular sign of strength. This, in fact, offers a high profit potential entry point.

ALERT: This signal is especially powerful if the CD value corresponding to a new price low is equal or greater than a previous CD value corresponding to a price 25% or more above the new price low.

    (3) A price breakout accompanied by a CD value breakout. This indicates a high level of strength for the stock and the anticipation of future new price highs. **This is a second possible entry point, which may be less profitable but offers lower risk than the one mentioned above.**

Using these techniques will be much clearer when you study the following real life example.

EXAMPLE 5: Neoware Systems (NWRE)

I have deliberately selected this stock even though it was already used to illustrate the Chaikin money flow and moving average indicators in Chapter 13. My purpose in doing this is two-fold: (1) To give a comparative analysis of the CD and CMF/Moving average indicators using this example and (2) to point out situations under which each of these indicators is best used.

Following are the closing prices for NWRE and the Nasdaq on the specified dates. The CD Value in the last column is the normalized value calculated for each data point.

Date	NWRE (price $)	NASDAQ	CD Value
05/04/2001	1.90	2192	8.67
05/07/2001	2.02	2107	9.59
05/14/2001	1.90	2199	8.64
05/21/2001	2.05	2251	9.10
05/29/2001	2.40	2149	11.17
06/04/2001	2.60	2215	11.74
06/11/2001	2.60	2028	12.82
06/18/2001	2.24	2035	11.01
06/25/2001	2.60	2161	12.03
07/02/2001	2.33	2004	11.63
07/09/2001	2.26	2085	10.84
07/16/2001	2.05	2029	10.10
07/23/2001	2.03	2029	10.00
07/30/2001	2.40	2066	11.62
08/06/2001	2.00	1956	10.22
08/13/2001	2.36	1867	12.64
08/20/2001	2.33	1917	12.15
08/27/2001	2.81	1905	15.57
09/04/2001	2.36	1688	13.98
09/10/2001	1.34	1423	9.42
09/24/2001	1.62	1499	10.81
10/01/2001	1.98	1605	12.33
10/08/2001	1.91	1703	11.22
10/15/2001	1.88	1671	11.25
10/22/2001	1.82	1769	10.29
10/29/2001	1.93	1746	11.05
11/05/2001	1.94	1828	10.61
11/12/2001	2.00	1899	10.53
11/19/2001	1.97	1903	10.35
11/26/2001	2.60	1931	13.46
12/03/2001	3.71	2021	18.36
12/10/2001	4.50	1953	23.04
12/17/2001	4.13	1946	21.22
12/24/2001	4.55	1987	22.89
12/31/2001	5.70	2059	27.68
01/07/2002	7.10	2022	35.11
01/14/2002	6.80	1930	35.23
01/22/2002	6.95	1938	35.86

Date	NWRE (price $)	NASDAQ	CD Value
01/28/2002	7.84	1911	41.03
02/04/2002	6.70	1819	36.83
02/11/2002	7.31	1805	40.50
02/19/2002	7.85	1725	45.50
02/25/2002	7.50	1802	41.62
03/04/2002	9.81	1930	50.83
03/11/2002	9.92	1868	53.10
03/18/2002	9.59	1851	51.80
03/25/2002	9.67	1845	52.41
04/01/2002	9.05	1770	51.12
04/08/2002	10.18	1756	57.97
04/15/2002	10.02	1797	55.75
04/22/2002	8.45	1664	50.78
4/29/2002	8.18	1613	50.71
05/06/2002	7.55	1601	47.16
05/13/2002	8.65	1741	49.68
05/20/2002	9.01	1661	54.24
05/28/2002	9.52	1616	58.91
06/03/2002	9.08	1535	59.15
06/10/2002	9.88	1505	65.64
06/17/2002	9.80	1441	68.00
06/24/2002	11.34	1463	77.51
07/01/2002	10.90	1448	75.27

We now perform the CD calculations in a manner similar to the previous examples:

(1) CD Value = NWRE closing Price/Nasdaq closing value
= 1.90/2192 = 0.0008667

(2) Multiply the CD value by a factor of 10,000 to bring the value to between 1 and 10.

(3) Plot the value on the Y axis of the Logarithmic chart on page 214.

(4) Repeat the above calculations for each data point and construct a hand-drawn smooth curve.

Notice that the price data for NWRE ranges between $1.34 and about $11, so we will use mainly the first cycle of the Logarithmic chart paper for the price curve. Multiplying the CD values by a normalization factor of 10,000 allows us to place the majority of the CD curve on the second cycle of the chart paper. This separation permits much easier interpretation of the data. Because we have a large amount of data, we will use each small square on the X axis to reflect one data point or a week of trading.

NWRE Chart Interpretation.

It is important to remember that we do not own the stock and our goal in this exercise is to decide whether and when to take a long position.

On the price chart NWRE remains in a trading range approximately between $2 and $3 during the period from 5/4/2001 to 9/4/2001. Points **A1**, **B1** and **C1** on the price chart reflect prices close to $2, but the corresponding CD values at **a1**, **b1** and **c1** show a steady rise in value. This is an indication that the stock is gaining strength relative to the Nasdaq even with a flat price.

We now wait for one of the buy signals discussed in the previous section to time our entry. Notice that a steep price drop from $2.36 to $1.34 occurred at point **B,** but the corresponding CD value at point **b** (CD = 9.4) is higher than that at point **a** (CD = 8.6) corresponding to a price of $1.90 at point **A**. This is an unmistakable signal of superior strength since even though the stock price dropped by 30% from point **A** to **B**, the corresponding CD value rose slightly between **a** and **b**.

This gives us our first buy signal based on the CD chart.

ALERT 1: I am certainly not a fan of catching falling knives and do not generally recommend buying stocks on steep drops since you do not know where that will end. In this case I take exception since a superior strength in the CD chart indicates a shake-out rather than a sustained drop and that a reversal is at hand.

ALERT 2: Notice that on the CMF/Moving average chart on page

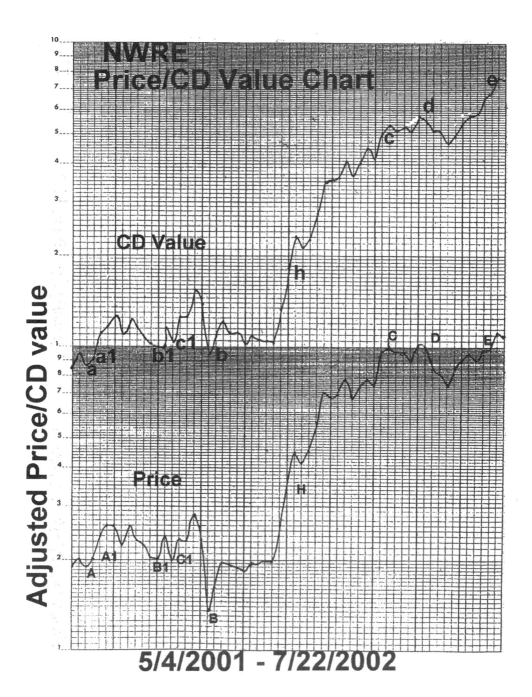

NWRE
Price/CD Value Chart

5/4/2001 - 7/22/2002

214

145 a buy signal was not given until point **1** with a price of about $2.5. It is interesting, however, to notice that between points **d** and **e** on the CMF chart the drop in the stock price was not accompanied by heavy selling which indicates relative strength of the stock. The CD chart interpretation above confirms this fact.

A clear price breakout occurred on 12/3/2001 when NWRE hits $3.71 at point **H** on the price chart. This was accompanied by a new high on the CD chart at point **h,** indicating that the strength of the stock relative to the index has hit a new high. This signals another possible higher price, lower risk entry point into the stock.

ALERT: Whether an investor buys at point **B** after a correction or **H** after a breakout is a personal choice. One option would be to buy part of the position at each of these points. Another possibility is to sell in the money puts at point **B** to use the option time value to mitigate a possible further drop in price.

After point **H**, the stock continued to rise until it reached around $10 at point **C**. Points **C, D** and **E** on the price chart designate another consolidation period around $10 as seen when the stock was trading at $2. The CD chart, however, continued its uptrend as seen by points **c, d** and **e**, indicating further strength in the stock and a signal to hold and not sell. In fact, NWRE eventually moved up to $20, giving us a profit of more than 1500% in a bad market.

ALERT 1: The CD chart strength between points **c** and **e** confirms what we have already seen using the CMF/Moving average chart on page 145. Notice that at point **g** on the CMF chart, money flow remained positive and the MA(10) failed to cross the EMA(20) to the downside.

Point to Remember: Deterioration in the CD chart is more often than not a sign of a long term trend reversal of a stock. Be sure to invest an hour or so a week constructing CD charts on an ongoing basis for your long-term holdings. All you need

to do each week is to calculate the CD value for each stock and add a single data point to each chart. By doing this and paying attention to the changes in the CD chart on a weekly basis, you will learn to recognize the warning signs discussed in this chapter and take action before it is too late. Keep in mind that in the world of investing, it is when you sell that counts.

CHAPTER 15

Using Option Concepts in This Book To Cash in on Special Situations

IN THIS CHAPTER I will show you how you can apply the concepts described in this book to specific situations. Please remember that the solutions I describe here are only examples of how the techniques in this book can be used and are by no means comprehensive. Try to think of this book as an illustrative design manual giving you the road map to create a final product. Use the concepts and examples in this book as guidelines and then add your own touch of creativity to adapt them to your own specific goals. This chapter is designed to make accomplishing this task easier.

Get Your Money Back From the Crooks on Wall Street

During the past couple of years I have assisted many investors to use the concepts described in this book to capitalize on market opportunities. One of the most common questions I have been asked is how to recover heavy losses of over 50% on a stock.

In the spring of 2002, a local investor asked me if there is a possible way she could recover a 90% loss on his investment in Lucent technologies. This person was devastated after she listened to her "expert" full-time broker who advised her to buy the stock at $40/share. As the stock declined, the advice was to hold on since Lucent is a reputable company with great prospects and solid fundamentals.

At this point, with Lucent at $1.00, this person was facing a $39,000 loss with little time to recover since she was within a few years of retirement. She indicated to me when I asked her what was her broker's advice that he suggested one of two options:

(1)Since she is in this for the long term, she just should hold on until the stock recovers. The problem with this is that she is within five years from retirement and the stock will have to go up 4000% in five years or 800%/year which is highly unlikely.

(2)The second option given to her was to average down since the stock is at a bargain low price. Having been burnt by this stock once, it is hard for any investor to throw in more of their own cash into a losing stock. In addition, a significant amount of cash will be needed to buy enough shares to reduce the average cost to a reasonable price.

My answer to this problem was to use a third approach that is lower risk and does not require spending more of her own cash. To implement this approach, we used the following stepwise procedure:

(1) Watch for signs of the start of an uptrend in Lucent as signaled by the moving average/CMF chart.

(2) Once an uptrend is confirmed on the stock, It is preferable to have this coincide with an uptrend in the market. Thus our next step will be to check whether the S&P 500 (index where LU trades) is in an uptrend. This is important since a more sustainable up move is likely to occur if the market as a whole is in an uptrend.

(3) Once 1 and 2 are confirmed, sell in the money puts on the stock at a far enough future date to receive a time premium that will mitigate an additional 25-50% drop in the stock price.

(4) The amount of shares you sell puts on will depend on the size of the loss you need to recover. It is advisable to sell options on enough shares to recover at least 50% of your loss.

(5) If the stock movement confirms the expected uptrend, use part of the proceeds from selling the puts to buy more stock. Although this is not necessary, it will allow you to recover your losses quicker.

By examining the Lucent chart page 220, it is clear that an upward reversal was signaled in the last week of October 2002 as seen at point **1** on the moving average chart and point **a** on the CMF chart. Notice how the MA(10) curved upward and crossed the EMA(20) in conjunction with the money flow moving from negative to positive.

We now check the general market by examining the S&P 500 index chart on page 184. As described in chapter 13, the market gave an upward reversal signal in October of 2002. It is thus clear that the strength in Lucent coincided with an uptrend in the market.

Our next step is to sell in the money puts on the stock to raise cash. With the stock at $0.80 (points **1** and **a** on the chart) we recognize that the January 2005 $2.5 strike puts are selling for $2.10 ($2.50 - $0.80 = $1.70 price value + $0.40 time value). This implies that we will receive $210 for each contract or 100 shares we sell.

ALERT: Notice that our actual price is $0.40 if the option were to be exercised, and we ended up buying the shares at $2.50. This will allow a drop in the stock by almost 40% before we will face a loss. This sizable time value as a percentage of the stock price is the main reason we picked an option far into the future.

Our next step is to decide on how many contracts to sell. By looking at the chart on page 220, we see that LU has a strong resistance at $2 as seen by the point **R** on the chart around September 2002. We believe that our target to lock in our profit will be around $2. This implies that the value of the option will be approximately ($2.50 - $2)= $0.50 (price value) + $0.40 (time value) or approximately $0.90. We thus approximate our potential profit at $2.10-$0.90 = $1.20/share or $120/contract.

Based on these calculations with the understanding that the $2

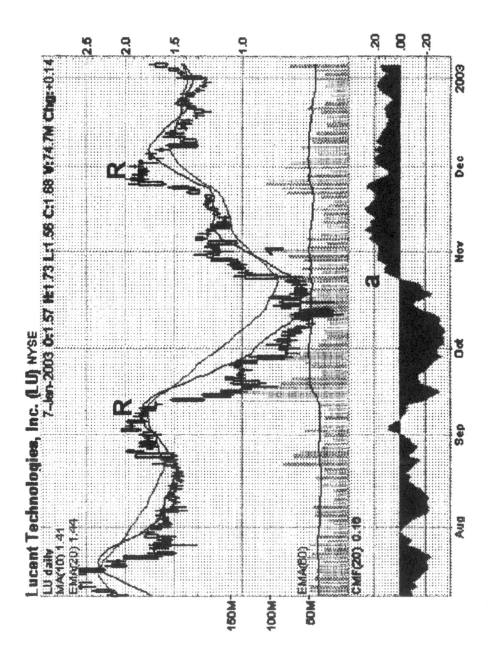

is just a guideline (we could exit anywhere between $1.75-$2) we will sell 200 contracts or 20,000 shares of LU Jan 2005 strike puts at $2.10/share for a cash premium of $42,000. Based on the above estimates, we expect to cash in $20,000+ on the option.

With the stock moving higher, we can opt to use part of the $42,000 to purchase more stock. As an example, we could buy 20,000 shares when the stock moves to $0.90 for $18,000 and have $24,000 in cash left.

ALERT 1: When selling a put option, the broker requires a certain amount of margin cash in your account to be able to buy the shares in case the option were to be exercised. In this case we will need $50,000 to buy 20,000 shares of Lucent at $2.50. However, since we received $42,000 in cash from selling the puts, our requirement in cash available will be $8000.

ALERT 2: It is important to understand that cash available does not have to be real cash but could be margin cash from other marginable stocks in your account. The broker will not use the cash but keep a hold on it until the position is closed, after which the cash is then released. Please be advised that different brokers have varied requirements; hence I would recommend you contact your broker to find their specific terms.

As expected, LU moves up and reaches $2 three times but fails to penetrate resistance in early December 2002. Since our main objective is to recover our loss, with LU at $1.90 we will buy back our 20,000 share January 2005, $2.5 strike puts for $1.10/share for a total of $22,000, netting a profit of $42,000 - $22,000 = $20,000. In addition, we will sell the 20,000 shares we purchased at $0.90 for $1.80, netting a profit of $0.90/share or $18,000. This will allow us to recover a total of $20,000 (puts profit) + $18,000 (stock profit) = $38,000 of our $39,000 loss.

Even if we decided not to purchase additional shares, we will have recovered $20,000 or 50% of our loss just by selling the puts.

In this case we will look to repeat the process with the $5 if the stock keeps looking strong.

ALERT: When you use this technique to recover losses, you should be true to your objective and close your position as soon as you see signs of fading momentum in the stock. Notice how we planned an exit strategy as soon as we sold the puts and we stuck by it and locked in our profits. If the stock were to break $2 and continue higher, we will have repeated the process with a $5 strike put, but we were sure to achieve our loss recovery goal first.

Take your revenge! Cash In on Bankrupt Stocks

As you are well aware, a stock price usually drops significantly on an announcement of bankruptcy. On page 96, I detailed an example involving Enron showing you how you can cash in on such situations by selling in the money puts. The question to be answered here is whether there is a common theme in bankrupt stocks that can allow you to cash in.

In fact, the rise in Enron from $0.25 to $1.25 within few days after its Chapter 11 bankruptcy announcement is not a coincidence and is a pattern common to many stocks going through that process. To decide whether a stock undergoing bankruptcy is a good short-term trade candidate, follow these steps:

(1) Check the amount of short interest on the stock. It is critical that a significant amount of short interest be present.

(2) As soon as the bankruptcy rumors start, be alert and ready to take action by buying the stock or selling the puts if you do not want to spend your own cash. Watch for the initial steep drop on heavy volume and take action as soon as the volume dries up to below average while the stock price is going down.

(3) With a large amount of short interest in the stock, the shorts will start covering sooner or later, since if the stock goes bankrupt and stops trading, the shorts will not be able to

lock in their profit. As soon as the short covering starts, the stock will move up on heavy volume. You should plan to close your positions and lock in your profit as soon as the volume starts dying down with an increase in the stock price.

This scenario has occurred with many stocks sporting large short interest such as Worldcom, Global Crossing, William Communications, Exodus Communications, United Airlines, American Airlines, Kmart and others.

Important Alert: What I mentioned here may seem to contradict the principle of going against the crowd by actually buying stocks with high level of short interest for large gains. Remember, however, that for this to be profitable you need to be sure that the shorts were betting against the technical strength of the stock. In cases of bankrupt stocks, the shorts were right since the price action of the stock as indicated by the CMF/ moving averages technical signals is negative. It is thus critical to remember that for a short squeeze to occur a high level of short interest must be accompanied by positive price action. If you ignore this, you will end up with the short end of the stick!

Heads or tails, You win!!

Good news for gamblers. Las Vegas casinos just introduced a new game where the odds favor the player. This is a simple coin toss game where the player bets an equal amount of money on each outcome (heads or tails).

In this game, the player does not get to pick the winning side, but that is decided by a coin toss after placing the bet. If the first toss is heads, that will be the winning side throughout the game. The first payoff for a winning throw is 2 to 1, but the player will lose his bet on the losing side. Let us assume we place a $1 bet on each side of the coin. The first toss is heads, and that is determined as the winning side with a payoff of $2; however, we lose the $1 we bet on tails. Technically we broke even; we bet $2 ($1 on each side) and now we have $2.

There is even better news! We can continue playing the game for a five-minute period, but to win we will have to throw heads every time. If we get tails, we will not lose more than the original $1 we bet. The catch is that if we throw heads, the payoff after the first toss will be determined by the dealer but could not be less than 5 cents on each dollar we bet. As you can see, this is a no-lose game, but the extent of our winnings is limited by time and the payoff determined by the dealer.

Believe it or not, these kinds of odds exist in the stock market. The trick is to pick the right stock at the right time to place your bets on. To find such stocks, you should look for the following features.

(1) The stock is trading within $0.10 of a strike price.

(2) A volatile stock, preferably Nasdaq technology related.

(3) The time to take action is within 30 days or less from earnings report. The closer the time is to earnings announcement the better, since this will allow you to reduce the amount of your bet.

Implementation of this process will be clearer when you study the example below.

We notice Intel trading at $17.40 on Monday January 13, 2003, $0.10 below the $17.50 strike price. Earnings are expected on Tuesday, and the January options are expected to expire on Friday, January 17, 2003. With Intel (INTC) being a volatile technology stock, this offers a perfect candidate for placing our bets.

Since we do not know what the earnings will do to the stock price, we will place equal bets on both possible outcomes as follows:

With the stock trading at $17.40 on Monday, January 13, 2003, we will buy 100 contracts (10,000 shares) Intel $17.50 strike call for $0.30 /share (time premium since price premium is zero) for a total of $3000. We will also buy 100 contracts Intel $17.50 January 2003 puts for $0.40/share ($0.10 price value + $0.30 time value) for a total of $4000. We will wait for earnings to take action with the following plan:

(1) If the earnings are good and the stock moves above $17.50, we will sell the puts for a small loss and sell the calls for a significant profit.

(2) If the earnings disappoint and the stock moves below $17.50, we will sell the calls for a small loss and the puts for a significant profit.

(3) If the earnings are neutral and little movement occurs, we will close both options with close to a break-even situation.

If you pick a volatile stock, this scenario will be very unlikely.

Intel comes out with a profit of $0.16/share, beating the $0.14 estimate on higher than expected revenues. The stock moves to $18 the next day, and the call option was worth $0.80 ($0.50 price value + $0.30 time value). The put option was worth $0.25 (time value). We sell both options on Wednesday morning, taking advantage of the earnings gap up for a total of $10,500. Our profit $10,500 - $7000 = $3500 or 50 % of our initial investment.

ALERT 1: The reason for the time value on the stock being high, even though we are within a couple of days to expiration, is the implied volatility of the stock near earnings time. If we picked a stock with low volatility, the option time value will be closer to $0.05/share. Detailing the relationship between option volatility and time value is beyond the scope of this book and is a book in itself. If you are interested, please consult other option books such as "Option Volatility and Pricing" by Nattenberg.

ALERT 2: I would recommend that you only bet 2% of the value of your trading account on any one position such as this. To bet $7000, the value of our account will have to be $350,000. This may be large but remember, no matter what amount you bet, your profit will have been 50% in a couple of days.

Up or Down the Channel, You win!

As you probably know, most stocks do not move straight up or down but move in a wave-like pattern within a price channel. The chart on page 227 shows the Moving Average Channel (MAC) for Cisco (CSCO) as it traded down from $17.5 to $10.

ALERT: Detailed explanation of a moving average channel can be found in detailed technical analysis books. For the purpose of this discussion, it is enough to know that the upper and lower moving average channels are obtained by calculating the moving averages of the daily price highs and lows respectively. The Middle MAC is determined by taking the moving average of the daily price mid-points.

Notice that as the stock is moving lower, the top and bottom prices remain within the price channel. In addition, when the stock reaches the middle, it tends to quickly move to either the top or bottom of the channel.

Our objective is to take advantage of the movement by buying both puts and calls with strikes near the lower and upper end of the channel. As an example, when CSCO is at point **3** on the chart, it is expected to either move to the upper channel near point **2** or back to the lower channel near point **1**. With the stock at point **3** and a price of $10, we will buy equivalent number of contracts of $12.5 calls and $7.5 puts. Since the market price of the stock is almost $2.5 away from the strike, we can purchase both options at low prices, allowing us to control a sizable number of shares.

Our strategy is quite simple: we will lock in our profit by selling the winning position as soon as the stock hits the top of the channel in case of a call or the bottom of the channel in case of a put.

As an example, let us say at point **3** we buy 5000 share $7.5 Cisco strike puts for a price of $0.20/share and 5000 share $12.5 calls for $0.20/share for a total investment of $2000 or $1000 per position. We will pick the same expiration day for both options.

To maximize our profit potential we will pick an expiration date so we can buy each option at no more than $0.20/share.

As you can clearly see from the chart on page 227, we will profit

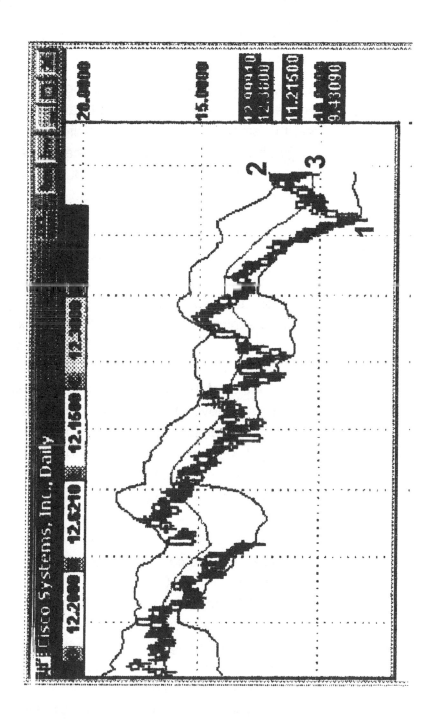

no matter which way the stock moves. If the stock moves to $12.50, the call price will show significant profit enough to more than make up for the loss in the put option and vice versa.

ALERT: By doing this, it is even possible to make profit on both positions by closing the profitable position first and wait to close the other position when the stock moves to the opposite side of the channel. This strategy should only be used if you have observed the $0.20/share limit on the option price, since one of the positions could result in a total loss if the desired move does not occur by expiration.

When Close to D-day, Bet Against the Majority

D-day for the option buyer is the third Friday of every month, also known as expiration day. When placing a bet on buying an option a few days before expiration, you should always check the open interest. Your objective is to assess whether there is an overwhelming sentiment one way or the other. If the call open contract volume is at least twice of that of the puts, then the majority is betting that the stock will close above the strike by expiration or vice versa. Consistent with the principles in this book, you should bet the other way by buying the position with the low open interest. From my experience, I have seen this to be true in most cases even when a stock is in an established uptrend as will be demonstrated in the example below.

By examining the table on page 230 showing Ciena (CIEN) January 2003 options, it is clear that the call open interest at a strike of $7.5 more than 4 times the put interest.

EUQAU: 8151 open contracts ($7.5 call)

EUQMU: 1898 open contracts ($7.5 put)

In other words, the overwhelming majority is betting that the stock will close above $7.50 by expiration on January 17,2003. As usually happens with most stocks, turning points coincide with extreme sentiment. With call volume running at four times put volume, we can easily conclude that we have an extreme level of bullishness on the stock.

The question is why will we want to bet against the CMF/moving average chart on page 231 which clearly shows an established uptrend since early November 2002.

ALERT: Can you recognize the buy signal on the chart page 231 at point **1** where the MA(10) crossed the EMA(20) accompanied by increasing money flow at point **a**? You should also be able to recognize that the drop in money flow between points **b** and **c** was just a correction since the MA(10) failed to penetrate the EMA(20) to the downside. In addition, notice how the last three days with price drops were accompanied by decreasing volume and with positive money flow, indicating that the uptrend will continue. If you cannot easily recognize these features, please re- read chapters 12 and 13 in this book.

Remember that we are placing a very short-term bet with high profit potential and low out-of-pocket cash. Three days before expiration we were able to buy Ciena $7.50 strike January 2003 puts for $0.25 and sell three days later on Expiration day (designated by **E** on the chart) for $1.25/share or 500% profit.

ALERT: There is a logical reason as to why the option with the most open interest close to expiration day tends to expire worthless. To ensure a smooth and liquid market, each stock option traded has a specialist that is required to sell whenever a buyer is looking to buy or buy whenever one wants to sell. It is thus to the advantage of the options specialist to have the majority of open options expire worthless to maximize profit by not having to buy back the majority of options they sold. The specialists do this by selling slightly larger blocks of the underlying stock than what they are buying to drive the price lower before expiration. If you believe this cannot happen, then you have been asleep for the past two years.

Expires After: Fri 17-Jan-03

Options: Jan-03 | Feb-03 | Apr-03 | Jul-03 | Jan-04 | Jan-05

CALLS							Strike Price	PUTS						
Symbol	Last Trade	Chg	Bid	Ask	Vol	Open Int		Symbol	Last Trade	Chg	Bid	Ask	Vol	Open Int
EUQAZ.X	3.80	-.060	3.60	3.90	21	938	2.50	EUQMZ.X	0.06	0.00	0.00	0.05	0	1,359
EIYAZ.X	1.50	0.00	1.15	1.40	0	22	2.50	EIYMZ.X	0.25	0.00	0.00	0.25	0	10
EUQAA.X	1.30	-0.50	1.15	1.30	244	18,108	5	EUQMA.X	0.05	0.00	0.00	0.05	0	5,906
EIYAA.X	0.20	0.00	0.00	0.25	0	219	5	EIYMA.X	1.00	-0.10	1.10	1.35	10	90
EUQAU.X	0.05	0.00	0.00	0.05	0	8,151	7.50	EUQMU.X	1.30	+0.50	1.20	1.35	52	1,898
EIYAY.X	0.10	0.00	0.00	0.15	0	95	7.50	EIYMU.X	3.50	0.00	3.50	3.90	0	0
EUQAB.X	0.05	0.00	0.00	0.05	0	3,786	10	EUQMB.X	3.70	+0.60	3.60	3.90	30	1,147
EUQAV.X	0.05	0.00	0.00	0.05	0	990	12.50	EUQMV.X	5.60	0.00	6.10	6.40	0	91
EUQAC.X	0.05	0.00	0.00	0.05	0	3,918	15	EUQMC.X	8.10	0.00	8.60	8.90	0	68
EUQAD.X	0.05	0.00	0.00	0.05	0	4,867	20	EUQMD.X	13.00	0.00	13.50	14.00	0	128
EUQAE.X	0.05	0.00	0.00	0.05	0	1,326	25	EUQME.X	18.00	0.00	18.50	19.00	0	17
EUQAF.X	0.05	0.00	0.00	0.05	0	7,003	30	EUQMF.X	22.90	0.00	23.40	24.10	0	5
EUQAG.X	0.05	0.00	0.00	0.05	0	471	35	EUQMG.X	27.90	0.00	28.40	29.10	0	4
EUQAH.X	0.05	0.00	0.00	0.05	0	6,810	40	EUQMH.X	32.90	0.00	33.40	34.10	0	1
EUQAJ.X	0.05	0.00	0.00	0.05	0	1,093	50	EUQMJ.X	42.90	0.00	43.40	44.10	0	100
EUQAL.X	0.05	0.00	0.00	0.05	0	1,568	60	EUQML.X	52.90	0.00	53.40	54.10	0	16

230

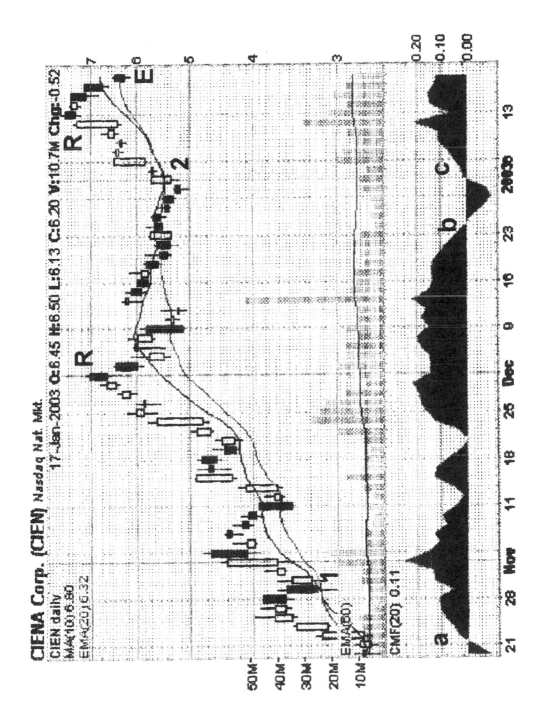

CIENA Corp. (CIEN) Nasdaq Nat. Mkt.

CIEN daily   17-Jan-2003 O:6.45 H:6.50 L:6.13 C:6.20 V:10.7M Chg:-0.52
MA(10):6.80
EMA(20):6.32

CHAPTER 16

Profitable Chart Patterns

IN CHAPTERS 12 and 13 we have learned how using the right mix of technical indicators, such as Chaikin money flow, moving averages, ADX, as well as others, can foretell future price direction of a stock. In this chapter we will complete the picture by demonstrating the usefulness of recognizing specific chart patterns as they form. These chart patterns not only can predict major trend reversals, but can also alert the trader into major pullbacks within an established trend.

By mastering the art of recognizing these chart patterns and combining it with the technical indicators discussed previously, you can further boost your trading profits.

Before going into specific details, it is important that you become familiar with two simple concepts: (1) Support and resistance, (2) Trend lines. Since information on these concepts is available on the internet and many other books, I will only discuss them briefly so you have a basic understanding to allow you to follow the rest of the chapter.

Support and Resistance

Have you ever remembered the price you paid for a stock that you made money on? Many investors will want to buy a stock that they profited on when the price falls again to their initial buy point. This is done in hope that the previous pattern will repeat itself, resulting in a profit. On the other hand, have you ever held a stock too long just to see it fall and your handsome profit disappear? Wouldn't you want to sell if the stock goes to that point again? Many investors are likely to do that to avoid the pain of loss.

These psychological actions by the majority of investors at certain price points create price congestion areas defined as support and resistance.

Support and resistance are hence established because people have bad memories of pain and regret, as well as good memories of being right. This point emphasizes the psychological factors in trading. In a perfect world, stocks will be priced at their intrinsic value defined by the fundamentals and profitability of the company. However, the stock price is usually determined by the perception of the company's success or failure. In cases of extreme optimism as seen in the 1990s, stock prices got ahead of their real values due to investors' perception of the future.

In a manner similar to the establishment of support and resistance, chart patterns are formed as a result of crowd psychological behavior. This is why recognizing such patterns is very important in successful trading. It is essential in looking at areas of support and resistance to recognize the strength and weakness of that area. There are three factors determining the strength of support or resistance:

(1) The amount of time a stock stays in the congestion area or width of support.
(2) Price range of support and resistance area relative to the price of the stock. This is the height of the price congestion area.
(3) The volume traded within the support or resistance area.

In the chart on page 235, it is clearly seen that chart A forms a stronger support than chart B due to taller height and wider width. This is, of course, assuming similar stock prices and trading volumes.

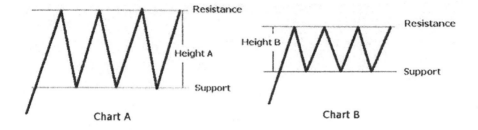

Chart A

Chart B

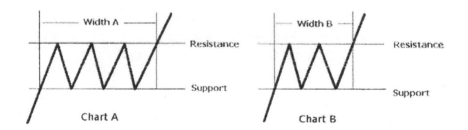

Chart A

Chart B

Trendlines

A trendline is formed when at least two price points are connected. To construct a lower trend line, you need to connect at least two support points, while an upper trend line is formed by connecting at least two resistance points.

A positive slope indicates a stock in an uptrend while a negative slope indicates a stock in a downtrend. When a stock is in an uptrend, the bottom or support line is more important. The uptrend is considered intact as long as the price does not break below this line. In case where the stock is in a downtrend, the upper or resistance line is more important. The downtrend is considered intact as long as this line is not broken.

Any break of the support line in an uptrend or the resistance line in a downtrend can signal a possible change in direction. This change can be a real reversal or a temporary direction change after which the original trend continues. Recognizing chart patterns in this chapter can help the trader decide whether the break of a trend line is real or just a temporary reversal.

The chart on page 237 shows an example of constructing the uptrend and downtrend lines for the Nasdaq. You can practice constructing trendlines on the stocks you hold to get more familiar with the concept.

Trend Reversals

Recognizing trend reversal is one of the keys to achieving significant trading profits. Profitable chart patterns signaling such an event are the PVP and VPV reversals.

PVP Down Reversal

PVP, or Peak-Valley-Peak reversal, is formed when a stock in an established uptrend goes through a trend reversal. A drop from the first peak above the uptrend line to an intermediate valley below it signals the first sign of a possible reversal. Subsequently a second peak is formed when the stock re-tests the uptrend line.

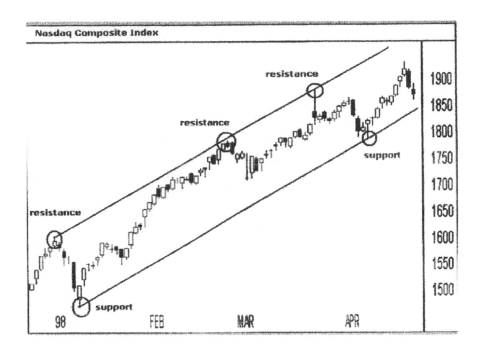

Nasdaq shown in both uptrend and downtrend using trendlines.
A trendline is formed by connecting at least two points. The more
points connected the more valid the trendline.

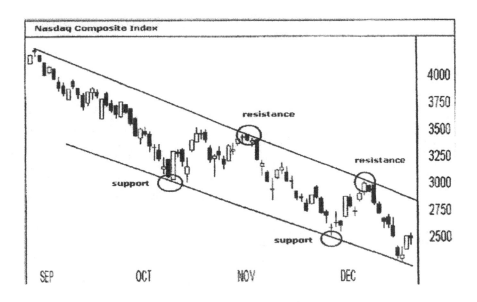

The stock then breaks below the valley to confirm the reversal.

Example 1: Nasdaq Index

By examining the chart on page 239, an uptrend line is drawn by connecting points **A** and **B**. The Nasdaq reaches a peak at point **C** before reversing and breaking the trend line at point **1** to reach a valley at line **D**. A test of the uptrend line at point **2** occurs, forming a second peak before finally reversing and breaking the valley support at point **3**.

The ideal trade in this case is to wait to enter a short position until the uptrend line is re-tested at point **2**. This allows for a high level of profitability with lower risk.

VPV Up Reversal

VPV, or Valley-Peak-Valley reversal, is formed when a stock in a downtrend goes through a trend reversal. A rise from the first valley below the trend line to a peak above it, subsequently followed by another valley, when the stock re-tests the downtrend line.

The stock then breaks above the first peak to confirm the reversal.

It is important to learn how to recognize reversals before they occur. It is hence valuable to be able to tell that a VPV or PVP reversal is in the making before the confirmation break actually takes place. This will increase your potential profit by getting in at the early stages of the advance or decline.

The examples below are taken from actual trades with the charts shown at the time of decision to enter the position. These are not synthetic positions and do not offer the benefit of hindsight. These examples also demonstrate that such reversals may involve the use of support and resistance lines as well as fan like multiple trendlines.

Example 2: Convergys Corporation (CVG)

Referring to the chart on page 241, the downtrend line is broken between points **1** and **2**, then re-tested at point **3**. Notice that a second re-test at point **4** occurred establishing the line connecting

Nasdaq Composite Index

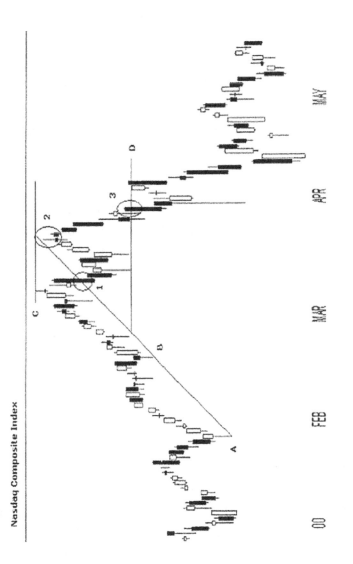

points **1**, **3** and **4** as strong support.

A most likely scenario is a break of the resistance line to complete the VPV reversal. This is reinforced by MACD oversold crossover and increase in the value of CMF as the second retest is complete. In addition, this stock passes the three times rule discussed in chapter 18. In summary, this rule requires that any stock undergoing a reversal break resistance by the third attempt.

VPV reversals are usually an indication of at a minimum a short term move to the next resistance level. While it is possible that this may be an indication of a long term trend, the stocks behavior will have to be monitored after the initial resistance is reached.

ALERT: Notice that the downtrend line was broken in late March but failed to be successfully re tested. The stock gapped down below the trend line at point **1**. It is thus important to wait for a re-test of the trend line before taking any position.

If a position was taken as indicated by the chart on May 20, 2005, a 40% profit will have resulted by December of 2005 when the stock moved above $18. As of the writing of this chapter, the stock trades at $21.

Example 3: EVC Corporation

This example shows a VPV reversal encompassing two trend lines forming a fan.

By examining the chart on page 242, the first downtrend line (lower fan blade) is broken between points **1** and **2** and re-tested at **3**. The second downtrend line (upper fan blade) is broken between points **3** and **4** and re-tested at **5**. The chart also shows that confirmation in this case has already occurred, breaking resistance at $7.40,

The VPV reversal pattern is also accompanied by positive CMF and MACD crossover as seen in the chart, indicating that a move to the next resistance is likely. This is, in fact, what happens, and the stock reaches $9 within one month. As opposed to the previous example, the stock in this case pulls back to $7.00 after reaching $9.

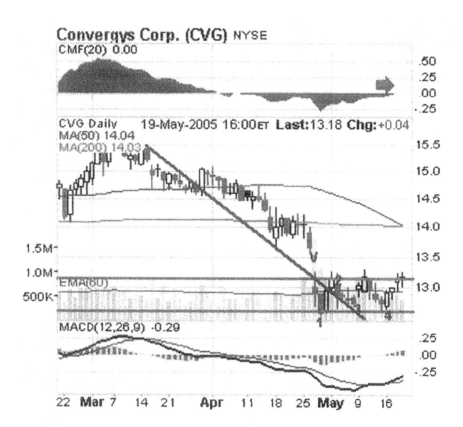

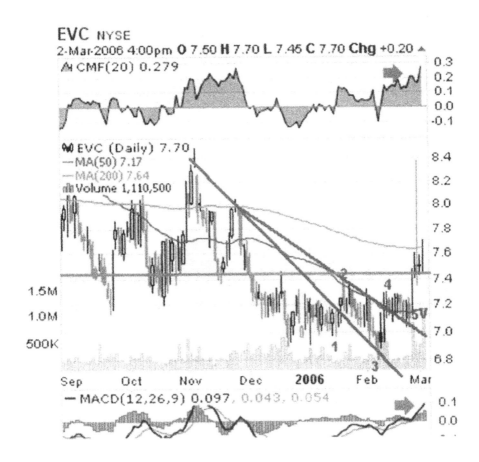

It is thus important to track the behavior of the stock once resistance is reached to decide whether the position should be exited or there is room for further advance.

Triangles

There are essentially three major types of triangle chart patterns: Symmetrical, Ascending and Descending triangles.

Symmetrical Triangles

Symmetrical triangles are continuation patterns and can be bullish or bearish dependent on the previous trend. This pattern is characterized by lower highs and higher lows, resulting in a narrower trading range as the apex is approached. In effect, each buying wave is met by a selling wave and each selling wave by a buying wave. The volume is usually low during the period of indecision within the pattern and increases on a breakout. An illustration of bullish and bearish symmetrical triangle patterns are given on page 244.

Example 4: Pancatos Pharmaceuticals (PANC)

The chart on page 245 clearly shows the symmetrical triangle formation following a double bottom. A break of the pattern takes place on increased volume with a re-test of the apex of the triangle. This pattern, combined with change in CMF from negative to positive and MACD divergence, indicates an imminent move. The stock moved quickly to $5.80 before correcting to $5.00 and then advancing to $6.80.

Example 5: Sciclone Pharmaceuticals (SCLN)

The chart on page 246 shows the formation of a symmetrical triangle and breakout on heavy volume at point **2**. In this case the stock moves to the edge of the down gap before meeting resistance as expected. This pattern, when occurring after an exhaustion gap, tends to result in filling of the gap. This is actually what took place, and the stock moved to $3.75.

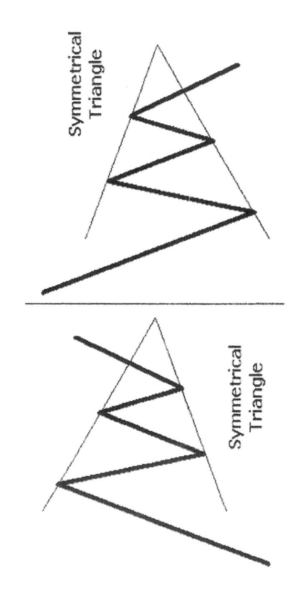

Symmetrical
Triangle

Symmetrical
Triangle

244

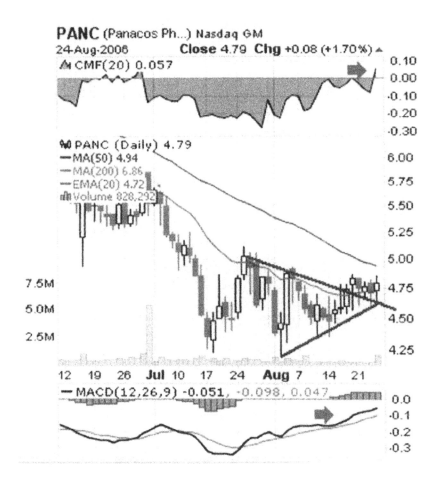

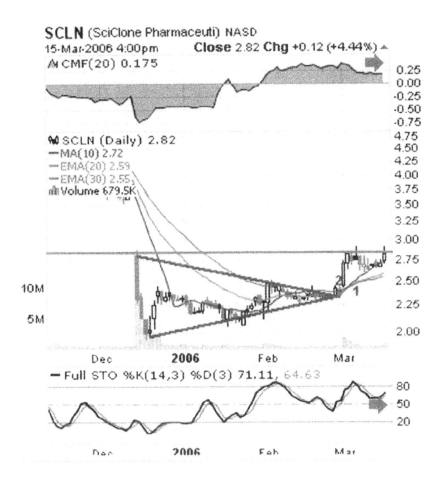

Ascending Triangle

An ascending triangle is a bullish continuation pattern that should mostly be traded if the stock is in an uptrend. The flat top part of the triangle defines price resistance. Whenever buying pressure builds, it is encountered by selling at the resistance line. The selling pressure weakens every time, resulting in a higher low, until eventually sellers are exhausted and a break above the resistance line takes place. Volume is usually low when trading within the triangle pattern and increases on breakout. A schematic of the ascending triangle can be found on page 248.

Descending Triangle

A descending triangle is a bearish continuation pattern and is more reliable when a stock is in a downtrend. The flat bottom part of the triangle defines support. Whenever selling pressure builds, it is encountered by buying pressure at the support line. The buying weakens every time, resulting in a lower high until eventually a break below the support line takes place. Volume is usually low when trading is within the triangle pattern and increases on breakout. A schematic of the descending triangle is presented on page 249.

Example 6: Vivo Participacoes (VIV)

The chart on page 250 shows a clearly defined ascending triangle pattern. The long line defines resistance as well as the upper arm of the triangle. Notice how the price hit against resistance where selling pushed the price back but to a higher level than the original low. The second attempt was successful in breaking resistance with a small gap up. Notice that this formation was also supported by positive CMF and MACD divergence, thus increasing the success potential of the trade.

Example 7: AVX Corporation (AVX)

A small ascending triangle with upper arm defining resistance

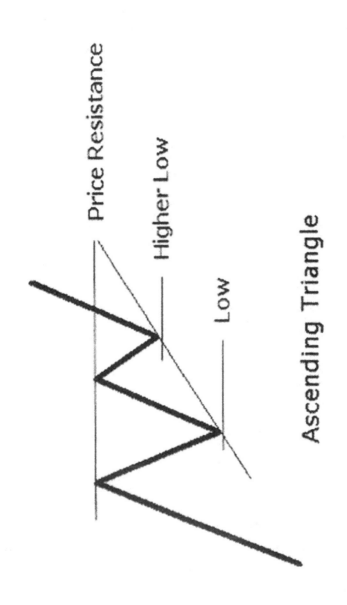

Price Resistance

Higher Low

Low

Ascending Triangle

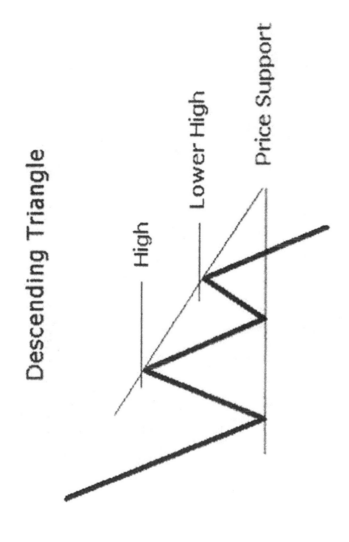

Descending Triangle

High

Lower High

Price Support

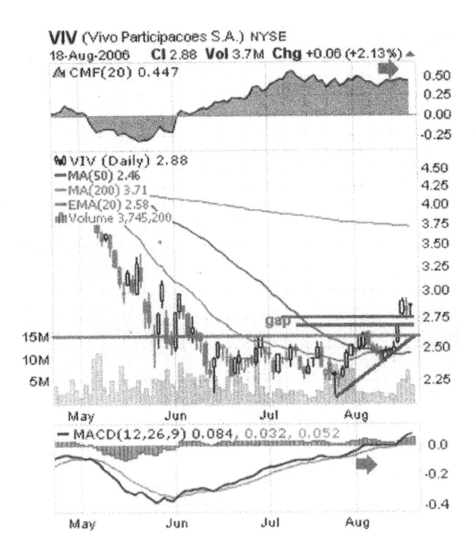

VIV (Vivo Participacoes S.A.) NYSE
18-Aug-2006   Cl 2.88 Vol 3.7M Chg +0.06 (+2.13%) ▲

CMF(20) 0.447

0.50
0.25
0.00
-0.25

VIV (Daily) 2.88
—MA(50) 2.46
—MA(200) 3.71
—EMA(20) 2.58
Volume 3,745,200

4.50
4.25
4.00
3.75
3.50
3.25
3.00
2.75
2.50
2.25

gap

15M
10M
5M

May   Jun   Jul   Aug

MACD(12,26,9) 0.084, 0.032, 0.052

0.0
-0.2
-0.4

May   Jun   Jul   Aug

250

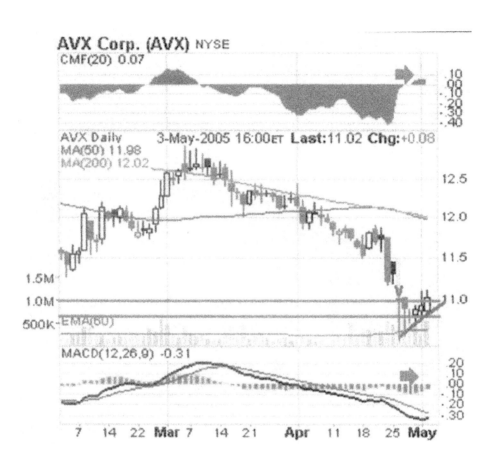

at $11.00 is clearly seen on the chart page 251. It is evident how the sellers get exhausted as the price hits resistance and then pulls back. This pattern is also reinforced by increase in CMF from negative to positive.

Wedges

There is a similarity between wedges and symmetrical triangles in that trend lines converge. The difference is mainly the noticeable slant.

A wedge, characterized by a downward slant defined by a lower high and a lower low, is considered a falling wedge. This chart pattern is bullish no matter whether the stock is in an uptrend or downtrend.

A rising wedge is characterized by an upward slant defined by higher highs and higher lows. This pattern is considered bearish whether in an uptrend or downtrend.

Volume usually stays low when the stock is trading within the wedge and increases on breakout, similar to a symmetrical triangle pattern.

Many traders believe that lower highs and lower lows are bearish indicators. In most cases this is true except for falling wedges and falling rectangles (to be discussed later). Falling wedges are one of the most bullish indicators that result in most cases in handsome profits.

Figures of the rising wedge and falling wedge are seen on page 253.

Example 8: Lionbridge Technology (LIOX)

The chart on page 254 clearly shows a falling wedge formation. As usual with this type pattern, falling wedges form after a sudden and sharp advance in the stock. This is where the stock takes a breather before continuing the advance. The chart shows a falling wedge supported by OBV divergence and positive CMF, indicating a likely significant advance. On our web site we entered

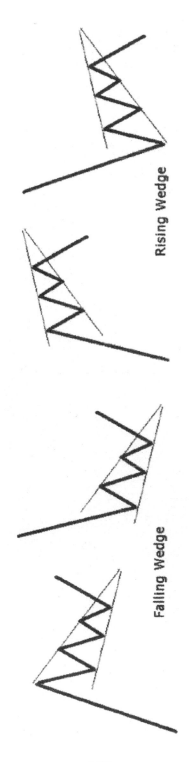

Rising Wedge

Falling Wedge

Lionbridge Tech (LIOX) NASD

CMF(20) 0.04

LIOX Daily
MA(50) 4.59
MA(200) 5.78

17-Jun-2005 **Close:** 4.52 **Chg:** +0.02

1 falling wedge

EMA(60)

OBV
MA(20)

a b

the stock on June 20, 2005 at $4.52 and sold on June 28, 2005 at $6.35 for a 40% profit in eight days.

Example 9: BSD Medical (BSM)

This is another example of the trademark of falling wedges. The chart on page 256 shows how a falling wedge is formed after a sharp and sudden advance in the stock. Notice how the drop from $9.00 to $4.00 during the formation of a falling wedge was accompanied by an essentially flat CMF. This indicates that as the stock was dropping the sellers were drying up. In addition, in the final stages of the falling wedge formation the stochastics were oversold. We entered the stock in our web site on September 23, 2006 at $4.55 and sold on October 5, 2006 at $5.35 for a 20% profit in 12 days. These are generally the kind of profits you expect from falling wedge formations.

Flags and Pennants

Flags and pennants are consolidation patterns that occur after a quick rise or drop in price. They are reliable continuation patterns where the stock is pausing for a short period of time before getting ready for the next move. This next move is usually in the direction of the original trend.

Flags are similar to wedges except the trendlines run parallel and do not converge. Lower tops and lower bottoms are characteristic of bull flags, while bear flags have higher tops and higher bottoms.

Pennants are mini-sized symmetrical triangles with a shorter duration. The stock is just taking a breather before the trend resumes.

Volume remains usually low during the consolidation period within the pattern and increases on breakout.

A figure of the different kinds of flags and pennants is shown on page 257.

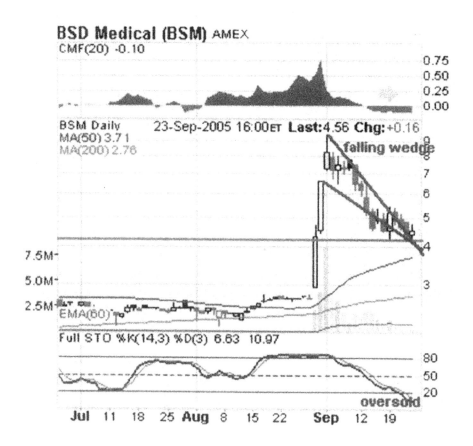

BSD Medical (BSM) AMEX

CMF(20) -0.10

0.75
0.50
0.25
0.00

BSM Daily   23-Sep-2005 16:00ET Last:4.56 Chg:+0.16
MA(50) 3.71
MA(200) 2.76

falling wedge

9
8
7
6
5

4

7.5M-

5.0M-

2.5M-
EMA(60)

3

Full STO %K(14,3) %D(3) 6.63 10.97

80
50
20

oversold

Jul 11 18 25 Aug 8 15 22 Sep 12 19

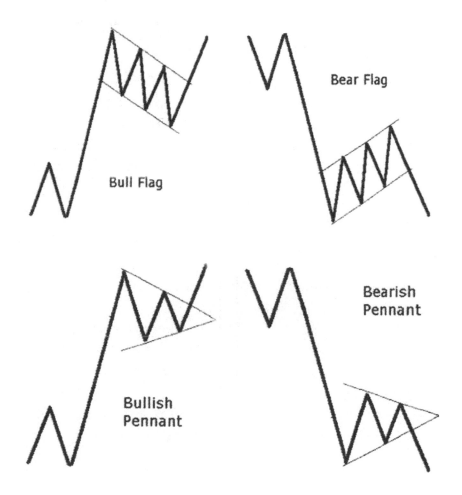

Bull Flag

Bear Flag

Bullish
Pennant

Bearish
Pennant

Example 10: Pier Imports (PIR)

The bull flag can be defined by the two small parallel lines shown on the chart page 259.

It is also evident that the bull flag appeared after a sudden and sharp rise in the stock. The chart shows a breakout of the flag with positive CMF indicating possible further advance. The stock moved from $6.60 to $7.25 within three days, demonstrating the strength of the bull flag as a continuation pattern.

Example 11 : KongZhong Corporation (KONG)

The bullish pennant is formed after a jump in price between points **1** and **2** as seen on the chart page 260. This is where the stock consolidates for a short period before continuation of the uptrend. Notice the increase in volume on breakout from the pennant formation.

Rectangles

A rectangle is defined by a resistance (upper line) and a support (lower line). Trading stays within the channel defined by these two lines, whereby any buying is met by selling or resistance, and any selling is met by buying or support. This continues until the channel is broken.

Rectangles are usually continuation patterns except in the case of falling rectangles where a reversal pattern is indicated. The following two examples demonstrate the unequaled power of falling rectangles as reversal patterns.

A schematic of the rectangle pattern is shown on page 235. This is the same diagram showing support and resistance.

Example 12: Talk.com (TALK)

The chart on page 261 clearly shows a falling rectangle. Both support and resistance lines are slanted down forming lower highs and lower lows. A break of the rectangle with positive CMF propelled the stock from $5.75 to $9.00 within a week.

In cases of falling rectangles, you should consider entering the stock on a pull back from a high volume test of the resistance (point

PIR (Pier 1 Imports, Inc.) NYSE
8-Sep-2006   Cl 6.67 Vol 801.0K   Chg +0.07 (+1.06%) ▲
CMF(20) 0.155

PIR (Daily) 6.67
—MA(50) 6.34
—MA(200) 9.03
—EMA(20) 6.29
Volume 891,900

MACD(12,26,9) 0.064, -0.052, 0.116

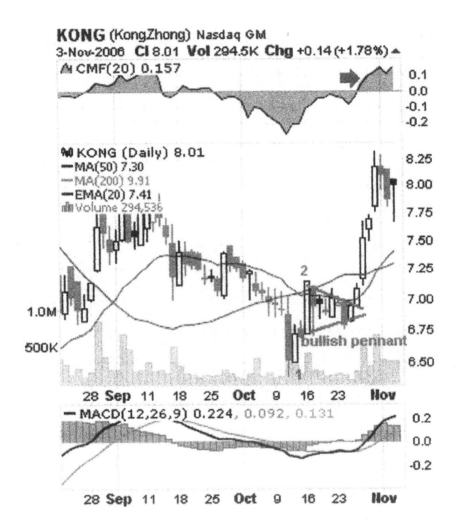

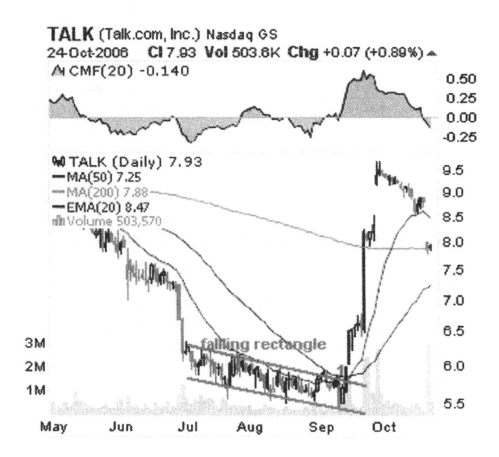

TALK (Talk.com, Inc.) Nasdaq GS
24-Oct-2006 **Cl** 7.93 **Vol** 503.6K **Chg** +0.07 (+0.89%) ▲

CMF(20) -0.140

0.50
0.25
0.00
-0.25

TALK (Daily) 7.93
—MA(50) 7.25
—MA(200) 7.88
—EMA(20) 8.47
Volume 503,570

falling rectangle

9.5
9.0
8.5
8.0
7.5
7.0
6.5
6.0
5.5

3M
2M
1M

May   Jun   Jul   Aug   Sep   Oct

1 on the chart). In such situations it is likely that the next move will result in a break of resistance.

Example 13: Vonage (VG)

A falling rectangle pattern can be clearly seen on the chart page 263. In this case the break of the rectangle occurs with negative CMF. This pattern is highly bullish that even in such cases the stock is likely to move to the next resistance before pulling back. In this case the stock moved to $9.00 before a pullback took place.

Falling rectangles are some of the most bullish indicators, especially when supported by positive CMF on breakout. Be sure to watch for them when scanning stocks to trade.

Rounded Tops and Bottoms

There are two kinds of rounded tops and rounded bottoms. One kind signals a reversal while the other signals a continuation pattern.

The reversal pattern requires a much larger consolidation period than the continuation pattern. Both consist of a long sideways move where the shape resembles that of a saucer.

The rounded bottom is usually a bullish signal while the rounded top is bearish. The rounded top is essentially an inverted rounded bottom.

The low of the rounded bottom should not be more than a 50% pullback from the high of the run (i.e., a 50% retracement). The higher the value of the pullback, within the 50% guideline, the stronger the breakout.

In both rounded top and rounded bottom, the wider the consolidation period, the longer the stock will run.

Figures of rounded tops and rounded bottoms are shown on pages 264 and 265.

Example 14 : Spirit Finance (SFC)

The curve under the line **ab** represents a rounded bottom as shown on the chart page 266.

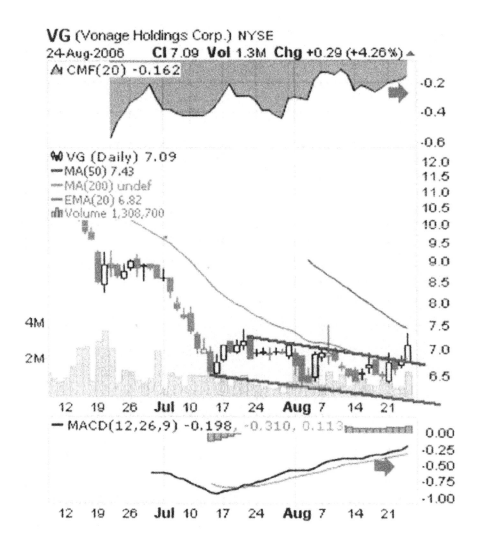

VG (Vonage Holdings Corp.) NYSE
24-Aug-2006   Cl 7.09 Vol 1.3M Chg +0.29 (+4.26%) ▲
CMF(20) -0.162

-0.2
-0.4
-0.6

VG (Daily) 7.09
MA(50) 7.43
MA(200) undef
EMA(20) 6.82
Volume 1,308,700

12.0
11.5
11.0
10.5
10.0
9.5
9.0
8.5
8.0
7.5
7.0
6.5

4M
2M

12   19   26   Jul 10   17   24   Aug 7   14   21

MACD(12,26,9) -0.198, -0.310, 0.113

0.00
-0.25
-0.50
-0.75
-1.00

12   19   26   Jul 10   17   24   Aug 7   14   21

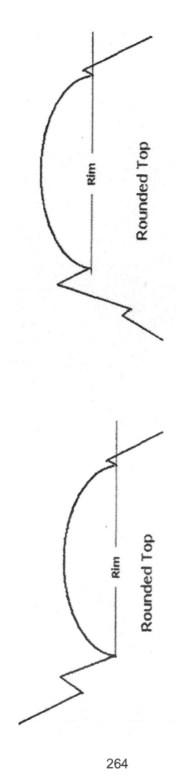

Rim

Rounded Top

Rim

Rounded Top

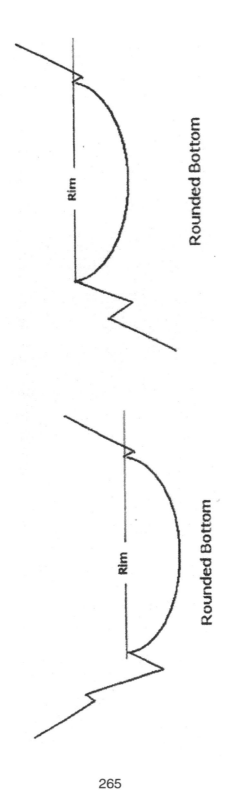

Note that before the rounded bottom formation, a break of the downtrend line **a3** between points **1** and **2** took place. The trend line was re-tested at **3** indicating a VPV reversal. The rounded bottom formation was completed at **b** accompanied by CMF changing from negative to positive.

The length of time taken to complete this pattern was almost two months, indicating a reversal pattern rather than a continuation pattern.

Even though rounded bottoms are bullish patterns, they are usually characterized by slower moves than falling wedges and falling rectangles. In this case the stock moved from $10.60 on May 24, 2005 to $11.25 on June 9, 2005, or 5% in 15 days. While this is still a significant move relative to the return for an average investor, it is meager compared to the highly bullish wedge and rectangle patterns.

Double Tops and Double Bottoms

These are some of the most basic patterns that even beginning traders are familiar with. They usually occur at the end of a trend and are considered trend reversal patterns.

The double top is an M-shaped bearish pattern that occurs after an uptrend. The second peak is characterized by a lower volume than the first peak. This is a major clue to the likely formation of a double top. The completion of the pattern comes with a break of support at the neckline.

The double bottom pattern is a W-shaped bullish pattern that occurs after a downtrend. The second valley is characterized by a lower volume than the first. This pattern is completed with a break of resistance at the neckline.

The figures on pages 269 and 270 show schematics of the double top and double bottom.

A classic example is the Nasdaq double top formation in 2000 shown on page 271.

Gaps

Other than common gaps that have no trading significance there are three kinds of gaps:

(1) Breakaway gaps. (2) Continuation gaps, and (3) Exhaustion gaps.

Breakaway Gaps

These gaps are the most significant for the trader since they offer potential quick profits. They are accompanied by high volume and signal the start of a new trend. Breakaway gaps can stay open for a long time and usually follow a period of consolidation.

While they offer high potential for profits, breakaway gaps can be tricky to trade. Anyone who has traded for a long period of time will tell you that any chart pattern can fail, In this case, however, failure can result in a refilling of the gap and thus a potential for large losses for the trader. On some occasions the market is intentionally bid up into the stops which are placed by short sellers, triggering buying activity at the market. This phenomenon is called stops running and can cause a temporary surge in price after which the stock moves lower.

It has been my experience that most breakaway gaps are followed by a minor pullback to the next support or the 20-day exponential moving average which has special significance in short term trading.

To control loss and reduce risk, it is best to wait for the stock to pull back to one of these support levels before taking a position. While there may be few situations where such a pullback may not take place, it is better to miss these trades than incur a significant loss.

Example 15: Charter Communications (CHTR)

The breakaway gap is clearly labeled in the chart page 272. The extremely high volume in conjunction with the gap can also be seen. As indicated previously, it is best to wait for a pullback to either the

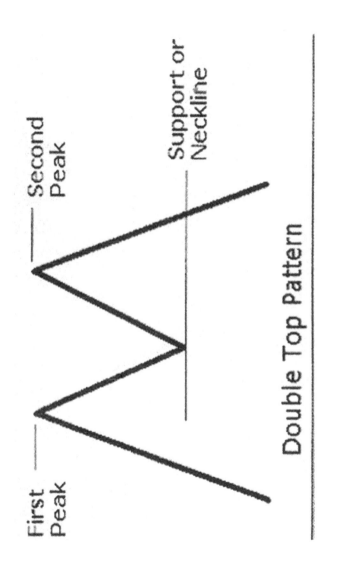

First
Peak

Second
Peak

Support or
Neckline

Double Top Pattern

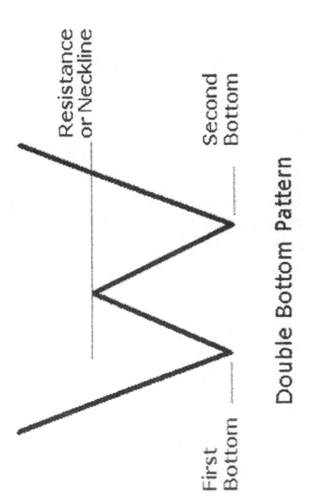

Resistance
or Neckline

Second
Bottom

First
Bottom

Double Bottom Pattern

270

Nasdaq Composite Index

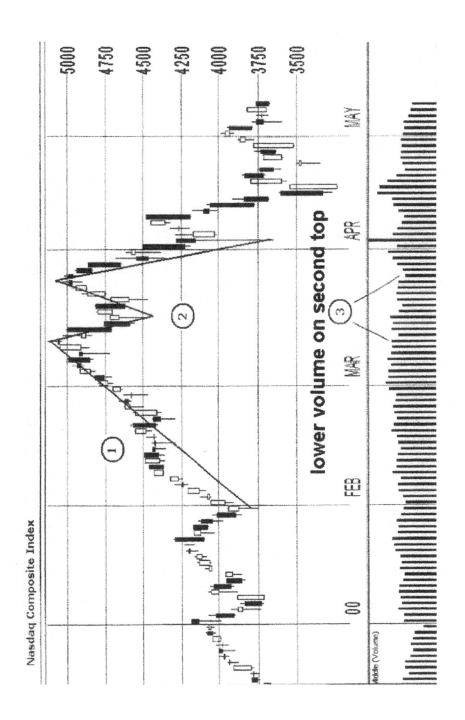

lower volume on second top

271

CHTR (Charter Co...) Nasdaq GM
27-Oct-2006　　CI 2.29　Vol 30.4M　Chg +0.17 (+8.02%) ▲

CMF(20) 0.316

CHTR (Daily) 2.29
—MA(50) 1.58
—MA(200) 1.26
—EMA(20) 1.82
Volume 30,415,628

breakaway gap

MACD(12,26,9) 0.150, 0.107, 0.043

20-day EMA or support before taking a position. In this case waiting for a successful test of the support line would have resulted in a highly profitable trade.

Example 16: Evergreen Solar (ESLR)

This is another example of a breakaway gap shown on page 274. Notice how the downtrend line is broken between points **1** and **2** on heavy volume. As explained previously, it is advisable to wait for a re-test of support before entry as depicted at point **3** on the chart. If you were to buy into the breakaway gap without waiting for a pullback, an immediate loss would have resulted.

Continuation Gaps

Continuation gaps are similar to breakaway gaps except they occur in the middle of a powerful trend. They are also accompanied by high volume as seen in the following example.

Example 17: Siga Technologies (SIGA)

The chart on page 275 shows a breakaway gap followed by a re-test of the support line. This is followed by a continuation gap on heavy volume taking the stock from $2 to $5.5. As of this writing, the stock is in the process of pulling back to the 20-day EMA as expected.

Exhaustion Gaps

Exhaustion gaps offer good trading opportunities in that they signal the end of a trend. These gaps may seem at first as continuation gaps since they are accompanied by heavy volume in the direction of the trend. However, the price fails to follow through in the direction of the gap. Exhaustion gaps are often accompanied by an increase in CMF as the gap is formed as is evident in the next example.

Example 18: Boston Scientific (BSX)

The exhaustion gap is clearly labeled on the chart page 276. Notice how even though the gap was accompanied by heavy vol-

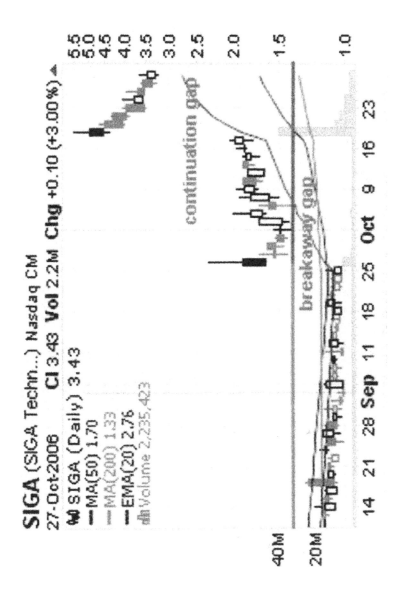

BSX (Boston Scientific) NYSE
27-Oct-2006 Cl 16.05 Vol 9.7M Chg +0.00 (+0.00%)
CMF(20) 0.255

BSX (Daily) 16.05
—MA(50) 16.02
—MA(200) 19.44
—EMA(20) 15.64
Volume 9,688,600

Exhaustion gap

MACD(12,26,9) 0.074, -0.062, 0.136

ume, the CMF increased as the gap was formed and turned posi-tive as the final bottom was established. In this case it was evident that a price reversal was about to occur.

Head and Shoulders Tops and Bottoms

The head and shoulders top usually occurs at the end of an uptrend and is a reversal pattern. This pattern consists of two minor peaks or shoulders and one major peak or head.

The left shoulder is formed on a breakout from the neckline. At the peak of the shoulder sellers are able to push the stock back to the neckline where buyers come in aggressively to push the stock up to a new high forming the head. Formation of the head comes with decreasing volume, indicating less buying interest. As buyers are exhausted, sellers are able to push the stock below the trend line to the neckline support where buyers come in again. In this case, however, there is not enough buying to take out the last high, resulting in the formation of the right shoulder. At this point new sellers drive the stock below the neckline to complete the pattern.

Note that the head, trendline and right shoulder form a PVP reversal pattern. Thus a trader will be able to recognize the reversal even if the formation of this pattern has not been identified early on.

A figure of the head and shoulders top pattern is shown on page 278.

The head and shoulders bottom or reverse head and shoulders is a bullish trend reversal pattern and appears at the end of a downtrend. The pattern consists of two minor valleys or shoulders and one major valley or head.

The left shoulder is formed by a major break below the neckline. At the bottom of the left shoulder buyers are able to push the stock to resistance at the neckline. Sellers then come in aggressively and push the stock down to a new low or head. As the new low is reached, selling volume tapers off and new buyers come in, pushing the stock back to resistance where sellers come in again. This time, however, sellers are unable to push the stock below the recent low forming

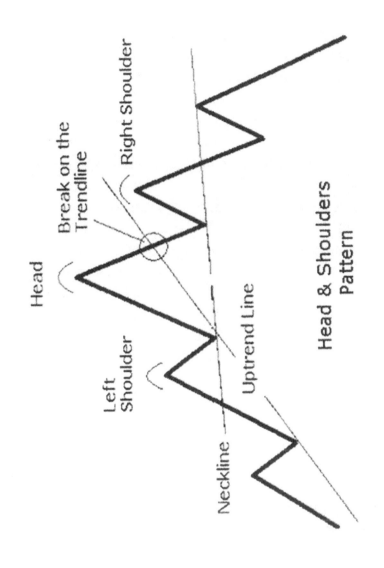

Head

Break on the
Trendline

Right Shoulder

Left
Shoulder

Neckline

Uptrend Line

Head & Shoulders
Pattern

the right shoulder. At this point buyers come in aggressively moving the stock above the neckline to complete the pattern.

Note that the head, downtrend line and right shoulder form a VPV reversal pattern. Paying attention to this makes it easier for the trader to recognize the reversal in case it was missed before.

A figure of the reverse head and shoulder or head and shoulder bottom is shown on page 280.

Cup and Handle

This is a continuation pattern made familiar by William O'neill, the founder of *Investor Business Daily*, and is described in his book, *How To Make Money in Stocks*.

This pattern is, in effect, a combination of two familiar patterns: the first is a rounded bottom or the cup and the second is a bull flag or pennant forming the handle. For this pattern to be profitable the stock must have established a prior uptrend.

For the breakout to result in a powerful run, the retracement to the bottom of the cup should be no more than 0.618, the Fibonacci number. The handle forms on a test of resistance and is usually either a flag or a pennant.

A schematic of the Cup and Handle pattern is shown on page 281.

A Final Word

It is important to make an effort to learn how to recognize the different chart patterns as they form. These patterns are followed by many traders and for that reason they work in the majority of cases. It is also essential to be prepared to exit a position or take protective measures using options such as selling covered calls or buying puts as explained in the earlier chapters of this book, if any of these patterns fail to hold.

Combining pattern recognition with CMF, moving averages, divergent signals, as well as other indicators described in Chapters 12 and 13, will increase your chances of success tremendously.

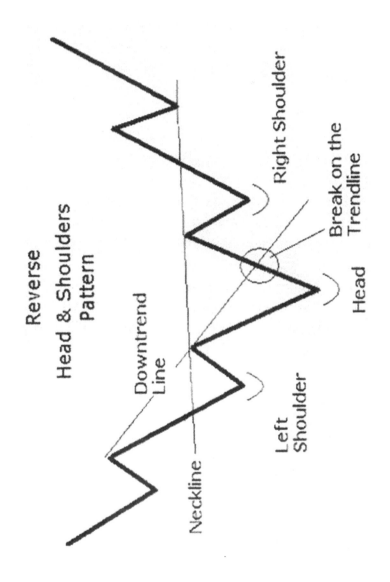

Reverse
Head & Shoulders
Pattern

Downtrend
Line

Neckline

Left
Shoulder

Head

Right Shoulder

Break on the
Trendline

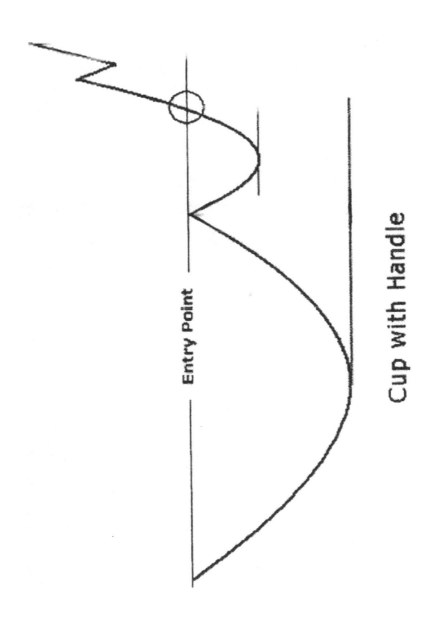

Cup with Handle

Entry Point

CHAPTER 17

Spotting Sudden Reversals

IN PREVIOUS CHAPTERS we discussed how using chart patterns combined with technical indicators can pinpoint trend continuations and reversals. In some situations whereby a stock has dropped or moved up quickly and significantly, no discernible chart pattern can be identified. These are usually called V reversals; however, by the time this fact is recognized, the trader is too late to the party.

An effective way to predict such reversals is using candlestick charts in combination with selected technical indicators discussed previously. In this chapter a short review of the most common candlestick patterns will be given to illustrate how they can be used to pinpoint sudden reversals.

It is important to point out that this chapter presents only the basic patterns. If you are interested in learning Candlestick charting in depth, please refer to any of the books by Steve Nison.

Basic Candlestick Features

Four price points are displayed: Open, close, highest price and lowest price. These prices can cover any time period, be it five minutes, one day, one week or one month.

Three types of patterns:

(1) Closed Candlestick: This is usually displayed in black or red and is a candlestick where the closing price is below the opening price.

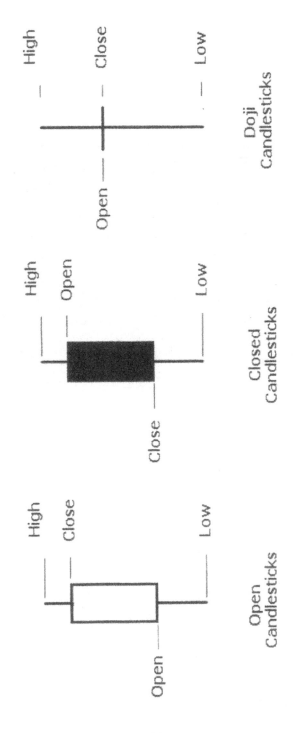

(2) Open Candlestick: This is usually displayed in white or green and is a candlestick where the closing price is above the opening price.

(3) Doji Candlestick: This is where the opening price and closing price are very close or the same and usually appears in the form of a cross or a spinning top.

A schematic of the different kinds of candlesticks is shown on page 284.

Heavy Buying Pressures

Periods of heavy buying pressures are displayed as a white marubozu candlestick. In this type of candlestick the open is located in the bottom 20% of the range while the closing price is located above the top 20% of the range.

A schematic of a white marubozu is shown on page 286.

Heavy Selling Pressures

Periods of heavy selling are displayed as a black marubozu candlestick. In this type of candlestick the open is located above the 20% of the range while the closing price is located below the bottom 20% of the range.

A schematic of the black marubozu is shown on page 287.

Both white and black marubozu candlesticks have special significance when appearing after an advance or a decline. A white marubozu appearing after a decline can signify an upward reversal while a black marubozu appearing after an advance can signify a downward reversal.

Indecision Periods

Dojis and their cousins, the spinning tops, have special significance in candlestick patterns since they indicate periods of indecision. These candlesticks provide important signals, especially when they appear in combination with others.

There are several types of Doji patterns shown in the diagram

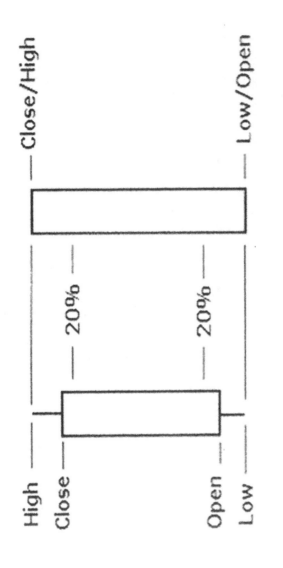

White Marubozu

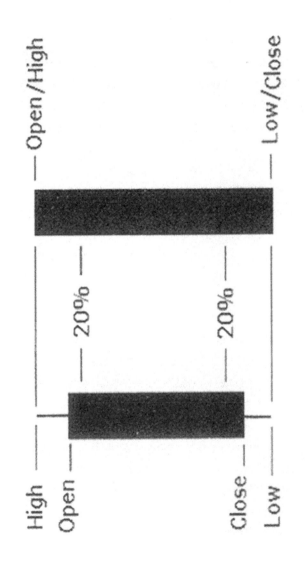

Black Marubozu

on page 289. The perfect Doji is where the opening and closing price are the same and the upper and lower tails are of the same length. In this case neither buyers nor sellers won at the end of a trading period. Long-legged Dojis are similar to ideal Dojis except that the tails are a lot longer. In this case also neither buyers nor sellers had the upper hand at the end of the period.

Spinning tops or hi waves are candlesticks similar to dojis characterized by a small body, long upper shadow and long lower shadow. This shows a standoff between bulls and bears at the end of the trading period.

These patterns indicate a loss of momentum in an advance or decline and the possibility of a reversal. This is especially true where a significant move with little consolidation or retracement has taken place.

A more detailed discussion of the different kinds of Dojis will now be given.

Hammer or Hanging Man

Both patterns are a form of Doji with a long lower tail and a small or nonexistent upper tail. The closing price should be near the open with both at the upper end of the period's range, resulting in a small body at the top of a long tail forming a hammer.

Whether the pattern is called a hammer or a hanging man is dependent on previous price movement. If this pattern is seen after a decline, it is called a hammer. This is a bullish signal indicating an upward reversal. This indicates that sellers were unable to keep the price at the lower end of the range even though they were present during the period. Buyers stepped in and moved the price to the top of the range at the end of the period.

If this pattern forms after an advance, it is called a hanging man. This is a bearish signal indicating a downtrend reversal. The long lower tail indicates that after a long advance sellers were present during the period, which may be a clue to possible exhaustion of the buyers.

Both hammer and hanging man require a confirmation candle-

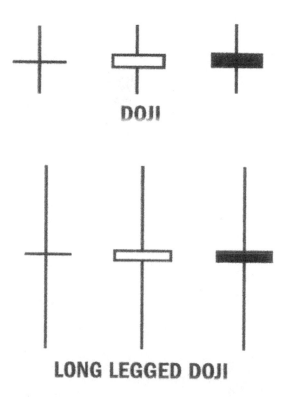

DOJI

LONG LEGGED DOJI

SPINNING TOPS

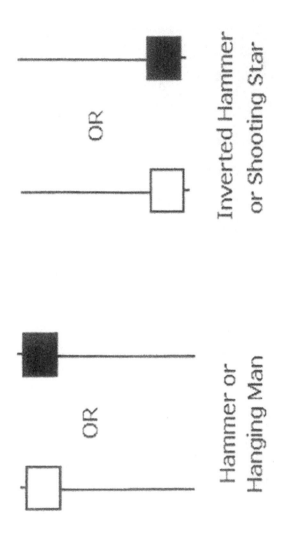

Hammer or
Hanging Man

OR

Inverted Hammer
or Shooting Star

OR

stick before taking action. This comes in the form of a white marubozu or a gap up in the case of a hammer. A black candlestick or a gap down is likely to appear in case of a hanging man.

The figure on page 290 shows a hammer or hanging man.

Shooting Star or Inverted Hammer

These patterns are essentially a hammer or hanging man turned upside down. They have a long upper tail and a small or nonexistent lower tail. The closing price should be near the open with both at the lower end of the period's trading range, resulting in a small body at the bottom with a long tail forming an inverted hammer.

Whether the pattern is named hammer or shooting star depends on the previous price movement. If the pattern is seen after a decline, it is called an inverted hammer. This is a bullish signal indicating a possible reversal. The long upper tail indicates that even though sellers prevailed at the end of the period, buyers were present. This presence of buyers should raise concern in case of a short position.

If the pattern is seen after an advance, it is called a shooting star. This is considered a bearish indicator signaling a potential downward reversal. The long upper tails indicate that buyers were present but sellers prevailed at the end of the period. This should raise concern in the case of a long position since the presence of sellers after a long advance indicates that momentum may be weakening.

In a manner similar to the hammer or hanging man, these patterns require confirmation before taking action. This comes in the form of a white marubozu or a gap up in the case of an inverted hammer and a black marubozu or a gap down in the case of a shooting star.

The figure on page 290 shows an Inverted Hammer and Shooting Star.

Gravestone or Dragonfly Doji

A gravestone Doji forms when the low, open and close are the same. This results in a long upper tail with an inverted T shape.

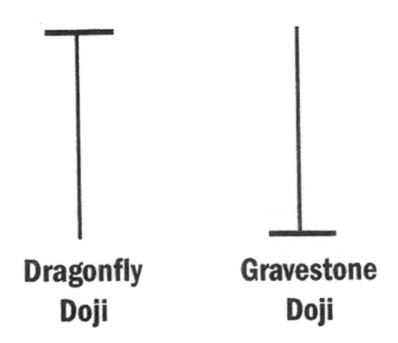

**Dragonfly
Doji**

**Gravestone
Doji**

This pattern implies that although buyers were present during the session, they were unable to hold the gains. Sellers were able to push the price at the end of the period to session lows. This pattern indicates a possible reversal especially after an uptrend. The long upper tail and the close near the low of the period indicate that buyers are exhausted and sellers have gained the upper hand.

A dragonfly Doji forms when the high, open and close are the same. This results in a long lower tail with a T shape.

This pattern indicates that although sellers were present during the session, they were unable to push the price lower. Buyers were able to push the price to the session high at the end of the trading period.

This pattern indicates a possible reversal especially after a downtrend. The long lower tail and the close near the high indicate that sellers are becoming exhausted and buyers are gaining the upper hand.

A schematic of the Dragonfly and Gravesone Dojis is shown on page 292.

Relative Candlestick Positions

The position of a candlestick relative to the one before carries special significance. There are two main classes of positions: (1) Star position and (2) Harami position.

(1) **Star position.** A candlestick is in a star position when its open gaps away from the previous candlestick. The "star" candlestick usually has a small body relative to the previous candlestick. If the gap is up, the star candlestick usually follows a white marubozu, while if the gap is down it usually follows a black marubozu.

The gap indicates that momentum has carried over to the next day but was mostly absorbed resulting in the formation of a small body. In effect, there is a close balance between buying and selling pressures. There are different types of star positions that can indicate bullish or bearish reversals and will be discussed later in this chapter.

(2) **Harami position.** Harami, or inside range candlesticks, form when the Harami candlestick has a body within the range of the previous candlestick. The Harami candlestick has a body smaller than the one preceding it.

It is preferable but not required that the upper and lower tail of the Harami candlestick be within the body of the previous candlestick. There are several Harami patterns that can give bullish or bearish signals and will be discussed in the coming sections of this chapter.

Illustrations of the Harami and star positions are shown on page 295.

Candlestick Combinations

The most reliable predictions are made by using candlestick combination patterns. These patterns are in most cases made of three candlesticks: the current period's, the last period's and the next period's, also referred to as the confirming candlestick. It is important to become proficient at recognizing such combinations if you expect to successfully predict future price trends.

In this section I will discuss the most prominent candlestick combinations.

Bullish Engulfing Pattern

This pattern usually occurs after a decline and indicates a possible reversal. The first candlestick is black indicating the continuation of the decline. The second candlestick is white with an open below the close of the first and a close above the first candlestick's open. The body of the second candlestick is hence larger than the first and completely engulfs it.

The first black candlestick indicates that sellers were still in control. This carried to the open of the next period with a slight gap down. The sellers, however, weakened throughout the period and buyers stepped in taking control by the end of the trading session. The buyers were so strong that the closing price exceeded the open of the previous session. This pattern is most reliable when used

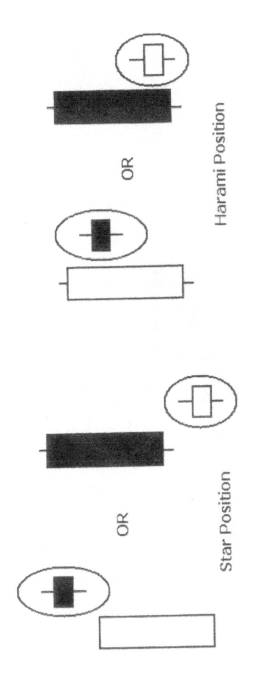

Star Position

OR

Harami Position

OR

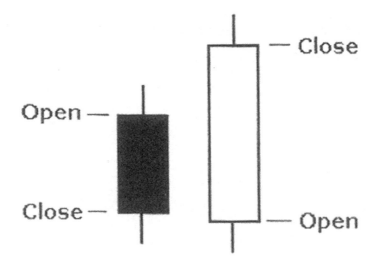

Bullish Engulfing Pattern

after a strong decline and in combination with oversold technical indicators such as MACD and stochastics.

The bullish engulfing pattern is shown on page 296.

Piercing Candlestick Pattern

This pattern is also a bullish reversal pattern not as strong as the engulfing pattern. This is why in this case a confirming candlestick is also needed. As with the engulfing pattern, the first candlestick is black indicating a continuation of the decline. The second candlestick is white with an open below the first and a close above the mid-point of the first. This is where the difference between the piercing and engulfing pattern lies. In this case the buying pressure was not strong enough to move the price above the open of the first candlestick. The third or confirming candlestick can be in the form of a white marubozu or a gap up.

A schematic of the bullish piercing pattern is shown on page 298.

Bullish Harami

In this pattern the second candlestick is in a Harami position which implies that it falls within the range of the first candlestick. The second candlestick has a small body relative to the first and can even be a Doji or a spinning top. In fact, the smaller the body of the second candlestick, the more bullish the pattern is. A Doji or a spinning top indicates a very high possibility of a reversal.

Of the four possible Harami combinations shown on page 299, the most bullish combinations **after a decline** are the black/black or black/white Harami. The first black candlestick indicates that the sellers are in control and were quite aggressive. The small body of the second candlestick indicates that the sellers were unable to push the price lower, and a fight between buyers and sellers ensued resulting in close to a draw. This is then resolved by a confirming white marubozu or a gap up to assert the reversal.

White/ black and white/white combinations are the most bullish signals. The first white candlestick indicates buying pressure during

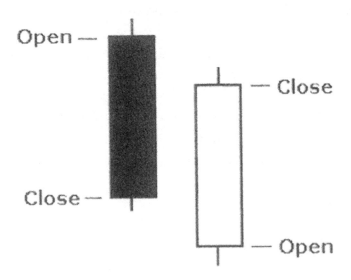

Open —

Close —

— Close

— Open

Piercing Pattern

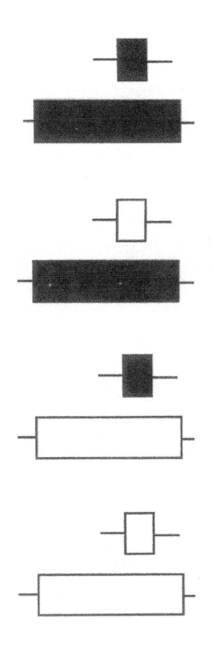

Possible Harami Combinations

the period. This is what you expect in a continuation pattern after a reversal has been confirmed. The second small bodied candlestick signifies consolidation before further uptrend takes place.

Three White Soldiers

This type of pattern usually occurs when a short squeeze is taking place. It is formed by three white Marubozu candlesticks in a row indicating that buying pressures have become extremely high.

The importance of this pattern is in its ability to predict possible break of resistance after the start of a reversal. If the three candlesticks have equal or increasing ranges, then a break of resistance is very likely. If, on the other hand, the range of the candlesticks is decreasing, this implies that buyers are becoming less aggressive and resistance may hold. This is especially true if the stock has already made a significant advance, in which case caution should be the order of the day.

A schematic of this pattern is shown on page 301.

Bullish Morning Star

This pattern usually appears after a downtrend and indicates a possible reversal. The first candlestick is a black Marubozu in the direction of the trend, while the third or confirming candlestick is a white Marubozu in the opposite direction of the trend. The middle candlestick is a Doji or spinning top. This indicates that after sellers were in control in the first period and at the open of the second period, they were unable to push the price lower. Buyers came in and put up enough of a fight to be able to push up the price near or above the close of the first day. The small-bodied middle candlestick indicates a standoff between buyers and sellers which is then resolved by the last confirming white candlestick.

Notice that the candlestick in the star position has part of its tail within the range of the first. This is what is known as the star position.

An illustration of the Bullish Morning Star is shown on page 302.

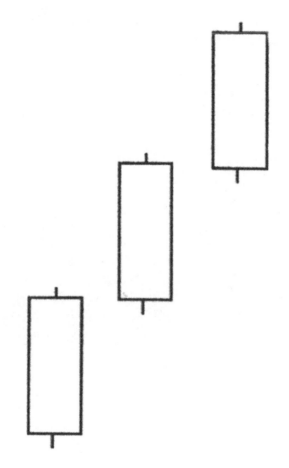

Three White Soldiers

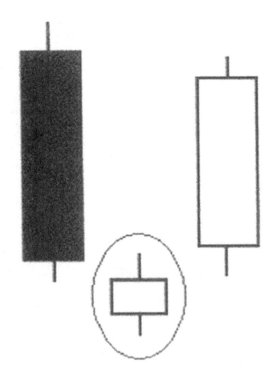

Morning Star

Bullish Abandoned Baby

This pattern is mostly similar to the bullish morning star, except that the middle Doji or spinning top gaps away from both the first and the last candlesticks.

The gap between the first and the middle candlestick indicates that significant selling pressure carries over to the next period. The small body of the second candlestick implies that those pressures were absorbed as buyers started stepping in. Reversal is then confirmed by the third white candlestick.

The diagram on page 304 shows a bullish abandoned baby.

Bearish Engulfing Pattern

This pattern usually occurs after an advance and indicates possible reversal. The first candlestick is white indicating a continuation of the advance. The second candlestick is black with an open above the close of the first and a close below the open of the first.

The body of the second candlestick is thus larger than the first and thus completely engulfs it.

The first white candlestick indicates that buyers were in control. This carried to the open of the next period with a small gap up. Buyers, however, weakened throughout the period, and sellers stepped in taking control by the end of the trading session. The sellers were so prevalent that the closing price was below the open of the prior period.

This pattern is most reliable when used after a strong advance and in combination with overbought technical indicators such as MACD and stochastics.

An illustration of the Bearish engulfing pattern is given on page 305.

Dark Cloud

This is a bearish reversal pattern not as strong as the engulfing pattern. This is why it is essential to have a confirming candlestick before action is taken. As with the engulfing pattern, the first candle-

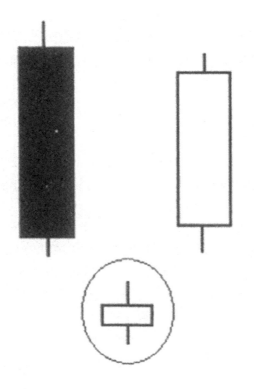

Bullish Abandoned
Baby

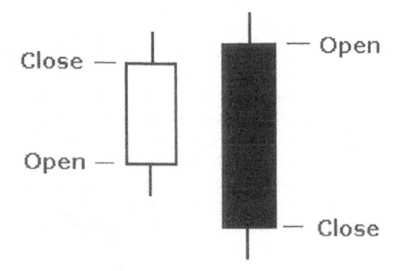

Close —

Open —

— Open

— Close

Bearish Engulfing Pattern

stick is white indicating the continuation of the advance. The second candlestick is black with an open above the close of the first and a close below the mid-range of the first. In this case the selling pressure was not strong enough to move the price below the open of the first candlestick. The third or confirming candlestick can be in the form of a gap down or a black Marubozu.

An illustration of this pattern is shown on page 307.

Bearish Harami

In a similar manner to the bullish Harami, the second candlestick falls within the range of the first. Also the second candlestick has a small body such as a Doji or spinning top.

Of the four possible Harami combinations shown on page 308, the most bearish is the white/black or white/white Harami. The appearance of this pattern after *an uptrend* can signal a possible downtrend reversal. The first white candlestick shows that buyers are still in control. The small body of the second candlestick combined with a slight down gap indicates a control shift from buyers to sellers with a struggle taking place. A confirmation in the next period usually comes in the form of a black Marubozu.

Black/white and black/black Harami combinations are the most bearish as continuation patterns. The first black candlestick indicates that strong selling pressures persisted during the period. The small body of the second candlestick signifies consolidation before a continuation of the trend.

Three Black Crows

This type of pattern usually occurs when a long squeeze is taking place. This is a situation where the stock shows deteriorating technical indicators with a low level of short interest indicating little fuel for further advance. This pattern is formed by three black Marubozu candlesticks in a row indicating that selling has become urgent.

The importance of this pattern lies in its ability to predict pos-

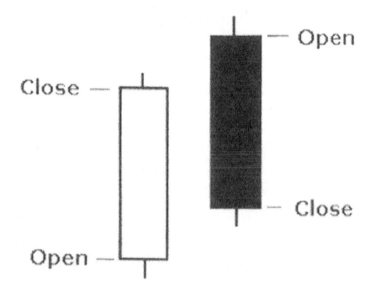

Dark Cloud Cover

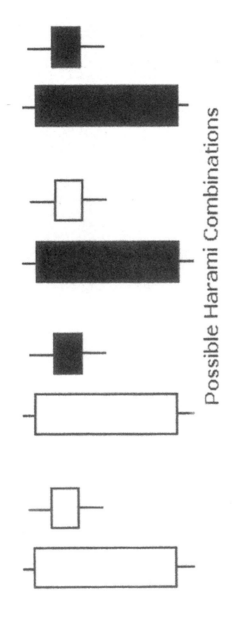

Possible Harami Combinations

sible break of support after the start of a down reversal. If the three candlesticks have equal or increasing ranges, then the break is very likely. If, on the other hand, the range of the candlesticks is decreasing, this implies that the sellers are losing momentum and the support may hold. This is especially the case if the stock has made a major decline. In this case a trader should exercise caution if a short position is in place.

A diagram of the three black crows is shown on page 310.

Bearish Evening Star

This pattern appears after an uptrend and is usually an indication of a downward reversal.

The first candlestick is a white Marubozu in the direction of the trend, while the third or confirming candlestick is a black Marubozu in the opposite direction of the trend. The middle candlestick is a Doji or a spinning top. This indicates that after buyers were in control in the first period and the beginning of the second, they were unable to sustain the advance. Sellers came in and were able to push the price near or below the close of the first day. The narrow range middle candlestick indicates that a fight for control between buyers and sellers ensued which was then resolved by sellers taking control as evidenced by the appearance of a black Marubozu.

Notice that the middle candlestick has part of its tail within the range of the first. This is what is known as a star position.

An illustration of the Bearish evening star pattern is shown on page 311.

Bearish Abandoned Baby

This pattern is similar to the bearish evening star except that the middle Doji or spinning top candlestick gaps away from both the first and last candlesticks.

The gap between the first and second candlesticks indicates that buying pressure carried over to the next period. The small body of the second candlestick indicates that buying pressures were ab-

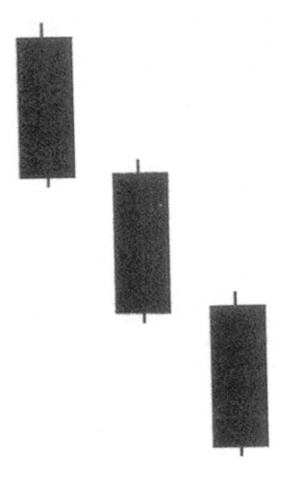

Three Black Crows

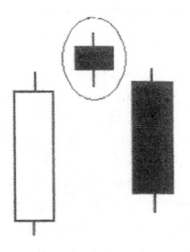

Evening Star

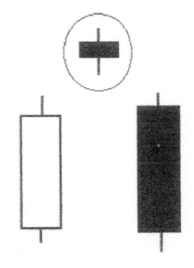

Bearish Abandoned Baby

sorbed and sellers started stepping in. Reversal is then confirmed by the third black candlestick.

A diagram of the Bearish abandoned baby is shown on page 311.

Practical Applications

As I mentioned in the beginning of this chapter, candlestick charts are most effective in predicting sudden reversals when combined with other technical indicators. It is important to keep in mind that your success in the market is highly dependent on your ability to utilize the random information the market generates in an effective way. Specifically, this refers to the type of indicators you should use and when to use them.

My trading experience has shown that the most profitable technical indicators to use in conjunction with candlestick charts are Stochastics and Moving Average convergence divergence or MACD. A sudden upward reversal is most likely to take place when the presence of a specific candlestick pattern is reinforced by an over-sold MACD <u>and</u> Stochastics. On the other hand a downward reversal is likely to occur when the candlestick pattern is accompanied by an overbought MACD **and** stochastics. In these situation the reversal is likely to continue for an enough time to result in a good profit.

In summary, look for a sudden reversal when the following conditions are in place:

(1) The stock is in a clear uptrend or downtrend.

(2) A candlestick pattern signifying a potential reversal appears

(3) Both MACD and stochastics are oversold. For the purpose of Candlestick signals, an oversold stochastics is defined as crossing over near the 20 line while an oversold MACD is defined crossing over near or below the zero line.

An overbought stochastics is a cross-over near the 80 line while an overbought MACD is a cross-over above or near the 0.1 point.

The use of these trading signals is best illustrated in real life examples.

Example 1 (MKTY)

Point **1** on the chart page 314 shows a bullish Harami with a confirming white candlestick and both MACD and stochastics highly oversold indicating an imminent reversal.

Point **2** shows a bullish engulfing pattern, however in this case the stochastics at point **B** is at 50 and not considered oversold. If you have not entered a position at point **1** you should not enter the stock based on these indicators alone.

ALERT: Even though point **2** preceded a major move, do not base your decision in such cases on candlestick charts alone since in many cases when both MACD and stochastics are not oversold an uptrend may not be sustainable as seen in other examples.

Point **3** shows a bearish Harami followed by a shooting star, with both MACD and Stochastics highly overbought, indicating a possible down reversal. This is, in fact, what happens, and the stock moved back to $1.80.

Point **4** shows a possible reversal with the appearance of a bullish Harami; however, the MACD has shown no cross-over yet. It is thus wise to wait for this to happen before taking action.

Example 2: Stem Cells (STEM)

Point **1** on the chart page 316 shows a gravestone doji followed by a white Marubozu in combination with highly oversold stochastics and MACD at points **A** and **a**. This is a definite indication of an upward reversal.

Point **3** shows a hanging man followed by a bearish Marubozu with both stochastics and MACD highly overbought as seen at points **C** and **c**. This results in a downward reversal as expected.

Note that points **2** and **4** should not be traded using candlesticks alone. At point **2** the MACD is highly oversold at point **b**, but the stochastics is highly overbought at point **B**. Even though the stock did move higher, an entry based on candlesticks alone would have violated our entry rules.

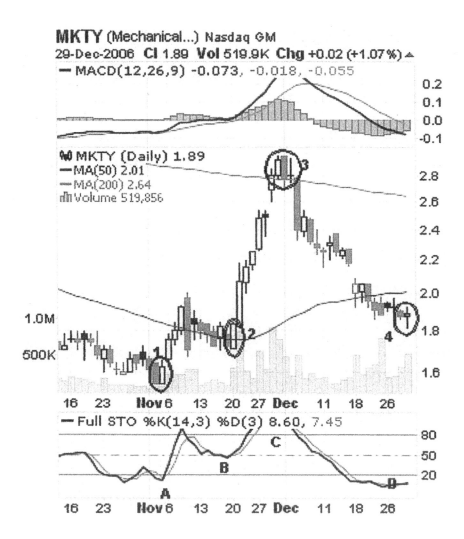

MKTY (Mechanical...) Nasdaq GM
29-Dec-2006 Cl 1.89 Vol 519.9K Chg +0.02 (+1.07%) ▲
— MACD(12,26,9) -0.073, -0.018, -0.055

0.2
0.1
0.0
-0.1

W MKTY (Daily) 1.89
—MA(50) 2.01
—MA(200) 2.64
Volume 519,856

2.8
2.6
2.4
2.2
2.0
1.8
1.6

1.0M
500K

16   23   **Nov** 6   13   20   27   **Dec**   11   18   26

— Full STO %K(14,3) %D(3) 8.60, 7.45

80
50
20

16   23   **Nov** 6   13   20   27   **Dec**   11   18   26

Point **4** shows a bullish reversal candlestick pattern with stochastics oversold at point **D** but the MACD is still overbought at point **d**. In this case not taking action was the right decision since the stock continued its downtrend after a slight move up.

ALERT: Points **2** and **4** clearly illustrate the danger of not following the rule that **both** MACD and stochastics should be oversold when trading an up reversal. Note that we were wrong at point **2** but right at point **4**. Trading is a game of probabilities, and our goal is to enter the high probability trades and not take 50/50 gambles.

At point **5** a bullish Harami with an engulfing white candlestick appear with both stochastics and MACD highly oversold at points **E** and **e**. This is followed by an up reversal as expected.

Example 3:   Sun Healthcare (SUNH)

Point **2** seen on the chart page 317 shows a bullish engulfing pattern with highly oversold stochastics at point **A** and MACD near the zero line. This indicates a likely reversal, and the stock moves from $10 to $13.

Point **1** shows a doji followed by a bearish engulfing pattern with both MACD and stochastics highly overbought. As expected a downward reversal quickly takes place.

At point **3** a bullish engulfing Harami appears (bullish Harami followed by a bullish engulfing pattern), in combination with highly oversold stochastics and MACD, confirms reversal and moves the stock back from $10 to $13.

Example 4: Frontier Airlines (FRNT)

Point **1** on the chart page 318 shows a bearish piercing pattern (a higher open but a close below the mid-point of the previous period). With both stochastics and MACD overbought at points **A** and **a** indicating a downward reversal. This results in a drop from $8.75 to $7.00.

Point **2** is a classic abandoned baby pattern, where a gap up

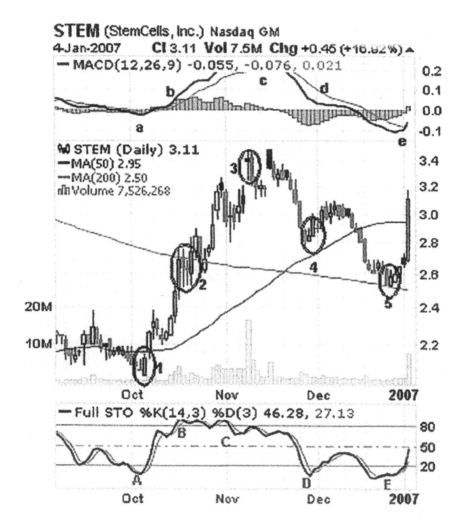

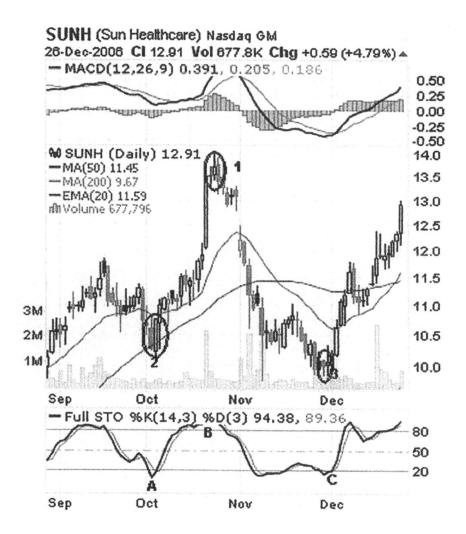

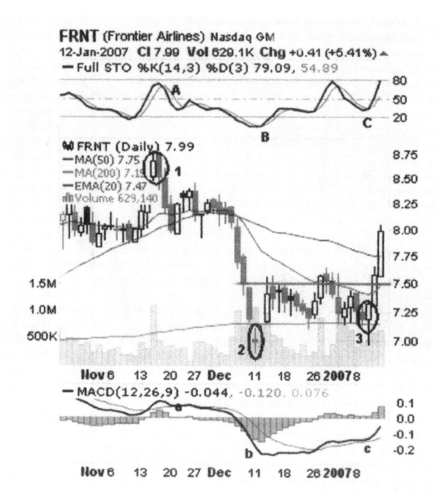

occurs confirming the reversal. In this case a Doji follows the abandoned baby before the confirming white Marubozu appears. As can be seen both stochastics and MACD are oversold at points **B** and **b.** This indicates a pending upward reversal.

Point **3** is a re-test of the low at **2** on less volume indicating the formation of a double bottom. This is also accompanied by a bullish engulfing pattern and oversold stochastics and MACD at points **C** and **c.**

ALERT: When trading, keep in mind the **Rule of Threes** mentioned earlier in the book. Notice between points **1** and **3** the high volume failed attempt to break the resistance line. This usually indicates that the third or next attempt is likely to be successful.

Example 5: US Concrete (RMIX)

Look at the chart page 321. Can you spot the tradeable reversal points using candlestick charts in combination with stochastics and MACD? If you guessed points **1**, **2** and **3** but not **4**, you guessed right.

Points **1** and **2** show oversold stochastics at points **A** and **B**, as well as oversold MACD at points **a** and **b.** Point **1** shows a bullish Harami while point **2** sports a bullish engulfing pattern. Point **2** acts as a retest of the bottom at point **1.**

At point **3** we can see a bearish engulfing pattern with both stochastics and MACD overbought at points **C** and **c** signaling a down reversal.

Point **4** shows an overbought MACD at point **d** but an oversold stochastics at point **D.** It is thus advisable not to take the trade based on these indicators alone. In fact, this stock is highly volatile on daily basis so any trader with longer time frame than few days (swing trader) should examine the weekly chart.

Final Word

The indicators in this chapter are to be used in cases where no discernible chart pattern is recognized. In most cases this happens with highly volatile stocks with V-type reversals. These type of stocks are most useful for swing trading with a time frame of few days. Keep in mind that as a trader you are likely to be subconsciously biased to your feeling about a stock. If you are bullish, you tend to see only positive signals, and if you are bearish, you tend to see only negative signals. It is critical to resist the urge to take a trade when only one of the indicators, stochastics and MACD are oversold or overbought. Will you miss some good trades? Of course, you will, but the trades you do enter will be overwhelmingly profitable.

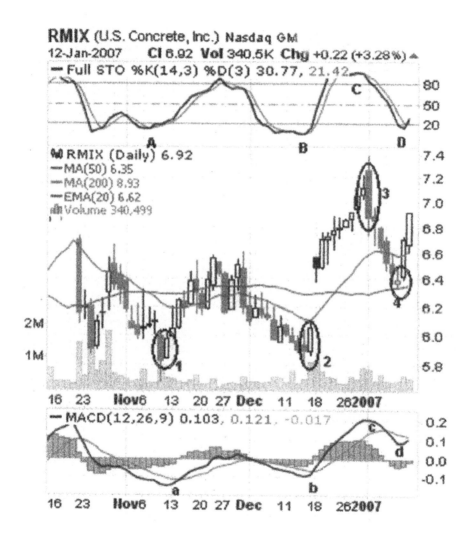

RMIX (U.S. Concrete, Inc.) Nasdaq GM

12-Jan-2007   Cl 6.92 Vol 340.5K Chg +0.22 (+3.28%) ▲

— Full STO %K(14,3) %D(3) 30.77, 21.42

80
60
20

A   B   D
                                                          C

⋈ RMIX (Daily) 6.92
— MA(50) 6.35   7.4
— MA(200) 8.93   7.2
— EMA(20) 6.62   7.0
▥ Volume 340,499

                                                    3
2M
                                                        4
1M   1   2

16   23   Nov6   13   20   27 Dec   11   18   262007

— MACD(12,26,9) 0.103, 0.121, -0.017   0.2
                                          c   0.1
                                            d   0.0
                                                       -0.1
              a   b

16   23   Nov6   13   20   27 Dec   11   18   262007

CHAPTER 18

Tricks of the Trade

IN THIS CHAPTER, I will discuss simple techniques that have proven effective in determining the short term direction of a stock as well as fine tuning entry and exit points. Some of these may be familiar while others may be new to you. These methods can be used in conjunction with chart patterns and technical indicators discussed previously to further improve your trading results.

When Is a Buy a "Low Risk" Buy?

Most investors look to buy at support levels or try to pick the bottom (52-week low), thinking that this will offer a sure way to profits. While these approaches work sometimes, who's to say that the support will not fail or the stock will not break the 52-week lows and establish new lows. For this reason it is important to refine your skills in identifying low risk opportunities.

My experience has shown that the safest and lowest risk opportunity offering a high profit potential is buying a stock on a retracement from a major up move. This major upswing demonstrates that the stock intends to move higher, while the retracement is just a pause to catch its breath before the move continues. Such retracements are evident in chart patterns as falling wedges, bull flags and pennants.

A medieval mathematician named Fibbonaci has come up with the most well-known and enduring retracement factor of 0.618. As an example, let us say that a stock makes a move from $5 to $9 after which a pullback starts taking place. To calculate the retracement number, multiply the magnitude of the move ($9 - $5 = $4) by 0.618 giving a result of $2.47 rounded to $2.5. You then subtract $2.5 from $9 to give a value of $6.5.

This implies that the stock should start to find support as it gets close to that price. This is a safe trade since you will buy as support is reached near this number and place a mental stop (to be discussed in chapter 19) just below it to limit your risk.

It is important to recognize that many stops are placed around the 0.618 pullback number. It is thus essential to place your stop below that to avoid being sold out due to stops being run. In addition, the stock may approach the 0.618 retracement but never actually reach it, in which case you will enter a position above the pullback number once support is established.

When and Where To Sell

Okay, so you found a stock that has retraced a recent major move and decided based on the analysis of chart patterns and technical indicators to enter a position. You then waited for support while approaching the 0.618 retracement number and entered a position slightly above it. How then do you decide when and in what price vicinity to sell?

In my many years of trading, there is a technique I successfully used to decide an approximate exit time and price. Of course, this method will not determine the exact high for the stock, but will give you an approximate price to get out at. You will then decide the exact time and price of exit based on other chart and technical indicators as this price is approached.

First you will have to measure the price difference between the low of the move to the high of the move. Say a stock moved from $3 to $5.50, the difference is $2.50 which is considered the first phase of the move.

As discussed previously, we will then wait for prices to consolidate after a pullback where we enter our position. Let us assume in this case that consolidation took place slightly above the 0.618 retracement number or $4.00.

An estimate of the sell point is obtained by adding the value of the move in the first phase to the entry price at consolidation. This will give us a sell price near $2.50 + $4.00 = $6.50.

To obtain the time of sale you will need first to determine the number of days it took for the first leg to be complete. Let us assume that the above stock moved from $3 to $5.50 in seven trading days. Next you will need to wait for a breakout of the consolidation phase that took place after the pullback. When the breakout occurs, that is considered day 1. You will then count the number of days in the first leg, resulting in a sell date approximately eight days after breakout of consolidation.

ALERT: It is important to stress that these numbers are not meant to be exact. If things were so simple, everyone will get rich trading. The purpose here is to be watching carefully for an exit as the stock gets closer to the price and time of sale. You can then decide based on the techniques learned in this book the exact time and price at which to exit.

How To Play Momentum

Many traders get burned playing momentum trades because they wait for the move to occur before taking a position. The trick here is to anticipate the move and take action before the stock actually takes off. Unfortunately, this is easier said than done since it is psychologically very difficult to get into a stock on its way down to 52-week lows or a new low.

To make a successful momentum play, you need to look for behavior that is not expected. An example will be a sudden intraday reversal after testing new lows and closing at the top of the day's range. This is what is called a key reversal day and predicts higher prices ahead.

Another indication of a momentum play is a stock that is moving down quickly. In this case you should watch the stock and look for a decrease in volume in conjunction with a slower rate of descent. Since the stock is likely to experience a consolidation period, you should look for a saucer-type pattern within this area as prices begin to move above support. Your entry should be within the consolidation period before volume picks up and a breakout occurs.

Yet another momentum play is what is known as "climactic volume play." In this case the stock is moving down on low volume when suddenly a pickup in volume occurs with a steep drop takes place. This behavior, when occurring at the end of a trend, indicates panic selling where all the weak hands have been flushed out. A reversal the next day indicates a clear momentum play since the stock is likely to bounce quickly.

ALERT: It is important that the "climactic volume" occurs close to the end of a downtrend. If the stock was moving up and a steep drop on heavy volume takes place, this is an indication of further significant downside. On the other hand, if the stock has been moving down and is getting near support or the 0.618 pullback number and a sudden drop on high volume occurs, this is a likely momentum play.

When you enter a momentum play, you should be aware of the "rule of three" that applies in many areas of the market. Most momentum moves are likely to last three days before a pullback. If you are trading short term, you want to watch carefully for a possible exit on the third day.

When Is a Bottom a "Real Bottom"?

Contrarian investing is based on the premise that the majority is always wrong at major turns. This applies to the top as well as the bottom of the market. In any market you will have both buyers and sellers; however, at inflection points the smart money takes the contrarian approach. At the bottom aggressive selling or distribution is usually met by intelligent accumulation.

You are surely familiar with the saying, "Do not catch a falling knife," indicating that trying to find the bottom is a fool's game since you can never be sure where the bottom is. While this may be true in some cases, there are signs that you can look for that signal a bottom and pending reversal:

Selling Climax: As a stock approaches a bottom, look for an orderly low volume drop to give away to heavy volume capitulation. This signals that most investors have given up in the stock and all the weak hands have sold. The bottom is reached when there is a lack of follow-through to the downside in the next few days.

Key Reversal Pattern: This is a pattern where a sell-off climax does not occur but rather a downtrend on low volume possibly in the earlier part of the day. This is followed by a more decisive move up in price on moderate volume later in the day.

When looking for this pattern, you need to check that last trades and not depend on the closing price. There is a trick called "last minute markdown" where a stock trades higher indicating key reversal, until the last tick when a few hundred shares are traded out of range to the downside. The market professionals know that the average investor is busy during the day and checks only closing prices. Seeing their stock going further down, they are likely to place a market order to sell the next day.

Rule of Three

You will usually observe multiple tests of the low before a reversal takes place. Based on experience, I have noticed that if the low is not broken after three attempts the stock is ready to reverse. Be sure to check if the low is penetrated on or before the third attempt; if not, the trend is likely to be up.

Price Rejection: If you are a trader who can watch the market intraday, you will observe that a stock is not likely to stay at the top or bottom more than a few seconds. This is essentially a price that is reached quickly and then "rejected." Price rejection usually occurs near stops whereby when the stock reaches that area and the stops are run, the stock spikes up or down to take out stops and then retreats.

Long-tailed candlesticks or price bars: The long tail can be either towards the top or bottom based on whether the stock is reversing from an upside or a downside. The long tail is in essence a price rejection and is best seen using candlestick charts. This phenomenon is characterized by a Doji, hammer, shooting star, hanging man or inverted hammer in candlestick jargon. Detailed discussions of candlesticks is beyond the scope of this book. If you are interested in more details, please refer to books by Nisson.

Measuring Short Term Strength

In Chapter 14 we have discussed CD (Convergence/Divergence) charts to predict the longer term strength of a stock. I strongly recommend that long term holders of stocks use these techniques to evaluate their holdings on a weekly basis. My experience has shown that it is worth the small amount of time you spend once a week to construct the charts.

In my trading experience, I have found that the most reliable method for measuring the short term strength of a stock is the five-day oscillator. The oscillator generates numbers between zero and 100. Results between zero and 30 are bearish, 30 to 70 are neutral and above 70 are bullish.

Since the oscillator is based on a small number of data points, namely five days, it is a direct measure of the short term strength of the stock.

The formulas for the oscillator are as follows:

A = Highest price in 5 days — Open 5 days ago

B = Last day's close — lowest price in 5 days.

Oscillator = [(A+B)100] / [(highest price- lowest price)2]

We will use a real life example to illustrate the use of the five-day Oscillator. KongZhong (KONG) is a Chinese internet company that has gone from $5.50 to $8.00, subsequently pulling back to around $6.50. It then rallied to around $7.00 forming a bullish pennant resulting in a run to $8.30 on by October 31, 2006.

The data presented here starts with the formation of the pennant.

Date	Open	High	Low	Close
10/18/06	7	7.02	6.84	6.97
10/19/06	6.90	7.00	6.87	6.85
10/20/06	6.85	7.08	6.85	7.01
10/23/06	6.94	7.02	6.94	6.96
10/24/06	6.97	7.00	6.76	6.79
10/25/06	6.82	6.95	6.81	6.94
10/26/06	6.93	7.12	6.93	7.08
10/27/06	7.17	7.67	7.11	7.52
10/30/06	7.60	7.72	7.50	7.69
10/31/06	7.81	8.33	7.76	8.17
11/01/06	8.17	8.29	7.96	8.10

Let us say that the day of interest is 10/26/06. Calculation of the oscillator requires five days of data from 10/20/06 to 10/25/06 which are shown in the above table. If we perform the calculation as indicated in the formula:

A = 7.12 - 6.85 = 0.27

B = 7.08 - 6.76 = 0.32

Oscillator = (0.27 + 0.32) 100/(7.12 -6.76) 2 = 59/0.72 = 82%

As you can see, the reading is above 70 which is bullish, and as expected the stock moved higher in the next few days. In essence this acted as a confirmation of the bullish pennant that formed before the breakout.

We are also interested in knowing the speed and direction of the move. After experimenting with many techniques, I found that the three-day difference of the five-day oscillator gives the best forecast. The formula for this is as follows:

3 day difference = Value of the five-day oscillator today - value of oscillator 3 days ago.

A positive value of the three-day difference indicates positive momentum while a negative number indicates negative momentum. A large number indicates that a substantial move is likely to occur in the near future, the direction of which depends on whether the three-day difference is negative or positive.

A highly positive number decreasing in value as the days pass indicates that the rally is slowing down and the stock may be ready to consolidate or reverse direction.

We will illustrate the use of the three-day difference using the example we used for the five-day oscillator (KONG). Our starting day is 10/26/06 which indicates that we will need oscillator data three days before that or on 10/24/06. Remember that to calculate the oscillator for 10/24/06 we will need stock price data five days before that or starting 10/18/06. This is why the previous table on page 329 contains data since then.

We will start calculating the three-day difference on 10/26/06, or start day and continue as long as we are holding the stock. For illustration purposes, in this example we will do that until 11/01/06.

We will need to calculate the oscillator starting three days before 10/26/06 and then each day thereafter. The calculations are as follows:

Date: 10/24/2006
A = 7.08 -7 = 0.08
B = 6.79 - 6.76 = 0.03
Oscillator = (0.08 + 0.03)100/(7.08 - 6.76)2 = 17%

Date: 10/25/2006
A = 7.08 - 6.90 = 0.18
B = 6.94 - 6.76 = 0.18
Oscillator = (0.18 + 0.18)100/(7.08 - 6.76)2 = 56%

Date: 10/26/2006
Oscillator = 82% calculated previously

Date: 10/27/2006
A = 7.67 - 6.94 = 0.73
B = 7.52 - 6.76 = 0.76
Oscillator = (0.73 + 0.76)100/(7.67 - 6.76)2 = 82%

Date: 10/30/2006
A = 7.72 - 6.97 = 0.75
B = 7.67 - 6.76 = 0.91
Oscillator = (0.75 + 0.91)100/(7.72 - 6.76)2 = 86%

Date: 10/31/2006
A = 8.33 - 6.82 = 1.51
B = 8.17 - 6.81 = 1.36
Oscillator = (1.51+1.36)100/(8.33 - 6.81)2 = 94%

Date: 11/01/2006
A = 8.33 - 6.93 = 1.40
B = 8.10 - 6.93 = 1.17
Oscillator = (1.40 + 1.17)100/8.33 - 6.93)2 = 92%

Three-day oscillator difference calculations are then completed as follows:

Date	Five-day Oscillator	Three-day difference
10/24/06	17	
10/25/06	56	
10/26/06	82	82 - 17 = 65
10/27/06	82	82 - 56 = 26
10/30/06	86	86 - 82 = 4
10/31/06	94	94 - 82 = 12
11/01/06	92	92 - 88 = 4

On 10/26/2006, our first day of calculating the three-day differ-ence we get a highly positive number of 65. This tells us that the stock has a very positive momentum and is likely to move higher three days from now. In that period the stock moves from $7.08 to $7.69. On 10/27/2006 we get a reading of 29 which is still strong, and the stock moves to $ 8.17 three days later. In the next three days, however, the value drops significantly, indicating a slowdown in the upward momentum in the near future. At this point we should keep a close watch on the stock for possible exit.

While the five-day oscillator and three-day difference numbers give an indication of the short term trend, they do not give a mea-sure of strength on a specific day. It is well accepted in trading that a strong close on the day is usually a bullish indicator for a stock.

We can use a simple strength indicator to measure the strength of a stock on a specific day. The formula is as follows:

Strength = (close - low)100/(high - low)

This gives a number between 0 and 100 and is interpreted in a way similar to the oscillator. Numbers below 30 are bearish; be-tween 30 and 70 are neutral, and above 70 are bullish.

Looking at the previous example (KONG), the strength index on 10/26/2006 is 79%, while on 11/1/2006 it drops to 44% indicating a move from positive to neutral. This change in bullishness is also confirmed by the three-day difference reading.

Five-day oscillator combined with three-day difference readings are very valuable timing tools for option trades since they are short term trend indicators. For instance, if you have high but diminishing oscillator readings combined with three-day difference readings mov-ing from highly positive to neutral or negative, a short term correc-tion is likely to occur. In this case you would sell covered calls to cash in on the short correction and then buy the calls when the correction is over.

The decision whether to sell calls or exit the position will have to be based on the potential profit left if you were to hold on the stock. If you check the chart and the next resistance is close to the current trading price, it is better to exit. On the other hand, if the next resistance is quite a bit higher than the current price, selling covered calls may be the way to go.

If we were to examine the chart for KONG, once the stock closes firmly above $8.00, there is little resistance until $11.00. In this case selling covered calls will be the choice if you intend to hold on to the position. When I am trading short term, I usually exit the position unless the next resistance is at least 10% higher, in which case I will sell covered calls and then exit the stock near resistance.

It is critical if you are trading short term that you do not turn every stock into a long term hold just to make a few extra percentage points. Once in a while, if there is significant profit potential left, it is wise to sell covered calls to capture some cash while the stock is pulling back. In the majority of cases, however, it is advisable to free the cash to get into another trade.

ALERT: It is important to understand the trading purpose of each of these indicators. The five-day oscillator identifies the trend, the three-day difference points to how far the current trend is likely to go, while the strength indicator can be used to get an indication of a good entry point.

Buy and Sell Envelopes

Previously in this chapter, we learned a simple method to forecast sell targets by adding the first leg of a move to the consolidation price after retracement. In this section I will present a more reliable but less simple method using buy and sell envelopes to determine buy and sell targets for a stock.

Buy and sell envelopes are invaluable in forecasting buy and sell price ranges based on averaged numbers. These ranges are then averaged again to give a final buy and sell price target.

The **Buy envelope** is determined by the following four parameters:

P1B = Trend Buy Reaction Number

P2B = Yesterday's low

P3B = Last Day's low - Averaged last three buy below numbers

P4B = Last Days low - Averaged last three decline numbers

The **Sell Envelope** is determined by the four parameters below:

P1S = Trend Sell Reaction Number

P2S = Yesterday's high

P3S = Averaged last three buy above days + last day's high

P4S = Averaged last three rally numbers + last day's low.

We will now explain how each of the terms defining these parameters are calculated.

Trend Buy and Sell Reaction Numbers

This is a simple formula that has been around for years that in essence produces buy and sell numbers on a daily basis. These numbers are just another support and resistance values.

The formula is as follows:

A = (high + Low + Close)/3

TBX = Trend Buy Reaction Number = 2A - High

TSX = Trend Reaction Sell Number = 2A - Low

Buy Below Number

This is a simple formula measuring the difference between today's low and yesterday's low.

BBN = Today's low - Yesterday's low

Decline Number

This measures how much a stock fell on a certain day compared to the day before.

DN = Yesterday's high - Today's low.

Buy Above Number

The buy above number is the difference between the last two

high prices. This number can be positive or negative dependent on whether today's high is higher or lower than yesterday's.

BAN = Today's high - Yesterday's high

Rally Number

The rally number measures how far did a stock move today relative to yesterday

RN = Today's high - Yesterday's low.

The best way to illustrate the use of Buy and sell envelopes is using an actual example. We will use the same example used previously, i.e., (KONG) with four days of data from 10/26/06 to 10/31/06. Our task here is to predict buy and sell points for the November 1 and a couple of days thereafter.

Date	Open	High	Low	Close
10/26/06	6.93	7.12	6.93	7.08
10/27/06	7.17	7.67	7.11	7.52
10/30/06	7.60	7.72	7.50	7.69
10/31/06	7.81	8.33	7.76	8.17

We will calculate the first parameter for the buy envelope P1B using the trend buy reaction formula:

A = (8.33+ 7.76 + 8.17)/3 = 8.09

P1B = TBX = 2*8.09 - 8.33 = 7.85. $\underline{P1B = 7.85}$

P2B = Yesterday's low = 7.76 $\underline{P2B = 7.76}$

Note that our calculations are being made for 11/1/06 so yesterday is 10/31/06; hence the low for that day was used.

Now we need to calculate the last three buy below numbers and average them as follows:

BBN1 = day 2 low - day 1 low = 7.11 - 6.93 = 0.18

BBN2 = day 3 low - day 2 low = 7.50 - 7.11 = 0.39

BBN3 = day 4 low - day 3 low = 7.76 - 7.50 = 0.26

Averaging these three numbers (0.18 + .39 + 0.26) /3 = 0.28

We can now calculate the third buy envelope parameter:

P3B = day 4 low - average 3 day BBN numbers = 7.76 - 0.28 = 7.48. $\underline{P3B = 7.48}$

We still need the fourth parameter to define the buy envelope. To obtain this we will need to average the last three decline numbers:

DN1 = day 1 high - day 2 low = 7.12 - 7.11 = 0.01

DN2 = day 2 high - day 3 low = 7.67 - 7.50 = 0.17

DN3 = day 3 high - day 4 low = 7.72 - 7.76 = -0.04

Averaging the three numbers we get (0.01 + 0.17 - 0.04)/3 = 0.046

The fourth parameter can be calculated as:

P4B = day 4 low - averaged three-day DN numbers = 7.76 - 0.046 = 7.71. P4B = 7.71

Now we are ready to calculate the **Sell Envelope:**

The first sell envelope parameter P1S = TSX

Trend sell reaction number

P1S = TSX = 2*A - prior day's Low = 2* 8.09 - 7.76 = 8.42.

P1S = 8.42

P2S = Yesterday's high = 8.33   P2S = 8.33

Again you should remember that the calculations are made for the time period starting 11/1/06, so the prior day is 10/31/06.

To calculate the third parameter, we need to first find the buy above numbers and average them for the prior three days:

BAN 1 = day 2 high - day 1 high = 7.67 - 7.12 = 0.55

BAN 2 = day 3 high - day 2 high = 7.72 - 7.67 = 0.05

BAN 3 = day 4 high - day 3 high = 8.33 - 7.72 = 0.61

Averaging these numbers we get (0.55 + 0.05 + 0.61)/3 = 0.40

PS3 = 0.40 + last day's high (8.33) = 8.73   P3S = 8.73

To calculate the final sell envelope parameter we need to determine the rally numbers for the last three days and calculate the average:

RN1 = day 2 high - day 1 low = 7.67 - 6.93 = 0.74

RN2 = day 3 high - day 2 low = 7.72 - 7.11 = 0.61

RN3 = day 4 high - day 3 low = 8.33 - 7.50 = 0.83

We now calculate the average as (0.74 + 0.61 + 0.83)/3 = 0.72

P4S = Last day's low (7.76) + 0.72 = 8.48   P4S = 8.48

Buy Envelope	**Sell Envelope**
P1B = 7.85	P1S = 8.42
P2B = 7.76	P2S = 8.33
P3B = 7.48	P3S = 8.73
P4B = 7.71	P4S = 8.48

We now average these numbers to get a single buy and sell number.

PBav = (7.85+7.76+7.48+7.71) /4 = 7.70 = **Buy Number**

PSav = (8.42 + 8.33 + 8.73+8.48)/4 = 8.49 = **Sell Number**

Applying Buy and Sell Targets to Real trades

As I mentioned before, the concepts in this chapter should not be used to decide whether to buy a stock or not. This decision should be based on chart patterns and technical indicators. Once the decision is made to buy, you can use the concepts in this chapter to fine tune your entry, and exit prices.

Let us say that you used a scanning program to look for stocks that are reversing from a down trend on heavy volume. Your system alerted you to KONG at point **2** on the price chart on page 260.

Do you buy the stock immediately? NO. This kind of trading is for amateurs who buy at the high. What we will do is wait for a retracement to one of three levels:

(1) EMA 20

(2) Next support below

(3) Fibonacci 0.618 retracement.

We watch KONG the next few days and we notice the formation of a bullish pennant clearly seen on the chart page 260. Since the stock is trading below the EMA 20, this cannot be used as a potential entry point. So our decision is limited to either the support below or the Fibonacci retracement.

A fall to the next support at $6.75 will result in breaking the bullish pennant formation which is not what we want to see, since if this happens it is likely the stock may go lower.

The Fibonacci retracement can be calculated as follows:
(price at point 2 - price at point 1) 0.618 = (7.25 - 6.50) 0.618 = 0.46

We can then estimate the retracement price at 7.25 - 0.46 = 6.79.

We will now wait to be sure that this price holds before entering a position. For the purpose of illustration let us say we wanted to be certain and waited to enter a position at a price of $7.00.

Our next step is to wait for a breakout from the pennant formation, which in this case happened rather quickly. The stock broke out of the formation on 7/26/06 and closed at $7.08.

We can now estimate the sell time and price using the simple method described early in this chapter.

Range of first leg = price at point 2 - price at point 1 = 7.25 - 6.50 = 0.75

Initial sell target: = 7.08 + 0.75 = 7.82.

To estimate the time of sale, we will add the number of days it took the stock to move from point 1 to point 2, which in this case was three days, to the day after the breakout.

Since the breakout occurred on 10/26/06, the sell date will be three days after that at a price of around $ 7.82.

After three days the stock closes above $8 but eventually pulls back near our sell target. This indicates that the stock is likely to go higher since our sell target has become support. Our next step is to re-calculate the next possible sell target.

If the stock were to fail in reaching the sell target or pulled back below it, we should seriously consider exiting the position, especially if that happens to be close to resistance. In this case the stock did not breach our sell point on the pullback so we hold the position and re-calculate the exit point.

ALERT 1: An important rule in the market is the Rule of Threes. This rule indicates:

(1) A stock is likely to rally for three days after a breakout from a consolidation pattern before pulling back.

(2) A stock should break out of a consolidation pattern after no more than three attempts.

Although these rules do not hold true 100 % of the time, you will be surprised how often they do.

ALERT 2: In this example it just happens that the time for the first leg took three days. If we had said five days for the move, the Rule of Threes will still apply. This implies that we would expect a pull-back after three days before continuation of the uptrend.

Notice that KONG pulls back after three days and consolidates before continuing the move.

To illustrate the use of Buy and Sell Envelopes, we will use buy and sell targets calculated using this method. In the last section based on data between 10/26 and 10/31 we calculated the sell target at $8.49 and the buy target at $7.70 for KONG. Since we already hold the stock and are trying to decide when to sell, the sell price carries more interest, although the buy price is still significant in that it establishes support.

Based on the above results, we expect the stock to reach the sell target within few trading days.

The question is how many days should we allow before we calculate the number again or decide to sell. Based on my experience, I will give the stock one week or five trading days to reach the sell target. I will follow these guidelines:
(1) If the stock fails to close above the sell price by the end of this period, I will exit the position.
(2) If the stock moves above the sell target intraday but closes below it, I would exit the position.
(3) If the stock closes below the buy number in any of the five trading days, I will exit the position the next day.
(4) If the stock is able to close above the sell number within the five trading days, I will recalculate the sell target.

Another important fact to pay attention to is that the sell number of the first leg is $7.82, while the buy number of the second leg is

$7.70. These numbers are remarkably close considering we used two different methods to calculate them. This is in a sense telling us that the sell number of the first leg has turned into support which is the buy number for the second leg. This is why we will exit if the stock closes below the buy number of the second leg as indicated in point (4).

The next week of data for KONG is as follows

Date	Open	High	Low	Close
11/1/06	8.17	8.29	7.96	8.10
11/2/06	8.15	8.15	7.80	7.87
11/3/06	8.05	8.05	7.67	8.01
11/6/06	7.95	8.48	7.95	8.33
11/7/06	8.17	9.23	8.10	8.27

Notice that the high on 11/6/06 was quite close to the sell number. In addition, the stock broke the sell number on 11/7/06 but failed to close above it.

It is common that the sell number is reached intraday. For this reason, one strategy I use successfully is to place a limit order to sell at or close to the high of the sell envelope, in this case around $8.73, for five trading days. In this case the trade would have been executed on 11/7/06, resulting in around 25% profit in two weeks.

Studying the chart for KONG, we see that there is no significant resistance until $11.00. It is thus likely in due time that the stock will reach that price. So why did we decide to sell?

Remember that the buy and sell numbers are short term targets and are good only for few days. If you are intending to keep the stock longer, you will need to calculate these numbers every five days or so to get new buy and sell targets. For long holding periods it is advisable to use CD charts described in chapter 14.

In the specific case of KONG, my decision would have been to sell for several reasons: (1) The intraday move to $9.23 failed to result in a close above the sell number. (2) This comes after three up days, and according to the rule of threes a likely correction will occur. (3) This also happened on a Monday which is a strong day for the market and is likely to be followed by a pullback on Tuesday which is a weaker day (explained in next section). The main reason for selling is that this stock was bought for my short term trading account. Having achieved 25% profit in a couple of weeks and with overwhelming sell signals short term, this is what should be done to stay true to my strategy.

Weekly Cycles

You probably heard the saying, "Buy in October and sell in May and go away." This refers to the seasonality of the market, indicating weakness starting the end of summer into October and subsequent strength into the new year. With the advent of the internet, the cycle has shortened significantly in recent years where selling is recommended in late February or March.

During my trading years, I have wondered whether there is a mini-cycle within the trading week. Are there any days of the week that are more often buy days than sell days? What is the best day to buy? Are there discernible intra-week trends based on the prior day's strength? And so on.

While it is not wise to generalize and make blanket predictions, I have found through my years of trading experience the following to be more often true than not:

Mondays are the strongest day of the week, especially after a weak Friday.

Tuesdays are sell days after a strong Monday. They are usually characterized by a choppy morning followed by a stronger afternoon. So if you are planning to sell on Tuesday, you are likely to get a better price later in the day. Tuesday mornings are considered a buy day after weak Mondays.

Wednesdays are usually choppy with no clear direction.

Thursdays are usually buy days, especially later in the day when they exhibit weakness. Thus, if you have decided on a stock to buy, Thursday may be a good day to do so.

Fridays usually have a minor downward bias in the morning with a stronger finish.

While these statements seem quite general, they are much more useful when combined with strength index and five-day oscillator readings.

In general terms, you will want to buy a stock on Monday if it was weak the previous Friday. You want to avoid buying a stock on Tuesday if Monday was a strong day. Tuesday will be a good buying day if on Monday the stock shows a five-day oscillator reading and strength index below 40. The reason for this is that you want to buy when the stock is weak and getting stronger, not at the top when the oscillator is showing a high reading and the only way to go is down.

With the exception of Monday which is the most profitable day for stocks, you should only buy on other days if the five-day oscillator is below 40. Friday is an exception where you will want to buy even if the five-day oscillator is above 40 in anticipation of a strong Monday. This is especially true if the general market index in which the stock trades was weak.

We will use the previous example (KONG) again to demonstrate how the use of the strength index and five-day oscillator in conjunction with weekly cycles can help in making buy decisions.

Day of the Week	Five-Day Oscillator	One-Day Strength Index
Monday (10/23/06)	32	25
Tuesday (10/24/06)	17	13
Wednesday (10/25/06)	56	92
Thursday (10/26/06)	82	78
Friday (10/27/06)	82	73
Monday (10/30/06)	86	86
Tuesday (10/31/06)	94	72
Wednesday (11/01/06)	92	42

Notice that the five-day oscillator was in the 30% range on Monday and significantly weaker on Tuesday. Remember that by looking at the chart for KONG page 260. We have already determined that the stock is ready to move higher due to the formation of a bullish pennant and the decision now is when rather than whether to buy. The low oscillator readings on Monday combined with a low strength index of 25% and an even lower oscillator reading of 17 on Tuesday give us a solid buying opportunity.

Contrast this situation with Monday 10/30/06 when the five-day oscillator reading was 86 and the strength index 86. This was certainly not a good buying opportunity. Remember that you want to buy when the stock is weak and getting stronger, not the other way around.

ALERT: This statement may seem in contradiction with what we stated before indicating that readings above 70 were bullish, but below 30 were bearish. Remember, if you are holding a stock, you would want to keep it as long as the readings are bullish and look into selling as they turn bearish. In this case, however, we are deciding when to buy. Buying when the readings are bearish and moving higher gives a much better profit opportunity since you are entering at the start of a trend.

Notice that the strength index from 10/30 to 11/01 started weakening, which in combination with high oscillator readings indicates that the stock is ready for a correction, not exactly a good time to buy.

A word regarding Friday, 10/27/06, this would have been a good buy day even with a high oscillator number since the Nasdaq (the index that Kong trades in was weak). This is an implication that a strong Monday for the index is likely and KONG is likely to carry its strength into Monday.

ALERT: The decision to buy should have already been made using chart patterns and other technical indicators. Using the day of the week strategy is only to pinpoint which is a better buy day. Do not make a decision to buy a stock on this strategy alone.

Final Word

It may seem that there are quite a few calculations to arrive at the indicators in this chapter. These calculations are repetitive and simple and can be easily programmed into an excel spread sheet. I recommend that you take the time to do this since you can then easily determine the trend of your stock, as well as approximate entry and exit points just by inputting price data into the spread-sheet.

CHAPTER 19

Risk Control and Money Management

THERE ARE four important elements to trading success. They are:
- (1) Psychological factors
- (2) Money Management
- (3) Risk Control
- (4) Trading System

Trader Psychology

It is common for people to be judgmental about everything. As an example, the sea may just be a large body of water for one person, but a breathtaking natural view where you can watch the sunset for another. It is common that past experiences affect future action; consequently, if you had a bad experience swimming or sailing in the ocean, you will view it in a negative or neutral light. On the other hand, if your memory of the ocean is of a romantic cruise that went perfectly, you are more likely to see only the positives. The same applies to trading; if your past experiences were bad in the market, fear and hesitation will control your actions. You will wait for a sure thing before you pull the trigger missing many opportunities, while sometimes you may just be watching unable to trade at all.

My experience has shown that usually if a trade appears as a "sure winner," it is likely to be a bad trade. Good trades are usually the hardest to take since they seem riddled with risk and danger. To be a successful trader, you need to free yourself from past experiences; otherwise they will control your actions, instilling fear in you to the point where trades that fit your system perfectly are hard to take. Think of yourself as a football or basketball player who has just lost a game but has to play again the next day. Most coaches will tell their players to focus on one game at a time, learn from their loss and move to the next one. That is, as a player you should not let your loss in one game affect your play in the next one.

Many beginning traders fall into a vicious cycle of success and failure, which ultimately results in them giving up. Most of the time a beginning trader feels confident, especially when the beginning trades are winners. Once a person runs into a string of losing trades, they feel the need to return to the learning stage and seek information. Another string of winners, and the trader feels that they now have the crucial information needed for success. As the trader starts expecting more and more that each trade should be a winner, every loss will result in a more determined search for information to stop the losses. These losses, however, never stop, and the trader eventually gives up.

To succeed in trading, you need to be able to make sense of the information and the conflicting signals the market generates. This is done by developing and sticking to a profitable trading system. This will allow you to extract the information you need to feed into your system to get the required output to make clear decisions that will allow you to act without hesitation.

Once you have developed a profitable system, the next challenge is to follow it. This unfortunately is easier said than done, especially on occasions when the system does not yield a profitable trade. Experienced traders know that the market is unpredictable and no system is 100 percent foolproof, so they admit the trade was a mistake, take the loss and move on. On the other hand, beginning traders start doubting the system they use just because a few trades fail and go on an endless quest to develop the non-existent perfect market system that never fails.

Profitable traders have four important personal behavior traits that are needed for success. They are: discipline, perseverance, patience and self-reliance.

As a trader, you must be disciplined and stick to your trading plan. You should only enter trades that based on your trading plan have the highest probability of success. You should not let your emotions control your actions by getting into trades before a signal is generated by your system.

Being able to continue trading after few losses takes discipline; entering trades at the right time requires discipline as well as taking profits and waiting for the right opportunity.

To be a successful trader you must have patience. Sitting on the sidelines is sometimes necessary if a good opportunity does not materialize. Many traders have difficulty doing that since in a regular job you are expected to be busy all the time, but in trading you need to be busy only at the right time. Remember that sitting on the sidelines and not trading at the wrong time is a strategy in itself. This strategy will actually save you from losing money on bad trades you may run into.

As a trader, you must be determined to succeed. This perseverance is necessary to get through periods where every trade you take seems to go the wrong way even though you felt it was the right move at the time. This can deeply damage your confidence, making you hold onto losing trades too long or hesitant in entering other potential trades. You need to get through the bad times, pick up the pieces and continue trading. With time as you persevere through the difficult challenges, success is likely to be close by.

Successful traders are self-reliant; they know that success comes from looking within and learning from their mistakes to improve their odds. If you blame someone else — an analyst, guru, relative or whoever it may be — for your losses, you will never acquire the knowledge you need to succeed.

In trading there will be good and bad times and you will have your share of losses. The system you use should be profitable with losses factored in. Successful traders are so confident that they are as comfortable about taking losses as they are taking profits. They believe that the next successful trade is just around the corner.

Money Management

Believe it or not, trading is a business and should be treated as such. Just as any entrepreneur in any business considers how to manage capital for maximum return, you will need to do the same in your trading business. A good example is casinos, which are in the gambling business, but in no way do they have a gambler's mentality. All the slot machines you play at the casino favor the house over time. In general they keep around two percent of the amount that you gamble, eventually ending with all your money if you play long enough. This is why the only people who come out as winners are the ones who stop gambling while they are ahead.

As a trader, you want to have the casino's edge by keeping the amount you place into a trade small enough that any loss or a string of losses will not deplete your capital. Just like the casino, your aim should be to make small to medium-size profits frequently so you can use the magic of compounding to build your account quickly.

Taking an excessively large position in a single trade is damaging in many ways. If you suffer a large loss, you will be more likely to encounter psychological barriers to taking the next trade which may end up being a big winner. If you keep your trading positions small, you are much less likely to stay objective and exit the position if it does not go your way. A large position is likely to cloud your judgment and you will hope that things will turn around.

Remember that at no time as a trader you should be saying to yourself, "I cannot afford to lose this money." If that occurs, you have definitely taken a larger position than you should and you are gambling, not trading.

Furthermore, there is no need to gamble to be a highly successful trader. Even a 3% per week or 15% per month profits compounded over a few years can turn a few thousand to several hundred thousand. Try to focus on taking small profits on daily, weekly or monthly basis and you will be surprised at how quickly your capital grows.

How then do you decide the amount to risk on each trade? My recommendation is to follow these steps:

(1) Calculate your potential loss on a trade. To do this you just subtract your "mental" stop loss point (to be discussed in the next section) from your entry point for a long position and vice versa for a short position.

We will apply this concept to (KONG), the example we used in a preceding chapter. By looking at the chart on page 260, we see the two support points. The first is at the lower arm of the pennant and the second which is a major support at $6.50.

We entered the position at $7.00 and, based on the information above, we have either a $0.20 or a $0.50 loss per share dependent on our exit point.

(2) Limit your potential loss per trade to no more than 2% of your total trading account.

Let us say you have a $25,000 trading account, in which case your loss should be no more than $500. Based on that, if you pick an exit at $6.80 with a potential loss of $0.20/ share, your maximum number of shares to buy is $500/0.20 = 2500 shares.

If you pick an exit at $6.50 with a loss of $0.50 a share, the maximum shares you should buy is $500/0.5 = 1000 shares.

By following this technique, you are essentially forcing yourself to pick the trades that have most profit potential. If you apply the concepts in this book, you will be able to fine tune your trading so only high profit potential trades are considered.

Risk Control

I am sure that even a beginning trader realizes that not all trades will be profitable. The important thing is to have a cumulative profit after losses have been factored in. Even if you have several losses for every winner, you should be able to be profitable if you observe the money management concepts discussed in the previous section and the risk control techniques discussed here.

The difference between novice and experienced traders is that experienced traders embrace risk while beginners try to eliminate it. Most investors enter a trade with no consideration for the potential downside. They have neither an idea what the potential loss is if they are wrong, nor an exit plan for the trade. In addition, they approach risk in light of their own financial circumstances. They ignore that the stock will move either way independent of the size of their pocketbook or of whether they can or cannot afford to lose their investment. The time to get out should be based on specific criteria you put in place, such as break of support level, violation of the chart pattern which was the reason for entry, and so on. You should not exit just because you cannot handle the temporary adversity in the price of the stock. In most cases the potential profit on a trade is dependent on your ability to withstand temporary adversity and not panic into exiting the position before your system dictates that you do so.

Practical Methods To Control Risk

You should make every effort to minimize your risk entering high potential trades and timing your entry as correctly as possible. Try to master the techniques described in chapter 17 and the chart patterns in chapter 16. Using these techniques in combination with technical indicators described in chapters 12 and 13 should reduce the potential for loss and thus the necessity of taking risk control measures.

On the other hand, it is well accepted that the market is unpredictable and even the best systems sometimes fail. For this reason you should be prepared to act whenever this occurs. In the next few sections I will discuss risk control situations that you can use when such adversity occurs.

Setting Stops

Stop loss orders are advocated to protect a position from significant loss. While this may be fine in theory, reality is frequently quite different. A stop loss order becomes a market order when the price falls below the stop loss price. This implies that the price at which the stock is sold may be quite a bit below the price you are expecting. The reason for this is that stop loss orders are usually concentrated in specific locations such as 52-week lows, 50-day MA, trendline break, support, among others.

Professionals and market makers are fully aware that the market will take a life of its own when stops are activated. This is what is known as "running the stops" in the market, and once this is started, selling will create more selling, causing the stock to drop temporarily. At this point the professionals who set up the run at the stops will come in and start buying right after you have sold your shares at the low of the day. If you do not believe this occurs, track the execution prices of your stop loss orders and you will find they are mostly near the low of the day.

In addition to running stops, there is another problem known as "front running." While this is not exactly legal, it is still widely practiced. This happens when a market maker or a floor specialist sees a big order from an investor coming, so he goes and purchases the stock for his own account and later sells it to the investor at a higher price from his, as well as other accounts. By allowing the order to be filled through multiple accounts, the specialist can make this appear a normal sale. This practice usually results in a profit of thousands of dollars to the specialist.

To avoid being a victim of "running stops," one of the oldest tricks around in the market, I recommend using one of the following options:

(1) If you are disciplined and can stick to your exit plan, use a "mental stop." This is a price filed in your head rather than with your broker. If the stock closes below this price, you should re-evaluate the position including charts and technical indicators. If they give a sell signal, you should be

ready to exit the next day.

(2) If you are not as disciplined and want to use an automatic stop, try to avoid using predictable prices where stops are usually bunched together. Instead of using support price, trendline break or 50-day moving average, try using a price just below the Fibonacci 0.618 retracement, near the buy or sell numbers, or at the top or bottom of the sell and buy envelopes discussed in chapter 17. Another option is using an average of the low for the past five days. This way if you are stopped out, you are likely to get a price close to what you expect.

Which option to use is a personal choice dependent on your level of experience and discipline.

Risk Control Using Options

We have learned in the early chapters of this book how to use basic option strategies to raise cash on stocks we own, as well as reducing cost basis on stocks we are intending to buy. Another benefit of options is their use as risk control vehicles in short term trading.

Let us say that you purchased a stock for a short term trade and you see the stock moving your way for few days. At some point your system indicates that a pullback is likely to occur; however, you believe it is just temporary and the stock will eventually resume its uptrend.

As I mentioned earlier, a trader's profitability in the market is dependent on their ability to withstand temporary price adversity without panicking and selling. This is where options can be useful as they offer you protection from an occasional pullback in an established trend.

There are three simple techniques that can be used with long positions to accomplish this objective.

(1) Covered Calls

(2) Inverted Collars.

(3) Bull Put Spreads

Covered Calls

I will illustrate how covered calls are used to control risk with a real life example. Again we will apply this technique using KONG.

As you may recall on page 338, we decided to purchase KONG at a price of $7.00 on 10/26/06 after breakout from a bullish pennant. Our calculations indicated an initial sell target of $7.82; however, the stock broke through the target so we decided to hold. Our five-day oscillator and three-day difference calculations indicated a possible short term correction after 10/3/06 when the stock closed at $8.17.

Our plan is to sell in the money $7.5 strike Nov 06 covered calls for around $0.80 which includes around a $0.15 time premium. Just in case the correction turns out to be a reversal, we will place a "mental stop" if the stock closes below the buy number for the second advance phase calculated using the buy and sell envelope method on page 337 at $7.69.

ALERT: We are placing a mental stop since we want to be sure not to end with a naked call. If the stock closes below the stop, we will exit the stock and buy the call back the next day. If, on the other hand, we place an automatic stop, the stock could be sold intraday at the day's low and bounce back at the end of the day. If this happens, we will end up being stuck with a naked call which is not advisable due to the large amount of risk involved, especially in an uptrending stock.

As seen on page 340, Kong closes at $7.87 on 11/2/06 and reaches an intraday low of $7.67 on 11/3/2006. At this point we can buy the call back and cash in the difference between the premium we obtained ($0.80) and the purchase price. In this case the time value of the option did not change much since the drop happened within a couple of days. Our profit is essentially the premium less the difference between the price of the stock at the time of the purchase of the call and the strike. Thus our profit is:

$0.80 - ($7.75 - $7.5) = $0.55.

In this case we were able to cash $0.55/share during a temporary pullback. This fact will definitely make us less likely to panic and exit the position prematurely. The stock eventually moved higher as expected and reached $7.94 on 11/14/2006.

ALERT: If you want to get the best exit day to buy back the option, you will need to calculate the five-day oscillator and the three-day difference at minimum every three days and preferably on a daily basis. You should close the calls within a day or two after these indicators signal an upward reversal. Alternatively you can exit when the stock gets close to the buy number or the strike. In this case, you may not get the best exit point, but you will still make a good profit.

The risk profile for the covered calls we sold is as follows:
Breakeven point = stock price - Call premium: = $7.00 - $0.80 = $6.20

This implies that the stock can drop to $6.20 before we suffer a loss. Of course, we will be out long before this happens.

Maximum Profit = (Strike - Stock Price) + Call premium = ($7.50 -$7.00) +$0.80 = $1.30.

This is our profit if we let the stock get exercised at a strike of 7.50 and not buy the call back which means we have an effective sale price of $8.30. Of course, our plan is to buy the call back since we believe the stock is moving higher.

Inverted Collar

This is a risk control strategy involving selling covered calls, but instead of using a stop loss to protect the downside we will buy puts. What we have in this case is a long put and a short call.

ALERT: In a regular collar trade you are selling out of the money calls and buying at or slightly out of the money puts. In this case, we are selling in the money call and buying out of the money puts, hence the name inverted collar. Regular collar trades are more effective for long term positions, but inverted collars are especially designed for short term situations.

Going back to the example above (KONG), after selling the $7.5 strike Nov 06 calls for $0.80, we will buy a $7.5 strike Nov 06 puts. Since the stock is trading at $8.15 far from the strike, the value of the put was limited to the time premium at around $0.15.

Buying the put is in essence similar to placing a stop at $7.50. If the stock falls below $7.50, we can exercise the puts and sell at $7.50. If, on the other hand, the stock approaches the strike at $7.50 but never drops below it, we can sell the puts for a small profit as did occur in this case.

This is a good strategy for traders who lack the discipline to observe a mental stop and exit the trade, although my preference is to train yourself to be a disciplined trader and not depend on such maneuvers.

ALERT: If we decide to exercise the put and sell the stock, we should buy back the covered call so we do not end up with a naked call. Remember that we are dealing with a temporary pullback, and the last thing we need is to hold a naked call on a rising stock.

The risk profile for the inverted collar trade is as follows:

Breakeven = Stock price - call premium + put premium = $7.00 - $0.80 +0.15 = $6.35

The stock can drop to $6.35 before experiencing any loss.

Maximum Risk = (stock price + put premium) - (put strike - call premium)

($7.00 + $0.15) - ($7.50 - $0.80) = $0.45.

This is the maximum risk of loss that we are likely to suffer. Note that if this number is negative it means you will have a risk-free trade.

Maximum Profit = Put strike + Put premium + Call Premium - Stock price

$7.50 +$0.15 + $0.80 - $7.00 = $1.45.

This is the maximum profit assuming that the put is exercised and the call expires worthless allowing us to keep both premiums.

This is not possible in this case since we have the same expiration month. The most likely scenario is that we will have to re-purchase the call, giving up part of the premium we obtained.

Bull Put Spread

In chapters 6 and 7 we learned how to use selling puts as a means of lowering cost basis on stocks you are looking to buy. The strategy, in brief, entails selling puts as the price is approaching support but the downward momentum is fading.

To reduce risk we have advocated using half put selling strategy, where you will sell puts on half the amount of shares you want to buy, collect the premium and then wait to see if the put is exercised. If the stock falls through the strike and the option is exercised, your cost is the strike less the premium. You will then sell puts on the other half of the shares at a lower strike above next support and collect a second premium. If you are careful in picking your strikes close to support, more often than not at least one of the puts will expire, allowing you to further reduce your cost.

What about if the support breaks and the stock just keeps falling? Although this is unlikely if you have done your homework, the market is full of surprises and it still can happen. This is where the bull put spread strategy is useful.

This strategy involves buying a put at a strike one step below the support you are intending to buy at. As an example, if you are intending to buy a stock near support at say $12.5, you will buy puts one strike below that around $10. As the stock moves towards $12.5, you will sell puts at the $12.5 strike.

We will use the JDSU example given on pages 54-55 to illustrate this technique. By examining the chart we found that the stock has established support at $13.00 on 4/4/2001, so we picked $12.5 as the strike to sell puts at.

The stock hit $12.40 on June 15, 2001, so we sold $12.5 strike July 2001 puts for $1.50. This is the first leg of the strategy, selling the puts on the stock so we can buy the shares at an effective price of $12.5 - $1.5 = $11.00 if the put was exercised.

To protect our downside, we will buy August 2001 $10 strike puts for $0.15. As mentioned previously, we will pick a strike one step below the one we sold the puts at. This will protect our downside, allowing us to exercise the puts and sell the stock at $10 taking a small loss or selling the put for a profit if the stock finds support.

JDSU traded around $9.50 on June 20, 2001, and the put option was valued at $0.75. If we believe based on evaluating the charts that $9.50 is a strong short term support, we can sell the puts at $0.75 and pocket a $0.60 profit. We can then repeat the process if the stock moves back toward resistance.

The advantage of using this strategy is that if bad news were to come out and the stock drop to $7.00, we can exercise the put and sell at $10.00. Our loss is $11.00 + $0.15 - $10.00 = $1.15 which is a much smaller loss than $4.00 if the stock dropped to $7.00.

The risk profile for the bull put strategy is as follows:

Breakeven: Higher strike -(sell put premium - buy put premium)= $12.5 - ($1.50 - $0.15)= $11.15.

This is the effective price of the stock if the $12.5 puts are exercised.

Maximum Profit: Sell put premium - buy put premium = $1.50 - $0.15 = $1.35

This occurs if both puts were to expire.

Maximum loss: (higher strike - lower strike) - (sell put premium - buy put premium)

($12.5 - $10.00) - ($1.50 - $0.15) = $1.15

This is the same number obtained previously if the $12.5 puts are exercised and we exercise the $10 puts.

Winning Trading System

You can have the psychological make-up of a successful trader and still fail. You can be disciplined, self-reliant, determined, cool and calm and still suffer one loss after the other. The reason for this is you need a winning trading system that you can stick to day in and day out. You need to then track the performance of this system, refine it as you go, adapt it to changing market conditions, and end up with a final plan that produces a good cumulative profit with losses factored in.

To develop a trading system, you need to first decide what kind of a trader you want to be — a day trader, a swing trader, intermediate term trader or a long term investor. This choice will dictate how you approach the market and what kind of charts and technical indicators you need to pay attention to. As an example, if you are interested in day trading, it is critical that you understand level II screens and their buy and sell signals.

This book is mostly geared towards short to intermediate term trading where holding periods are from a couple of weeks to a few months. Subsequently, our interest should be mainly focused on daily charts occasionally supplemented by longer weekly time frame charts when necessary.

The next step is to form a mental image of the kind of trading you are interested in. This involves deciding whether you want to trade long or short or both sides of the market, the stock price range you are interested in, and what kind of general chart pattern you want to focus on.

It is advisable to trade both long and short since going long when the market is in a downtrend will make profits more difficult to come by. On the other hand, if your discipline is not yet as good as it should be, sticking to long trades may be better since short trades carry unlimited loss potential. Do not be discouraged if you feel comfortable only trading on the long side of the market, since even in the worst days there are stocks in their own bull market. The trick is to pick a system that is inherently low risk when you are on the long side in a weak market. In general this means avoiding momentum trading and stocks that have already had a significant run

The price range of stocks you decide to trade should mainly depend on two factors: (1) The size of your trading account, (2) The time you are able to dedicate to your trading.

To be able to limit your loss to 2% of your account, a small account (below $25,000) necessitates that you trade low-priced stocks (below $15, preferably below $10). This will allow you to hold multiple positions with enough shares to have a meaningful return if the stock moves in your direction. Another reason for focusing on lower price stocks is that they are likely to move quickly, thus building your trading capital much faster.

You should understand that due to the volatility of low-priced stocks you will need to devote more time to managing your trades. You will have to keep track of your trades on a daily basis to plan your next day moves. If you cannot dedicate the required time, then you should stick with stocks above $15.00 with the understanding that your profits are likely to be lower in terms of absolute dollar numbers.

Lastly, you need to have an idea of the general pattern you need to trade. Trading in the market is like any other career where you can be more successful if you specialize. In the same way that you cannot be a good mechanical, electrical and civil engineer at the same time, you cannot be a momentum trader, trend trader, bottom fisher and reversal trader and be an expert in any of them. If you try to be an expert in everything, you will be good at nothing and mediocre in all. Remember that you are trading against market professionals and there is no place for mediocrity in the market. The good trader finds his own area of interest and strength, develops it and becomes so proficient at it that he can pick a stock conforming to his system with a glance at the chart.

Now you have the basic elements of a trading system put together. Your next step is narrow the field of thousands of stocks to the ones that are candidates to trade.

Notice that I used the word candidates, since our goal is to narrow these further on close examination of the charts. Our objective is to initially end with around 25, but no more than 50 stocks for chart review.

To do this, we will need to translate the general criteria comprising our trading system into specific conditions that can be entered into a scanning software program to pick out the stocks that meet your system parameters.

There are many scanning software programs available to traders. The only requirement is that the software should allow you to enter your own filtering criteria into the program. This should narrow down the stock candidates to the ones fitting your own system. Once you confirm that this feature is available, you can pick the program you are most comfortable using.

Your last step is to study the chart for each stock that the scanning program filters in. You then place each stock into one of the following categories:

(1) Stocks eliminated from consideration
(2) Stocks placed on daily watch for possible future entry
(3) Stocks for entry the next couple of days.

Stocks Eliminated from Consideration

Since our objective is to find stocks with the highest profit potential and lowest risk, we will eliminate the following candidates from consideration:

(1) Stocks that have already run up before our screening system picked them. Although they can run up further, remember that our goal is to identify a low risk buy.

(2) Stocks that are highly volatile on both daily and weekly charts. These require too much time to manage the position; otherwise a profit can easily turn into a loss.

(3) Stocks exhibiting a negative CMF divergence. If the price is going higher but the CMF is going lower, it is likely that the run-up is temporary and is likely to be followed by a reversal. This situation is usually encountered with stocks showing a downtrend on the weekly chart but an uptrend on the daily chart.

(4) Stocks showing an unclear chart pattern. Try to pick stocks that clearly show a pattern in your own eyes. If you cannot clearly see the pattern, do not trade the stock. Even though

a more experienced trader can see what you cannot, remember that is your money you are trading and your responsibility to manage the position.

Stocks Placed on Daily Watch for Possible Future Entry

Can you remember times when you picked a stock that did nothing for a few days or a couple of weeks just to take off after that? This is why daily tracking of some stocks is necessary until a viable entry point is identified or the stock is eliminated.

These are stocks that show bullish charts but indicate a possible short term retracement. Our objective is to watch the stock on a daily basis until we believe the retracement is close to complete before entering. These are the most difficult stocks to trade since the ability to pinpoint whether a retracement will occur and its extent can only come with experience. Broad guidelines include:

(1) Stocks that show a significant one-day price increase on heavy volume. These are likely to pull back before continuing the uptrend.

(2) Bull flags, pennants, rectangles and ascending triangles. These are likely, in most cases, to pull back to the support defined by the specific chart pattern. A pullback may not occur if the OBV shows a heavy positive divergence. That is, up days have a much higher volume than down days during formation of the pattern.

(3) VPV reversals. You will need to be sure that the downtrend line has successfully been re-tested. If that has not occurred, watch the stock on a daily basis for an entry point.

Stocks for Entry the Next Couple of Days

Stocks that show highly bullish chart patterns and extremely bullish indicators should be considered for trading the next day or the day after. These include:

(1) Falling rectangles
(2) Falling wedges

(3) Breakaway gaps. In this case you may want to wait until the day after just to be sure that any pullback will be minor.

(4) MACD Histogram divergences.

Normally, our entry will be dictated by a breakout from the pattern on increasing volume. In case of the highly bullish falling rectangle pattern, we can enter before a breakout occurs if the following conditions apply.

(a) A recent failed breakout move on heavy volume occurred.

(b) A subsequent pullback on decreasing volume took place.

(c) The current move is either the second or third attempt of a breakout.

Remember the rule of three: a breakout should be successful on the third attempt or the pattern is likely to fail. My experience has shown that in over 95% of cases a falling rectangle pattern results in a breakout and massive bullish move. You should always keep your eyes open for this pattern.

Practical Application

How will a trader then go about developing a stock scanning system that suits his own objective? This is best illustrated with an example.

Keep in mind when reading this section that this shows just one approach out of many that can be used. It is meant to demonstrate a systematic way to scan stocks and look at charts. If you have your own system already in use, you can incorporate any ideas presented here to further improve it if you find them useful.

Let us say you are a beginning trader with $20,000 trading account looking to set up a stock screening system. You define your main objectives as:

(1) You are only comfortable with long trades.

(2) You want to get the maximum bang for the small account you have.

(3) You want to reduce risk by picking stocks in the early stages of a move.

To accomplish this, the chart pattern you want to look for is a heavy volume reversal from a downtrend. The reversal indicates that you are more likely than not to get in on a start of a move, while heavy volume points to a high level of participation pointing to a serious and sustainable move.

We will have to translate this concept into specific condition that can be entered into a scanning software to narrow down our choices. The following conditions define such a system:

Stock Price Parameters

(1) Price between $5 and $10.

It is known that stocks below $5.00 do not attract much institutional interest so we will pick stocks above $5.00. We will keep the price below $10.00 to get maximum return on our small account.

(2) Price today > Price Yesterday

We want to be sure that the price is moving higher and the stock is in an uptrend.

(3) Percent Price Change < 50

We want to be sure that the stock has not moved so much in price that we end up buying just before a correction. We will thus limit the move to 50%. The reason for this will be clearer when volume criteria are discussed.

Stop Price Parameters

In a previous section I stressed the importance of having a stop set when managing a trade to reduce risk. It is thus evident that you will not want to enter a trade if the stock is trading below its stop price. The question remains as to what specific stop price you want to use.

If you currently do not have a specific scanning software, I recommend that you use one that calculates its own stops and incorporates them into criteria selection. This will make things a lot easier for you, especially if you are a beginner.

If you need to program your own stops, you can use the EMA (20) or numbers determined by the buy and sell envelopes. Alternatively, a multi-day or multi-week moving average can be used dependent on your trading time frame. The important thing is that you use a stop in your scanning criteria and use the same one consistently.

We will define the stop price parameters as follows:

(1) Stock price yesterday < Stock stop price yesterday

(2) Stock price today > Stock stop price today.

Since by definition a stock should be sold if it trades below the stop but may be bought if it trades above it, these two conditions clearly define the start of a reversal.

In effect, what this indicates is that the stock changed from a sell candidate yesterday to a possible buy today.

(3) Stop price today >Stop price yesterday

This condition guarantees that not only the stock price is moving higher but the stop price is also moving higher. In essence, this is a trailing stop following the stock as it inches higher.

Volume Parameters

(1) Average volume > 250,000

This condition insures sufficient liquidity.

(2) Percent volume change > 25%

This is to insure that the move is occurring on heavy volume. Combining this condition with a price move of less than 50% results in stocks that are moving on heavy volume, but have not made such a large price jump that a correction is imminent. In fact, the best candidates are stocks showing a volume spike with small to moderate price movement.

(3) Volume today > Volume Yesterday

We want also to be sure that the move is not only taking place on heavier than average volume but on increasing volume.

In summary, our scanning criteria are as follows:

(1) Price > $5
(2) Price < $10
(3) % price change <50
(4) % volume change >25
(5) Volume >250,000
(6) Price today > Price yesterday
(7) Volume today > volume yesterday
(8) Stop Price today > Stop price yesterday
(9) Price yesterday < Stop price yesterday
(10) Price today > Stop price today.

By running this criteria using our in-house scanning program, the stocks shown in the table below are picked as candidates.

Heavy Volume Reversal Scan(9/13/2006)

Symbol	Price	Volume	Average Volume	% Volume Increase
AUY	9.68	3969900	2361800	68
CHU	9.63	815900	474400	197
BE	8.82	4916900	1195200	311
SCI	8.67	685100	515900	33
MFA	7.65	906100	471500	92
RNAI	5.79	446931	303000	47
TALK	5.69	430193	283300	52
FORD	5.50	1319066	505200	161
SIX	5.25	2682600	1571500	71

The effectiveness of such a scan is seen in the low number of stocks picked. Your goal should be to narrow the choices as much as possible so you can end up with the best trading opportunities.

Our next step is to place each of these stocks into one of the three categories we mentioned before:

(1) Elimination
(2) Daily Watch
(3) Entry in the next couple of days.

We will now study the chart for each candidate. Note that the date the scan is run (9/13/2006) is designated by an X on the chart of each stock.

AUY (chart page 367)
This stock will be eliminated for the following reasons:
(1) MACD negative divergence between points 1 and 2
(2) Stock already ran up before we picked it

BE (chart page 368)
This stock will also be eliminated because:
(1) High volatility
(2) Stock already run up

CHU (chart page 369)
This stock will be a trade candidate in the next couple of days since:
(1) Breakaway gap on extremely heavy volume
(2) Highly positive CMF
(3) MACD oversold with crossover.
We will want to wait a day or two before entry just to be sure the gap is not closed. A good entry would have been around $9.50

FORD (chart page 370)
This stock will be eliminated because of
(1) Stock has run up from $4.50 to $5.50 before we picked it.

MFA (chart page 371)
This stock is a daily watch candidate due to:
(1) Ascending triangle formation
(2) Highly positive CMF
This stock was picked before a breakout of the ascending triangle pattern took place. We will thus wait for a breakout above the upper arm before entry. A good entry would be around $7.25.

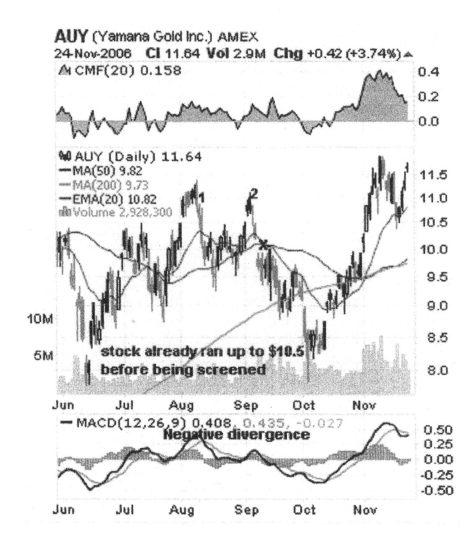

AUY (Yamana Gold Inc.) AMEX
24-Nov-2006 Cl 11.64 Vol 2.9M Chg +0.42 (+3.74%) ▲
CMF(20) 0.158

0.4
0.2
0.0

AUY (Daily) 11.64
MA(50) 9.82
MA(200) 9.73
EMA(20) 10.82
Volume 2,928,300

1
2
X

11.5
11.0
10.5
10.0
9.5
9.0
8.5
8.0

10M
5M

stock already ran up to $10.5
before being screened

Jun   Jul   Aug   Sep   Oct   Nov

MACD(12,26,9) 0.408, 0.435, -0.027
Negative divergence

0.50
0.25
0.00
-0.25
-0.50

Jun   Jul   Aug   Sep   Oct   Nov

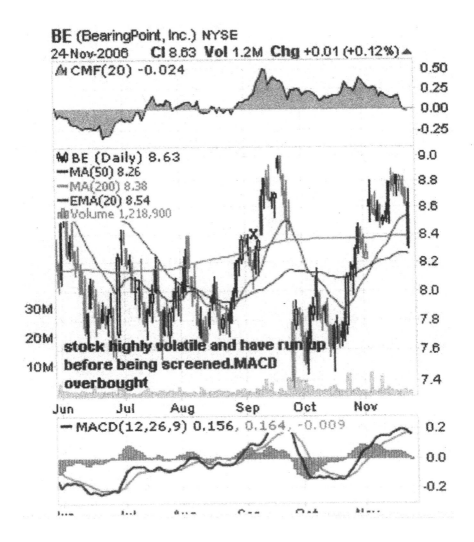

BE (BearingPoint, Inc.) NYSE
24-Nov-2006 **Cl** 8.63 **Vol** 1.2M **Chg** +0.01 (+0.12%) ▲
▲ CMF(20) -0.024

0.50
0.25
0.00
-0.25

W BE (Daily) 8.63
—MA(50) 8.26
—MA(200) 8.38
—EMA(20) 8.54
▯Volume 1,218,900

9.0
8.8
8.6
8.4
8.2
8.0
7.8
7.6
7.4

30M
20M
10M

stock highly volatile and have run up
before being screened.MACD
overbought

Jun   Jul   Aug   Sep   Oct   Nov

—MACD(12,26,9) 0.156, 0.164, -0.009

0.2
0.0
-0.2

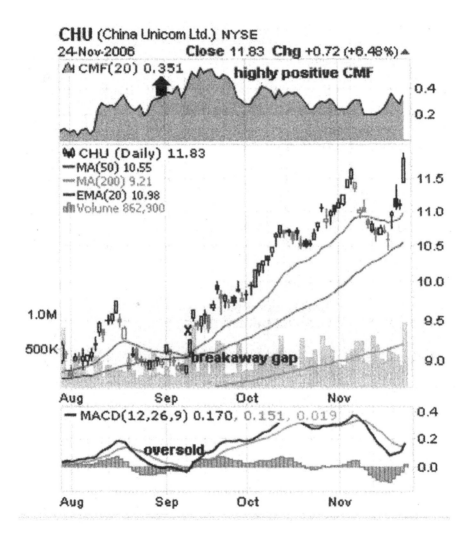

CHU (China Unicom Ltd.) NYSE
24-Nov-2006   Close 11.83 Chg +0.72 (+6.48%) ▲
CMF(20) 0.351   highly positive CMF

0.4
0.2

CHU (Daily) 11.83
—MA(50) 10.55
—MA(200) 9.21
—EMA(20) 10.98
Volume 862,300

11.5
11.0
10.5
10.0
9.5
9.0

1.0M
500K

X
breakaway gap

Aug   Sep   Oct   Nov

MACD(12,26,9) 0.170, 0.151, 0.019
oversold

0.4
0.2
0.0

Aug   Sep   Oct   Nov

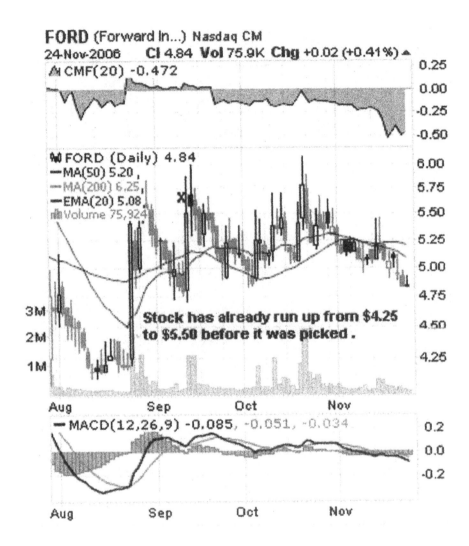

FORD (Forward In...) Nasdaq CM
24-Nov-2006   Cl 4.84 Vol 75.9K Chg +0.02 (+0.41%) ▲
CMF(20) -0.472

0.25
0.00
-0.25
-0.50

W FORD (Daily) 4.84
— MA(50) 5.20 ,
— MA(200) 6.25 ,
— EMA(20) 5.08 ,
Volume 75,924

X

6.00
5.75
5.50
5.25
5.00
4.75

3M

2M

1M

Stock has already run up from $4.25 to $5.50 before it was picked .

4.50
4.25

Aug   Sep   Oct   Nov

— MACD(12,26,9) -0.085 , -0.051 , -0.034

0.2
0.0
-0.2

Aug   Sep   Oct   Nov

370

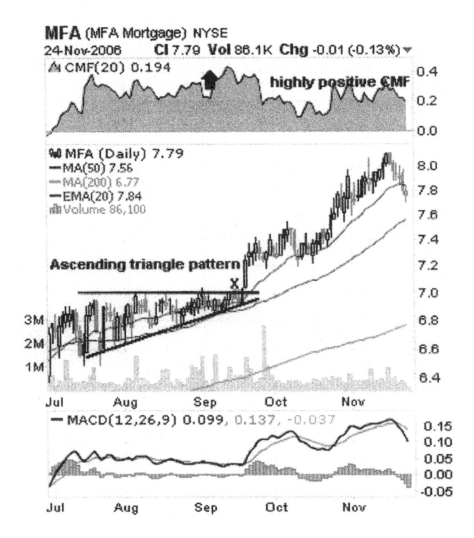

MFA (MFA Mortgage) NYSE
24-Nov-2006   **Cl** 7.79 **Vol** 86.1K **Chg** -0.01 (-0.13%) ▼

CMF(20) 0.194   highly positive CMF

0.4

0.2

0.0

MFA (Daily) 7.79
—MA(50) 7.56
—MA(200) 6.77
—EMA(20) 7.84
Volume 86,100

8.0

7.8

7.6

7.4

7.2

7.0

6.8

6.6

6.4

Ascending triangle pattern

X

3M

2M

1M

Jul   Aug   Sep   Oct   Nov

—MACD(12,26,9) 0.099, 0.137, -0.037

0.15
0.10
0.05
0.00
-0.05

Jul   Aug   Sep   Oct   Nov

RNAI (chart page 373)

This stock will also be placed on daily watch since we have:

(1) VPV reversal formation

(2) Highly positive CMF

In this case we will wait for a re-test of the downtrend line before entry. A good entry would have been around $6.00 early October. This means that you would have had to check the chart every day between 9/13/06 and early October when the trade was entered.

This is another reason why it pays off to narrow the candidates as much as possible.

The VPV reversal may have been difficult to spot by a beginning trader, and the CMF may have not been clearly positive throughout. This may have resulted in the stock being eliminated and the gap to $13.00 missed. If this situation happens to you, do not get discouraged; remember there are thousands of stocks and there are always new candidates.

SCI (chart page 374)

This stock may either be eliminated or placed on daily watch. There are reasons to do either:

(1) The stock has already run up from $7.25 to $8.50 which makes it a candidate for elimination.

(2) Stock is breaking out of a rectangle with highly positive CMF which make it a possible watch candidate.

In such a case the best thing to do is to wait to study all the charts. If we have better candidates, we will eliminate such a stock. This is what we decide to do in this case.

TALK (chart page 375)

There should be no doubt in your mind that this is a top candidate for entry the next day.

This is reinforced by:

(1) Falling rectangle pattern.

(2) MACD divergence during pattern formation.

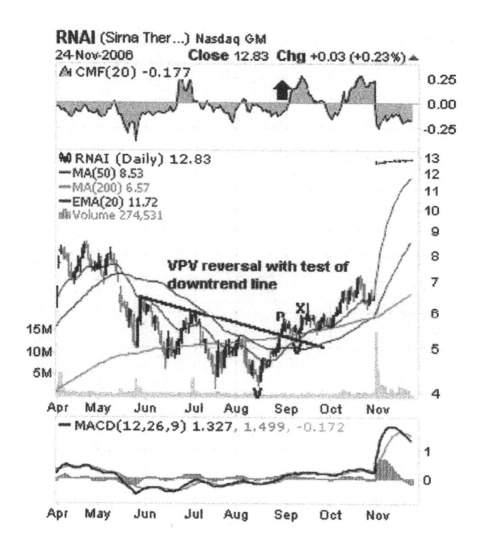

RNAI (Sirna Ther...) Nasdaq GM
24-Nov-2006   Close 12.83 Chg +0.03 (+0.23%) ▲

CMF(20) -0.177

0.25
0.00
-0.25

RNAI (Daily) 12.83
—MA(50) 8.53
—MA(200) 6.57
—EMA(20) 11.72
Volume 274,531

VPV reversal with test of
downtrend line

13
12
11
10
9
8
7
6
5
4

15M
10M
5M

Apr May Jun Jul Aug Sep Oct Nov

—MACD(12,26,9) 1.327, 1.499, -0.172

1
0

Apr May Jun Jul Aug Sep Oct Nov

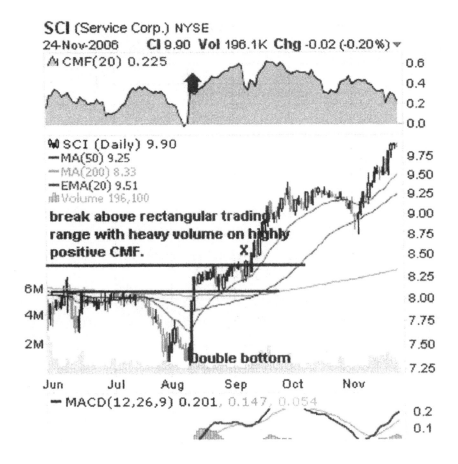

SCI (Service Corp.) NYSE
24-Nov-2006   **Cl** 9.90 **Vol** 196.1K **Chg** -0.02 (-0.20%) ▼
CMF(20) 0.225

0.6
0.4
0.2
0.0

SCI (Daily) 9.90
—MA(50) 9.25
—MA(200) 8.33
—EMA(20) 9.51
Volume 196,100

break above rectangular trading range with heavy volume on highly positive CMF.

X

8M
4M
2M

Double bottom

9.75
9.50
9.25
9.00
8.75
8.50
8.25
8.00
7.75
7.50
7.25

Jun   Jul   Aug   Sep   Oct   Nov

—MACD(12,26,9) 0.201, 0.147, 0.054

0.2
0.1

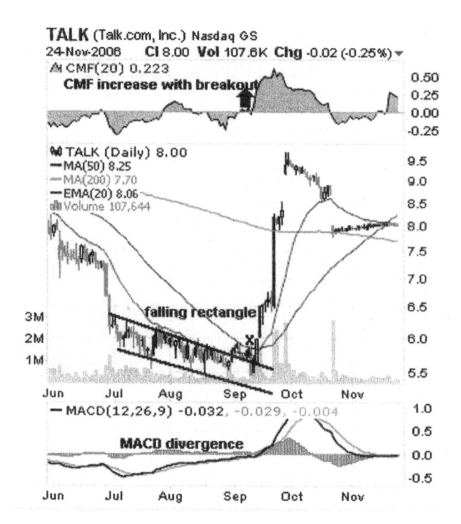

Our entry into this stock will be at the next day's open as long as it is within 2% of the close. We will place a limit order if we cannot watch the open.

SIX (chart page 377)

This stock will be eliminated due to:

(1) No clear identifiable chart pattern

(2) High volatility.

Remember what I said before; if you are in doubt then you should opt out of the stock.

In summary we thus have:

(1) Entry in the next two days: CHU, TALK

(2) Daily Watch: RNAI, MFA

(3) Elimination: AUY, BE, FORD, SCI, SIX.

This is what you should want to end with when you perform a stock scan. Most of the stocks should be eliminated with only a handful of candidates left. If your scan gives too many candidates, it is likely that your conditions are too broad and should be narrowed down.

Remember that the smaller the number of candidates you get, the more time you can spend studying each chart. This is sure to make you less likely to miss good trading opportunities.

Final Word

In my experience coaching and helping traders improve their results, I have found two common practices. The first is most traders tend to place their stop loss points in expected areas where they can easily be run over by market professionals. By picking more unique stop loss points as described in this chapter, a trader is more likely to get out at a price close to the stop rather than the low of the day.

The second is that the majority of traders when using a scanning program to pick stocks either trade the stock or eliminate it, but never place it on a daily watch list.

I have encouraged most traders I have coached to try making a list of stocks from every scan that can be possible future entry candidates. I suggested that they should then check the charts daily on each of these stocks and decide whether to enter or drop the stock.

Many traders were very pleasantly surprised by the results. Not only were they less likely to miss profitable trades, but they had a list of trading candidates always available to them. In addition, I have heard comments to the effect that the decision-making experience of looking at each chart and deciding entry or elimination was an invaluable education process. Please be sure to try this when using your own scan to identify stocks for trading.

CHAPTER 20

Thinking Outside the Box

I FIRMLY BELIEVE that the only way to deal with new challenges such as the present market is to be creative and think outside the box.

If you were to read most available option books, they teach the standard approach, which is:

You profit from a falling market by buying puts and protect your profit by selling calls. In addition, under no circumstances should you be selling puts in a falling market.

Our objective in this book focuses on raising cash in addition to protecting profits. To achieve this, we had to think outside the ordinary by using reverse crowd psychology. When a stock is moving higher, the price of call options is moving up at an accelerated pace since most of the crowd is buying them in anticipation of higher stock price. Our philosophy is just the opposite; we can get maximum cash premium by selling calls when everyone is buying. On the other hand, when a stock is moving lower, call options are going down in price while put options are going higher. In this case we buy back our call position at a profit and sell a put at a high premium.

One other important point is the perceived risk associated with options. The reason for this is that over 75% of all options expire worthless. By thinking outside the box we have turned this statistical fact into an advantage. This system allows you to make maximum profits by allowing the option to expire worthless and keeping the premium.

To limit risks and maximize profits, we stress the importance of carefully picking strike prices and expiration dates. Most importantly, we recommend that you formulate a plan of action on how to handle all possibilities when you enter a trade as we did in the case histories described here.

While writing this chapter, I could not help but recall my day trading experience. I have noticed that most seasoned and successful traders use only a handful of technical indicators that work well for them. On the other hand, inexperienced traders are more likely to blame their losses on lack of information. They subsequently go and search for more techniques to incorporate into their system making it more complex, confusing and less reliable. They eventually give up, thinking that trading is a losing game and few make money at it. To be successful in investing, you must resist the conventional wisdom of needing to know everything before taking the plunge.

Remember that both general practitioners and heart surgeons are doctors, but heart surgeons who are specialists enjoy more success. My goal is for you to become a specialist rather than a practitioner by developing a simple system with few technical indicators and become proficient at it. Use your own imagination and creativity to build on the concepts introduced in this book to put together that magic system that works for you.

Remember that the market is the wind and you are the sailboat. You cannot control the wind, but you can adjust your sails. This book shows you how to do that to be profitable in this difficult market.

Epilogue

I AM SURE you are wondering whether I personally have used the techniques in this book. In fact, between April 15th and May 18th 2001 (option expiration date) I was able to generate $11,500 in cash by using a combination of the techniques in this booklet on just four stocks. These are: Applied Micro Circuits (AMCC), JDS Uniphase (JDSU), LSI Logic (LSI) and Qualcomm (QCOM). This was equivalent to 50% annual cash return based on the present value of these stocks. I then repeated the process on the first three stocks and was able to generate an additional $9,750 between May 21 and May 30, 2001, which was equivalent to 175% annual cash return. In fact, the total cash I generated using this system between April 15 and July 18 is $45,600 on six stocks; they are (AMCC, GX, JDSU, LSI, QCOM, SFA).

In 2002, I was able to average over $15,000/month in my long-term account with an investment portfolio of only eight stocks by using option strategies described in this book.

If you have a portfolio of several stocks, you can pick the best candidates to sell covered call and put options on each month and generate impressive amounts of cash without selling any of your holdings.

As in the case with learning any new technique, it will take some practice to be able to pick the right stocks, timing, strike prices and expiration dates as well as put/call combinations to maximize your returns. On the other hand, this is not rocket science and within two–three months you will become proficient. However, to facilitate the learning process, I recommend you read each example carefully and follow the thought process.

In addition to using options to generate significant amounts of cash on stocks, I have presented approaches that, in my experience, were useful in timing the sale and purchase of stocks.

To achieve superior stock market returns, it is advisable to combine using options to generate cash on long-term holdings with short-term trading to grow your investment capital. It is in the latter case where technical analysis concepts presented in chapters 12 and 13 of this book are most useful.

Although I firmly believe that each investor should develop the style that serves them best, I will share with you my own approach that have successfully returned over 20% per month in the past two years.

My investment funds are divided into two accounts, a long-term holding account and a short-term trading account. One-third of the total available dollars are dedicated to the trading account and two-thirds to the long-term holding accounts.

The objective of the long-term account is to hold no more than eight stocks for a period of months and possibly over a year. Stocks in this account are purchased based on long-term technical indicators as well as fundamental analysis of the business sector and specific company's prospects. Purchases are made either by selling puts or outright stock buying dependent on the specific situation. The stock is sold when technical indicators as demonstrated by the long-term CD charts discussed in chapter 14 show weakness. When a stock is sold, it is replaced by a stronger candidate.

In this account selling covered calls is essential to continuously raise cash, and selling puts is used to add to strong stock positions. This ensures a healthy return even when the market is stuck in a trading range.

The trading account focuses on the outright purchase and sale of stocks with a holding period of a few days to a few weeks. Options can be used to enhance profitability, but they must be very short term to allow profit taking. Stock purchases are strictly decided on technical indicators discussed in chapters 12, 13, 16, 17 and 18. Special attention is given to stocks exhibiting a potential of short or earnings squeeze due to the possibility of quick and sizeable profits. The goal of this account is to generate compounded profits of at least 10% per month.

During a sideways market, my focus is mainly on generating cash in my long term account by selling options. In a trending market, I employ short-term trading strategies to build capital in my short-term account. By using this balanced approach, I am certain to achieve healthy returns in any market.

At the request of many investors who purchased the first printing of this book, I have started a subscription website, namely: **www.generatethousands.net**, where I share my stock picks with investors using concepts in this book. If you are interested in following the stock recommendations this system generates, you are welcome to become a member. On the other hand, this book has all the information you need to be successful on your own without having to be a member of the site.

In this book, I have provided you with a simple low risk system to generate cash on your stocks whether they are winners or losers. I have used it myself successfully in a tough market and have shown by actual case histories that it works. DO NOT let anyone, including your friends, broker or financial advisor, talk you against taking advantage of this opportunity. If they think it does not work, that is only an indication that they can't do it.

389

391